FULLY
REVISED
AND UPDATED

The
SIMON & SCHUSTER

Pocket Guide to

CALIFORNIA
WINES

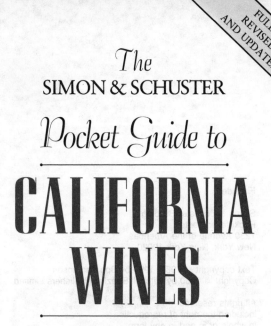

BOB THOMPSON

A FIRESIDE BOOK
PUBLISHED BY SIMON & SCHUSTER INC.
NEW YORK LONDON TORONTO SYDNEY TOKYO

Fireside

Simon & Schuster Building
Rockefeller Center
1230 Avenue of the Americas
New York, New York 10020

Designed by Barbara Marks
Printed and bound in Malaysia

10 9 8 7 6 5 4 3

Library of Congress Cataloging in Publication Data

Thompson, Bob, date.
   The Simon & Schuster pocket guide to California
wines / Bob Thompson.
       p.   cm.
   Rev. ed. of: The pocket encyclopedia of California
wines. Rev. ed. 1985.
   "A Fireside book."
   1. Wine and wine making—California.   I. Thompson,
Bob, date. Pocket encyclopedia of California wines.
II. Title.   III. Title: Simon and Schuster pocket guide to
California wines.   IV. Title: Pocket guide to California
wines.
TP557.T49   1990
641.2'2'09794—dc20   89-26006
                                                                             CIP

ISBN 0-671-66897-8

FOR EMMETT WATSON
WHO SHOWED ME
THE GULF BETWEEN
SKEPTICS AND CYNICS
AND TAUGHT ME WHICH SIDE
TO CHOOSE

Contents

Acknowledgments

To California's winery owners and their staffs, a blanket thanks for patiently answering questions and thus filling this book with facts.

To Dr. Maynard A. Amerine, William Bonetti, Ken Brown, Tucker Catlin, Jack Davies, Dawnine Dyer, Greg Fowler, Joe Heitz, Zelma Long, Louis Martini, Michael Martini, Michael Mondavi, Robert Mondavi, Tim Mondavi, Phillip Posson, Richard Sanford, and Dr. Vernon L. Singleton, extra applause for advancing my understanding of what makes certain wines special.

To Dan Berger, Don Carano, Bob Foster, Craig Goldwyn, Nancy Johnston, Rebecca Murphy, Rich Thomas, Bill Traverso, Jim Wallace, and Wilfred Wong, my gratitude for repeatedly offering me the opportunity to taste wines in the rigorous atmosphere of major competitions.

To Harolyn Thompson, affectionate thanks for helping me taste almost as much at home as I do at the competitions (and for voicing her own useful opinion in both circumstances).

To Hugh Johnson, a bow for engineering the book's first appearance.

And to Carole Lalli and Kerri Conan, my editors at Simon & Schuster, appreciation for their kindly but unwavering insistence on clarity of thought in every sentence of this third edition.

Foreword

When my publishers asked me to write a book on
California wines as a companion volume to my
Pocket Encyclopedia of Wine I had to answer that it could
not be done from England. Far too much is going on in
California for anyone to follow it in detail from a distance.

There was only one person who I believed could do the
job perfectly: my friend Bob Thompson, who from his home
in the Napa Valley has kept a cool, appraising eye on the
frenetic California wine scene since many of its present pro-
tagonists were under age for tasting.

The following pages speak for themselves. Rely on them
and you will not be disappointed. In using them you will
pick up a thorough working knowledge of the most exciting
wine region in the world.

Hugh Johnson
Essex, England

Introduction

·—————·

Way back, when Hugh Johnson wrote the first *Pocket Encyclopedia of Wine,* he called it an exercise in crowding angels on a pinhead, or students into a telephone box. When the first *Pocket Encyclopedia of California Wines* joined the series in 1980, I said my effort more resembled taking a census in a rabbit warren. By the time of the second edition, 1985, rabbits no longer seemed prolific enough to convey a clear idea of how fast vineyards and wineries were springing up in California.

From the first edition to the second, the winery count increased from 300 to 500. From then to now the number has climbed to 680, maybe 700, and continues to climb. But let us be content with the image with rabbits. There is no point in straining for effect.

While wineries proliferate, the market for wine remains dead flat, or in slight decline. That being the case, why all the new hopefuls, and who are they?

Tastes have changed toward drinking higher-quality wine, but less of it. The audience for jug Burgundy and Chablis is dwindling with age. Old-line makers of run-of-the-mill varietals are losing—or have lost—their support to trendier new names. Annual sales at Almaden Vineyards, for example, dwindled from a peak of more than 13 million cases to fewer than 7 million between 1975 and 1987, when Heublein, Inc. bought it, sold off all its properties, and turned it into a penny-saver brand. The Almaden story has echoes in other quarters.

These shifts have opened the door to scores of new players offering small volumes of prestigious varietal types at lofty prices. A few larger firms offer similar rosters of varietals at rock-bottom prices (the new jug trade, better known as the "fighting varietal" market).

Most of the new names have built wineries to anchor themselves to their dreams. Many more hope to build. (Many new labels belong to moonlighting winemakers with entrepreneurial hopes but not enough cash or cachet to invest in land or a building, and many more belong to vineyardists who hope they have planted in superior ground, but want to defer the cost of a winery until they are surer.) Yet another source of new names is the "second" label. More and more established wineries are working themselves into either higher- or lower-priced segments of the market than their original label attracts by adding a new name.

Newcomers of every stripe have been tempted into the game by the vast number of vineyards planted during the boom years from 1964 through 1980, when wine grapes shot from 129,700 acres to 336,850. (In terms of wine produced, the increase was from 40 million cases a year to 106 million.) Since 1980, plantings have dropped back to 323,500 acres without discouraging new entrants in the field. They are now lured by the opportunity to replant existing vineyards to more marketable varieties. Chardonnay is the prime example. Between 1970 and 1985, when every variety was expanding, its acreage shot from 1,600 to 22,000. Since 1985, Chardonnay has reached 37,000 acres, but these recent increases are at the expense of almost every other variety, red and white. Among reds the story is a bit different. Cabernet Sauvignon plantings increased from 4,000 acres to 22,600 between 1970 and 1985, but have expanded little since. Pinot Noir and Zinfandel have posted the gains in red grapes since 1985, though upward pressure is not tremendous. Red wine accounts for only 14% of all table wine sales these days.

All of this change—one is tempted to say chaos—has created a market situation peculiar to California wine. While arbiters of vinous taste want the certainties of the Classification of 1855 in Bordeaux, they seem to want novelty, more novelty, and nothing but novelty from California. No trend can be too hot, no name too new. Old wineries change their labels, even their names, in bids for attention. Courting such a torrid rate of change comes pretty close to lunacy, considering that it takes a vineyard twenty vintages to show what it will do, and almost that many for a winemaker to settle into his craft.

With logic out the window, conscientious wine merchants present us year after year with shelf after shelf of fresh bewilderment. And year after year the great majority of wine drinkers ignore the arbiters and cling to any old favorite. Good old, sensible old great majority. Wineries endure by making wines that taste good bottle after bottle.

However, there is something to say for not getting completely stuck in the past. If we had all stayed with Dixieland, we would not have heard Duke Ellington, let alone all who have come along since.

On most nights each year I hurry past the new labels in my cellar in favor of an old favorite I know is going to fit my mood and the meal. But it is on those other nights, when my courage is up, that I earn the stunning rewards of discovery. Sometimes they come in the form of novelty, sometimes in the form of a classic reinvented. In short, this book is an express invitation to cling to old favorites much of the time and haunt the frontier during the rest.

All of the opportunities are here. The listings take no pity on those who do not live where the mainstream flows. The newest, tiniest, and most obscure join with the oldest, largest, and most famous. Well, almost all of the chances are here. In the tumult a number of cellars have slipped through the net. Also, regional and local merchant labels do not appear. With few exceptions—mostly winemaker labels—each entry is anchored to property: a winery building, a vineyard, or both.

Except for the following few paragraphs, this guide is as bereft of generalizations as I can make it because generalities are not worth much when it comes to wine. And the sweeping statements that follow are offered only as underpinnings to details in the body of the text.

• On average, I taste and note between 2,000 and 3,000 California wines a year at dinner, at informal tastings, and at formal competitions. Wines that have made consistent impressions are described; wines that have not, are not. The descriptions are, I hope, simple and consistent enough so that other tasters will be able to identify wines of kindred character. No description is meant to be the last word. Winemakers change their minds, their sources of grapes, and their places of employment too often for that. More to the point, each of us tastes every wine a little differently.

• In these changing times, a willful winemaker often matters more than a vineyard does. When an opinionated enologist leaves one cellar behind for another, he or she is apt to continue making wines very similar to the old in whatever new surroundings. At the same time, the successor may do something entirely different with the original property.

• The avalanche of new cellars and vineyards has begotten the beginnings of an appellation system, a recent development in California (and the rest of the United States). These appellations draw close attention throughout the text, though little or nothing is known about many of them. The simple fact is, what we find out about where grapes ought to grow in California will be defined by them, so they might as well be learned. These appellations, dubbed "American Viticultural Areas" by their inventor, the Bureau of Alcohol, Tobacco, and Firearms, are mapped on pages 197–217.

• In thinking about appellations and California, keep one grand generality in mind: Europe is no place to look for a geographic and climatic model for California. A persistent range of mountains runs parallel to California's north-south coast, shutting off the flow of Pacific Ocean air to the interior in all but a few places. These corridors mark the finest growing conditions for distinctive wines whether they are north or south of any reference point. The cool spots where Pinot Noir might turn out well are dotted here and there from Mendocino County south almost all the way to Los Angeles, and these are cheek by jowl with warmer spots better left to Cabernet Sauvignon. In other words, there are no such things as Burgundy and Bordeaux in California. The climatic, and thus vinous, fragmentation caused by these coastal mountains will not go away. It will not even be understood clearly for a long time to come, especially in districts where the oldest vines will not yield their twentieth vintage until the early 1990s.

HOW TO READ ENTRIES

T wo alphabetizing conventions:

- When the winery name is the name of a person, the listing is under the family name (Pradel for Bernard Pradel, etc.).
- When the winery name includes a definite article in a foreign language (La Paloma, etc.), listing is governed by the definite article.

1.	2.	3.	4.

DUGWELL CELLARS Napa T,S $8–$15

1. Winery names are printed in red to separate them from merchant labels, winemaker labels, and grower labels, as well as technical and legal terms. Names so printed indicate the existence of an independent producing winery.

2. County name locates the winery, though not necessarily the vineyards that supply it.

3. D (dessert wine), S (sparkling wine), and T (table wine) indicate classes of wine produced by the winery.

4. $–$ The least- and most-expensive wines, per 750ml bottle, 1989 prices to consumers at the cellar door. The price range shows the relative market position of each winery. Prices elsewhere may vary radically owing to different tax rates in states outside California, or to merchant pricing programs in and out of California. However, what is cheap in the home market should be comparatively cheap in all others.

Not incidentally, each variety of wine has an anchor point at which fine quality may be expected. The anchor points (using 1988–89 cellar door prices) are $10–$14 for Chardonnay, Cabernet Sauvignon, Merlot, and Pinot Noir; $6–$8 for Gewürztraminer, Riesling, and Sauvignon Blanc; and $6–$9 for Petite Sirah, Syrah, and Zinfandel. Chenin Blanc, French Colombard, and modestly characterful generics should fall in the $4–$6.50 range.

1.   2.
→* **Cabernet Sauvignon (herbaceous, supple)** 79 81
83 84.

1. Author's personal assessment of quality and style.
- • Wine untasted, or tasted too seldom to form solid
  opinion.
- * Everyday wine.
- ** Average to above-average wine of its type and
  region.
- *** Excellent wine of its type and region.
- **** Outstanding wine.
- **→*** Approaching next-higher class.
- [ ] Excellent value in its class.
- NYR Not Yet Ranked; fewer than five vintages to as-
  sess.

2. Author's choice of vintages of better-than-average quality for the house in question. Also see general vintage notes
on pages 186–188.

Availability. Embedded in the text of almost every entry is
an annual production figure in cases (of 12 standard bottles). When the federal government repealed Prohibition, it
gave the individual states power to govern commerce in
beverages containing alcohol. In these circumstances every
state is its own sovereign market. One winery will claim
"national distribution" by sending three cases to New York
and two to Chicago, while another will make no such claim
in spite of sending several thousand cases outside California's boundaries. With this in mind, use case volumes to
assume:

- 1,000 cases or less. It is best to live close to the cellar or
  know its owner.
- 5,000 cases. It helps to live in California, but a handful of
  stores in the top ten metropolitan wine markets are likely
  to have small rations.
- 10,000 cases. Most major urban centers in states without
  severe impediments to wine sales will have at least one
  stellar merchant with supplies.
- 20,000 cases. In states with active wine audiences, a few
  skilled merchants beyond the major urban markets may
  be expected to stock at least some types from a winery's
  list.
- 40,000 cases. Most states with active wine audiences will
  have limited to good supplies in most cities and some
  outlying areas.
- 100,000 to 500,000 cases. Wines are almost sure to be
  available even in the most regressive government-
  monopoly states, and they will surely be available in all
  the rest.
- 1 million cases or more. There is enough for everybody.

LEARNING FROM THE LABEL

United States law demands that labels carry a useful minimum of information about the wine in the bottle; voluntary disclosure by wineries often tells a great deal more.

1. Brand. Mandatory. The single most important clue to quality and style, though in cases of wineries with several brands it must be compared with the bottler's name (*see* 7).

2. Wine type. Mandatory. Basic possibilities are varietal and generic. By law varietal wine must be a minimum 75% of the grape variety giving it its name (51% for wines bottled before 1983). Though most fine wines have a higher proportion, it is a mistake to assume that 100% automatically makes the best wine. Most varieties can gain by discreet blending. A whole class of proprietary (coined) names on extremely expensive wines based in Cabernet Sauvignon is one clear demonstration of this point. Generic names impose no requirements as to grape variety and only very dim ones as to style or character. This does not stop excellent wines from being offered under generic names, but does make useful generalizations difficult. There are also proprietary names for inexpensive wines otherwise qualified to be generics.

3. Specific character. Optional. Several label terms modify types to indicate color, degree of sweetness, or other qualities. Definitions are in the A–Z. For table wines: Late-harvest, Dry, Off-dry. For sparkling wines: Natural, Brut, Extra Dry, Sec. For sherry types: Dry, Cocktail, Golden, Cream. For port types: Ruby, Tawny, Vintage.

4. Region of origin. Mandatory. Several layers of names are in current use. Most general is California; to use it, state law requires 100% of the grapes to be grown in California. Traditionally, counties have been the most-used smaller unit; federal law requires a minimum 75% of the grapes in a wine to have been grown within the county named. Increasingly, federally approved American Viticultural Areas are supplanting county appellations; to use one of these, federal law requires 75% of the grapes to have grown within the AVA and that the minimum 75% varietal requirement be from the given AVA. Most AVAs fall within the larger boundaries of a single county; a few overlap the boundary between two counties. All current AVAs are listed with the maps, pages 197–217, and described in the text.

5. Individual vineyard. Optional. Augments the AVA system. Properties may be owned by the winery or an individual grower. Federal law requires that 95% of the grapes in a vineyard-designated wine come from that vineyard, and that the vineyard be within an AVA also identified on the label (*see* 4). A less precise alternative is "Estate Bottled," which may be used for all vineyards owned or controlled by a winery and lying within the same AVA as the winery itself.

6. Vintage. Optional. States the year in which the grapes were grown (and generally, the year in which the wine fermented). If used, federal law requires 95% of the wine to come from the stated year. The allowance permits practical topping of casks during the aging.

7. Bottler. Mandatory. Small type at the bottom of a label must give the name of the bottler and the bottler's business (not necessarily winery) location. The line may say "bottled by," in which case the firm could buy wine one day and bottle it the next. "Cellared and bottled by" (or similar) indicates that the bottler has blended or done similar— sometimes invaluable—work to put his stamp on the wine. "Made and bottled by" can be used if the bottler fermented a minimum 10% of the wine in the bottle. "Produced and bottled by" may be used only if the bottler fermented a minimum 75% of the wine. "Grown, produced and bottled by" guarantees complete control of 100% of the wine from vineyard to corker.

8. Alcohol content. Mandatory. The legal limits for table wine are 7% to 14%. The alcohol can be stated as a percentage of volume, with a permitted allowance of 1.5% above or below the actual content, or the words "table wine" or "light wine" can appear instead. If the alcohol content exceeds 14%, that figure or the exact volume must be given. For sherry types the alcohol limits are 17% to 20%, and for port types 18% to 20%, with a permitted allowance of 1% from actual.

9. Sparkling wine. If the word "champagne" appears on a label, it must be accompanied somewhere on the package by a statement noting the exact technique used to produce the effervescence. These include *méthode champenoise* ("*méthode champenoise*" or "fermented in this bottle"); transfer process ("bottle fermented" or "fermented in the bottle"); and Charmat process ("bulk process" or "Charmat process"). Descriptions of the processes are in the A–Z.

10. Contains sulfites. Mandatory. Advisory directed to certain severe asthmatics who suffer allergic reactions to these sulfur-based compounds.

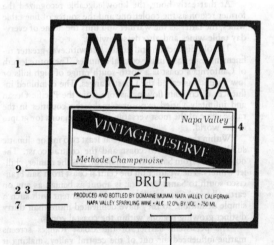

CALIFORNIA WINE DISTRICTS

————•————

The map shows every California county with more than 1,000 acres of grapes, or ten wineries or more. Most qualify on both counts, but a few on only one or the other.

As a quick glance shows, vineyards are pervasive everywhere save in the rainy north coast, the mountainous interior, and the desert south.

The state is far from one piece. By the 1880s, scholars and growers alike had divided California into its two main vineyard regions: the coastal counties and the central valley.

At that early hour, the knowledgeable recognized the former region as the cooler one and the source of fine table wines, the latter as the warmer and thus the home of everyday table wines and also dessert wines.

The old distinction still holds, but with ever-greater refinement, especially in the coastal counties. The entire length of California's coast is a north-south range of high hills or low mountains called the Coast Ranges. The combined influences of cool air flowing ashore from the Pacific Ocean and infinitely varied exposures make the counties in the range some of the most versatile growing regions for grapes in the world.

Within the coast counties are at least two major climatic subdivisions, the north coast and the central coast. The north coast, from San Francisco north, has the rainier, chillier winters. The weather on the central coast from San Francisco south to Santa Barbara, is about as benign as any on earth all year. Growers have not been content with such a simple definition, so they have delineated more than thirty distinct growing regions within the coastal zones.

The persistent barrier of the Coast Ranges screens marine-influenced air out of the central valley, making it reliably warm and dry from end to end. A comparatively few distinct viticultural districts have been identified in this more homogenous zone.

More detailed maps on pages 197–217 cover all the major growing regions. With these maps are lists of wineries for quick reference.

A–Z OF CALIFORNIA WINE

ACACIA Napa T $15–$24
Acacia set out in 1979 to make its name on Carneros Chardonnays and Pinot Noirs. The original partnership was well on the way to its goal when, in 1986, its members sold the label and a winery built in 1981 to Chalone, Inc. The new owner has kept the original focus, including several individual-vineyard bottlings. Annual production averages 25,000 cases, the planned level.
*** Pinot Noir–Iund Vineyard (firmly varietal but also well marked by new oak flavors, slow to mature); Pinot Noir–St. Clair Vineyard (ditto as Iund and in more plentiful supply); Pinot Noir–Madonna Vineyard (fleshier, a shade more forward than Iund and St. Clair); Pinot Noir–Carneros District (ditto as the Madonna) 82 84 85.
** Chardonnay-Carneros, Chardonnay–Marina Vineyard (both markedly woody, often a bit harsh in youth). Also: Vin de Lies (the bargain, meant for quick consumption).

ADELAIDA CELLARS San Luis Obispo T $8–$10
With grapes from their 10-acre vineyard in the westerly hills of Paso Robles AVA, plus others purchased from independent growers nearby, owner/winemakers John and Andree Munch produce 4,500 cases a year of just two wines. The first vintage: 81.
[**] Cabernet Sauvignon (typical varietal flavors but unusually soft, forward).
** Chardonnay (ripe, quickly mature).

ADLER-FELS Sonoma T,S $7–$18
At a hilltop hideaway just n. of the Sonoma Valley, David Coleman and Ayn Ryan buy only Sonoma grapes to produce 7,000 cases of wine per year. The label began with a 79 Napa Cabernet, a type since dropped; the winery dates from 1981.
** Chardonnay–Nelson Vineyard (uneven; appealingly varietal in 83 84); Sauvignon Blanc (full of Sonoma grass flavors; steady); Gewürztraminer; Mélange à Deux (ripely fruity but bone-dry, champagne-method blend of Riesling, Gewürztraminer).
NYR: Pinot Noir (added with 82; thus far quite uncertain).

AHERN WINERY Los Angeles T $7.50–$10
Since 1978, Jim Ahern has drawn primarily upon San Luis
Obispo vineyards to produce always steady, sometimes dis-
tinctive wines at his cellars in the San Fernando Valley.
Current production is 6,200 cases a year.
*** Edna Valley Chardonnay (toasty style, richly flavored).
** Paso Robles Chardonnay; Paso Robles Sauvignon
Blanc; Paso Robles and Temecula Cabernet Sauvignons, and
Paso Robles and Amador Zinfandel.

AHLGREN VINEYARDS Santa Cruz Mountains T
$9–$13.50 Dexter and Valerie Ahlgren make 1,800 cases
per year at their winery in Boulder Creek. Once split between Napa and Central Coast grapes of half a dozen varieties, the roster has more recently been narrowed to three
varietal types, all from bought-in Central Coast grapes. The
first vintage was 76.
** Monterey (Ventana Vineyard) and Santa Cruz Mountain Chardonnays; Santa Cruz Mountain and Santa Clara
Cabernet Sauvignons, and California Semillon (all husky,
well-wooded).

ALDERBROOK VINEYARDS Sonoma T
$6.50–$9.75 A swiftly rising star with all three of its
white wines, all from Dry Creek and Russian River Valley
vineyards anchored by 55 partner-owned acres adjoining
the cellars at Healdsburg. Production is about 18,000 cases
per year on the way to 30,000; the first vintage was 82.
[***] Chardonnay (splendidly specific varietal; off-dry in
85 but usually dry) 84 86 87; Semillon (understated, firmly
textured, ever more complex with bottle age) 83 84 85 86
87; and Sauvignon Blanc (lean, almost austere) 84 85 86 87.

ALEATICO
A little-planted black grape closely resembling some of the
dark-skinned Muscats, and rarely, its varietal wine. Acreage
in California is down to 54, most of it in Tulare and San
Bernardino counties. One tiny patch in Sonoma yields a
varietal wine for Trentadue.

ALEXANDER VALLEY AVA
Encompasses the Russian River drainage from Sonoma
County's n. boundary down to Healdsburg, then s. and e.
beyond that town. Versatile growing conditions—Sonoma's
warmest—encourage Cabernet Sauvignon, Sauvignon
Blanc, and Zinfandel, and permit Chardonnay, Gewürztraminer, and Riesling, especially late-harvest styles of the latter two. Most of the vineyards lie within the river's flood
plain between Cloverdale and Healdsburg, but the e. hills
support some vineyards important for their acreage, their
quality, or both. Plantings exceed 6,500 acres; a score of
wineries lie within its boundaries.

ALEXANDER VALLEY FRUIT & TRADING CO.
Sonoma T $6–$10 Sound, fetchingly rustic varietal
wines come from the 12,000-case winery of Steve and
Candy Somers, most of them from the family-owned, 40-
acre vineyard surrounding the cellar, the Sauvignon Blanc
and Chenin Blanc from a neighbor. The first vintage was 82.

NYR: Cabernet Sauvignon (spot-on herbaceous flavors); Zinfandel (a shade lighter than most); White Zinfandel; Sauvignon Blanc (purely varietal); and Chenin Blanc.

ALEXANDER VALLEY VINEYARDS Sonoma T
$6–$12 Due e. of Healdsburg, the 60,000-case winery and rolling 250-acre vineyard of the Henry Wetzel family have gained steadily in critical appraisals since the first vintage, 75. Production has climbed to 50,000 cases, the capacity of the vineyard. This drove the owners to buy grapes from neighbors for the first time in 1988 and will likely lead to separate estate and nonestate bottlings of Cabernet Sauvignon and Chardonnay from the 88s onward.

[***] Cabernet Sauvignon (dark, firm to hard, full of berry aromas young; able to age into rich older wine, especially from cooler vintages) 78 79 81 84 85.

→* Chardonnay (for years leaner and tarter than its region promises; vintages from 86 onward suggest a drift toward a riper, fuller style) 81 83 84 87.

** Johannisberg Riesling (fat, soft); Gewürztraminer (same vein as JR); and Dry Chenin Blanc (well-wooded).

NYR: Pinot Noir (dark, tannic, heady); Merlot (still tiny production but programmed to grow as new vines mature); and Zinfandel (new with 85, as a replacement for earlier heady monster called Sin Zin).

ALICANTE BOUSCHET
Black grape and its varietal wine. Little planted now—almost half of the 2,850 acres are in Fresno County—it was prized for its inexhaustible color and tough skin by Prohibition-era home winemakers, who could get 600 gallons per ton by macerating the skins over and over with sugared water. However, the wine's tendency to fade in color and its common flavors have seldom charmed commercial vintners. It is rarely offered as a varietal.

ALMADEN Madera T $3.50–$6
One of California's most famous historic names is wearing an almost completely new face these days. Heublein, Inc. bought the name in 1987, moved winery operations to Madera, and sold off or abandoned the previous owner's three wineries and 5,800 acres of grapes in Monterey, San Benito, and Santa Clara counties. As a historic winery, Almaden's oldest roots in the Santa Clara Valley go back as far as 1852. Wines of the old regime say "produced and bottled at San Jose" at the foot of their labels; those from the new era have California appellation and say "produced and bottled at Madera."

NYR: Cabernet Sauvignon, Chardonnay, Sauvignon Blanc, Riesling, Chenin Blanc, French Colombard, Grenache Rosé, White Barbera, White Zinfandel, Zinfandel, White and Red.

ALTA VINEYARDS Napa T $8–$12
When Benjamin Falk sold the winery and vineyard he started in 1979 to Schramsberg, he kept the label and continued to make wine in leased space. Currently Falk and winemaker Jon Axhelm buy Napa and Knights Valley grapes to make 2,000 cases a year.

** Napa Chardonnay.

NYR: Knights Valley Sauvignon Blanc (deft new-wood note in 85). Napa Gamay may rejoin the roster with an 89.

ALTAMURA VINEYARDS Napa T $15
A family-owned, 2,000-case winery and 60-acre vineyard near Stag's Leap began as a specialist in Chardonnay with an 85. The Altamuras were planning to add a Cabernet Sauvignon after crushing about 800 cases of that variety in 88.
NYR: Chardonnay (first effort well-wooded, quite buttery).

AMADOR FOOTHILL Amador T $5.25–$9
Owner/winemakers Ben Zeitman and Katie Quinn use their own 10 acres and bought-in Shenandoah Valley and Fiddletown grapes to make 12,000 cases a year, some of the Zinfandels vineyard-designated. Zeitman's first vintage was 80.
** Zinfandel, Zinfandel–Grand père, Zinfandel Eschen (all hearty, heady, from old vines.)
*→** Fumé Blanc (typical Amador floral perfumes, weighty) and White Zinfandel.
NYR: Cabernet Sauvignon (tiny bit from own 4-acre patch).

AMERICAN VITICULTURAL AREA (AVA)
A fledgling system of appellations of origin is administered by the Federal Bureau of Alcohol, Tobacco, and Firearms. AVAs set physical boundaries and require that 75% of a wine carrying an AVA name must be of fruit grown within the prescribed region. The rules impose no limits on varieties that may be grown or on characteristics of the resulting grapes or wines. The more than 55 approved for California to date are listed in this book under their individual names.

AMIZETTA Napa T $16
A 3,000-case grower/producer specializing in Cabernet Sauvignon from 20 estate acres in hills above Lake Hennessy, e. of St. Helena. The winery made its first public appearance with an 84 Sauvignon Blanc but has dropped that variety to concentrate on the red.
NYR: Cabernet Sauvignon (85 86 distractingly minty).

ANDERSON VALLEY AVA
Mendocino County's westernmost AVA follows the cool, fog-beset course of the Navarro River from the town of Boonville w. to the hamlet called Navarro. Within it grow 1,200 acres of grapes. Gewürztraminer and Chardonnay have performed particularly well since modern-era planting began in the early to mid-1970s; Pinot Noir and White Riesling come up to nearly the same level; the characteristic tartness of Chardonnay and Pinot Noir grown in the region has given great hope for sparkling wines. High up the valley's w. hills are some splendidly flavorful patches of Zinfandel. A dozen mostly small to tiny producers make wine here.

ANDERSON VINEYARDS, S. Napa T,S
$12.50–$18 The proprietors of a 32-acre vineyard e. of Oakville make an estate Chardonnay and blend their own grapes with Chardonnay and Pinot Noir bought from neigh-

bors for champagne-method sparklers. The debut vintage: 80. Current production nears 15,000 cases per year. The figure will go up as a 68-acre Carneros ranch purchased in 1988 comes into play.
→* vintage Brut (boldly flavored to slightly rough-hewn and full-bodied to outsized); vintage Blanc de Noir (even bigger than the Brut).
** Tivoli (nonvintage, mostly press-wine, outmuscles both of its running mates and yet manages to charm as much or more.) Chardonnay (big, ripe, woody, toasty).

ANDERSON WINE CELLARS Tulare T
$3.99–$7.99 A family-owned winery near the town of Visalia. Its owners make 2,000 cases of wine a year, the Colombard from their own vines, the Ruby Cabernets from a neighbor's, and the Chardonnay from bought-in fruit, typically from Monterey. Sales are almost entirely at the tasting room.
NYR: French Colombard, Chardonnay, Ruby Cabernet Blush, and Ruby Cabernet.

ANDRÉ
Label for E. & J. GALLO–produced Charmat sparkling wines.

ANGELICA
The oldest name for California-produced dessert wine pays tribute to Los Angeles, where the type was first produced by Franciscan missionaries in the early 1800s. Early commercial bottlings were a now-illegal blend of fresh grape juice and brandy patterned after the commonest style of wine made in the missions. Since the repeal of Prohibition, nearly all wines thus named have been made in much the same way as cream sherry, many of them from Muscat grapes. Some of the well-aged, intelligently blended examples have been memorable. A dwindling number of traditionalists still offer Angelicas to a shrinking population of cognoscenti.

ARCIERO WINERY San Luis Obispo T $4.50–$8.50
The Arciero family built a 150,000-case cellar in 1984 to make wine from 525 acres (soon to be 700) of estate vineyards. Arciero's plantings—most of them still coming to maturity—scatter in several parcels across rolling grasslands e. of Paso Robles. Production nears 60,000 cases.
NYR: Chenin Blanc, Sauvignon Blanc, Chardonnay, White Zinfandel, Cabernet Sauvignon, Nebbiolo, Petite Sirah, and Zinfandel (thus far, all agreeable middle-of-the-roaders).

ARGONAUT WINERY Amador T $5–$6
A tiny winery, run by a partnership of eight, makes only reds from Sierra-foothills grapes, primarily for local sale. The first vintage was 76; the 1,000-case volume will not expand until one of the principals retires from other work.
*→** Barbera, Syrah, Zinfandel (all husky, heady in the Sierra-foothills tradition).

ARROWOOD WINERY & VINEYARDS Sonoma T
$17–$20 The longtime winemaker at Chateau St. Jean has established his own winery and vineyard near the Sonoma Valley town of Glen Ellen while continuing in his

old job just a mile or two up the road. Richard Arrowood's winery went up in 1987, but his debut Chardonnay comes from 86, and his inaugural Cabernet Sauvignon from 85. Both are blended from several vineyards belonging to independent Sonoma growers. Initial volume is 8,000 cases; the goal is 15,000.
NYR: Chardonnay (understated fruit, firm textures); Cabernet Sauvignon (conventionally styled first vintage).

ARROYO SECO AVA
Centered on the town of Greenfield is a randomly shaped, fog-cooled, windblown, seldom-rainy sub-AVA of MONTEREY. Nearly all of it lies on valley floor between the Salinas River and hills to the e., but a skinny arm runs into hills w. of the voluminous but almost completely underground Salinas River. The district contains fewer than half a dozen wineries but nearly 8,500 acres of grapes, all planted since 1972. White Riesling has surpassed other varieties, but Chardonnay, Pinot Blanc, and Gewürztraminer do ever better as growers learn to deal with the local climate's curious demands.

ARROYO WINERY, VINCENT   Napa T $5.75–$10.50
A grower/producer with 60 acres near Calistoga, Arroyo launched his estate label with three reds from 84 and a white from 85. Current production is 1,200 cases.
NYR: Chardonnay (big, well marked by wood); Cabernet Sauvignon (big, rustic, thunderously oaky 84); Petite Sirah (ditto); and Gamay Noir.

ARTHUR VINEYARDS, DAVID   Napa T $13
On the same hill as Chappellet and Long Vineyards, this family winery was a newcomer with the vintage of 85. The only wine is an estate Chardonnay; current production is 2,500 cases; the vineyard's potential is 6,000.
NYR: Chardonnay.

ASHLY   Santa Clara T $16.50
The partnership leases space to make an annual 1,000 cases of Monterey Chardonnay. The first vintage: 84.
NYR: Chardonnay (to date, dark-gold, ultratoasty heavyweight).

ATLAS PEAK VINEYARDS   Napa ·T $?
Under development by Great Britain's Whitbread, Italy's Antinori, and France's Bollinger is a 300-acre vineyard high up on Atlas Park, and an estate winery tunneled into the same hill e. of Napa city. The firm has crushed some trial lots, but the earliest possible release date for any wine is 1991. The winemaker is Dr. Richard Peterson (ex-Monterey Vineyard). The roster of wines may include one of California's few varietal Sangioveses to date but will be anchored in a Cabernet Sauvignon–based red, a Sauvignon Blanc–Semillon blend, and a Chardonnay.

AU BON CLIMAT   Santa Barbara T $13–$25
Partners Adam Tolmach and James Clendenen make 5,000 cases per year of the great Burgundian varietals, both from bought-in Santa Barbara grapes. Of late they have been working on the run after a rented winery near Los Alamos

was bought out from under them before their new one on the Bien Nacido Vineyard was ready; they made the 89s in their permanent home. Their first vintage was 79.

→** Chardonnay (definitely of the toasty school); Reserve Chardonnay (the regular only more so; to come from Benedict Vineyard from 87 onward); Pinot Noir (complex with fruit, wood; has been its most attractive early).

NYR: Pinot Noir–Benedict Vineyard (starts with 88); Pinot Noir–Bien Nacido Vineyard (also starts with 88).

AUDUBON CELLARS Alameda T $4.50–$13.50
The winery is the outgrowth of a label designed to raise funds to preserve wildlife, first used on 84s. Audubon became the whole identity of the Berkeley winery after a 1987 change of ownership. Under the direction of Hubertus von Wulffen, all of the grapes are bought-in from Napa, Sonoma, and San Luis Obispo counties. Yearly volume: 30,000 cases.

NYR: Sonoma Chardonnay–Sangiacomo (attractively rich 86); Sonoma Chardonnay–Wilson (just off the pace of its sibling); Napa Sauvignon Blanc–Pope Vineyards; Napa Cabernet Sauvignon; San Luis Obispo Zinfandel; Pinot Noir Blanc; blanc and rouge.

AUSTIN CELLARS Santa Barbara T $4–$25
After several vintages at Firestone Vineyards, brash Tony Austin opened his own winery in 1981 and forthwith set out to define the styles of Santa Barbara wines for himself and his peers. Austin has not done that, but it has achieved some intriguing results. Thus far all of his wines have come from bought-in Santa Barbara grapes; an estate vineyard is in the works in rolling country not far from his original employer's vines. The production goal is 20,000 cases.

→** Pinot Noir (variable; at its best an enticing synthesis of varietal, regional, and wood flavors) 83 84; Botrytised Sauvignon Blanc (rich in flavor and texture alike, and able to age to greater complexity than the early flavors promise) 84 86.

** Sauvignon Blanc (well off-dry, definitively vegetative); Gewürztraminer (also off-dry, perfumey), and Chardonnay.

BABCOCK VINEYARD Santa Barbara T $6–$16
A 40-acre, family-owned ranch on s.-facing slopes in the lower Santa Ynez Valley was first planted to vines in 1979. The label began with an 83 Johannisberg Riesling made in leased space; a permanent cellar went up in time for the 84s. Production is at 7,000 cases, all from estate grapes.

NYR: Johannisberg Riesling (usually off-dry but some dry, barrel-fermented lots); Gewürztraminer (same program as Riesling); Sauvignon Blanc; Chardonnay (regular and reserve bottlings); and Pinot Noir. All steady, sound.

BAILY VINEYARD Temecula T $6–$10
Phil and Carol Baily grow Riesling and buy local grapes for the rest of their annual 1,800 cases. The first vintage: 86.

NYR: White Riesling (dry and off-dry); Chardonnay; Sauvignon Blanc; Late Harvest Sauvignon Blanc; Muscat Blanc; White Cabernet; and Cabernet Sauvignon–Nouveau.

BALDINELLI VINEYARD Amador T $5–$7.65
One of a very few estate wineries in the Shenandoah Valley draws on 70 gently sloped acres just e. of Plymouth, more than half of them Zinfandel planted in the 1920s, the rest Cabernet Sauvignon and Sauvignon Blanc planted in 1972. Ed Baldinelli's first crush was 79; annual production has since quadrupled to 16,000 cases.
→* Zinfandel (big but balanced and polished) 80 83.
** Cabernet Sauvignon (burly, conventional); Sauvignon Blanc (typically ripe, weighty); White Zinfandel (off-dry, pleasantly fruity).
NYR: Reserve Zinfandel (gigantic in its 86 debut).

BALLARD CANYON Santa Barbara T $5.75–$12
The 10,000-case winery of Dr. Gene Hallock and family draws on their 45 rolling acres n. of Solvang for every variety except Sauvignon Blanc. From the first wines, 78s, there has been a proclivity toward sweetness and light. In 1988 the winery established a series called Candlelight for less expensive wines sold only in 1.5-liter bottles.
** Johannisberg Riesling (soft, off-dry, appealingly flavored); Muscat Canelli (same vein as Riesling); Chardonnay (sound, reliable); Chardonnay–Dr.'s Fun Baby (the sweet edition); Fumé Blanc (strongly varietal and well off-dry, dropping into "Candlelight Series" jug line as of 1989); Rosalie (originally Rosalie's Blushing Brunch, a sweet, pink wine from Cabernet); Cabernet Sauvignon (pungently vegetative in the regional way).

BALLATORE
The name of an outstanding sparkling muscat by E. & J. GALLO.

BALLING
The prevailing measure of sugar and thus potential alcohol in grapes corrects errors in the BRIX scale; the latter, however, remains the commonly used name.

BALVERNE VINEYARDS Sonoma T $6–$12
On the lower slopes of Chalk Hill, in the Chalk Hill AVA, the 200-acre vineyard and 20,000-case winery has focused ever more sharply since its founding. The first wines were 80s. Since then Johannisberg Riesling, the proprietary Healdsburger (Riesling and Gewürztraminer), and an off-beat German varietal called Scheurebe have been rooted out of the white wine roster; Zinfandel is the red casualty.
** Chardonnay (has had ups and downs, but splendidly understated and balanced for long life in its finest year, 81); Gewürztraminer (dry, fully flavored); Sauvignon Blanc (at times melony-ripe, at other times intensely herbaceous); Cabernet Sauvignon (has tended toward the dark and tannic).

BANDIERA Sonoma T $4–$7
The name goes back to the repeal of Prohibition, when it was a family-owned small cellar at Cloverdale. An investment group called CALIFORNIA WINE CORPORATION bought the property in 1981, swiftly enlarging the cellar to its current

175,000-case capacity. The grapes come primarily from leased vineyards in Sonoma County and Napa's Chiles Valley.

*→** Chardonnay, Fumé Blanc, White Zinfandel, Cabernet Sauvignon.

BARBERA

A black grape with origins in Italy's Piedmont, and its varietal wine. Of 13,400 acres, almost 12,000 are planted in the San Joaquin Valley, where the reliably acidic variety has its main role as a backbone of jug red wines, but sometimes appears in low tannin, off-dry varietals. A few acres of Barbera grow in the coastal counties, where the style is dry, wood-aged wine meant to be long-lived. Barbera wines produced in the coastal counties often have a proportion of Petite Sirah for the extra dollop of tannin and the extra layer of flavor.

BARBERONE

An almost-disappeared name of generic red wine based in Barbera and styled after its lower-priced forms.

BAREFOOT CELLARS

The label goes on wines somewhere between merchant and winery-produced, but made for the price conscious in any case. Volume reached 150,000 cases in 1989, and is programmed to go to 400,000. The mostly Sonoma-appellation, $3.99–$4.99 roster includes Sauvignon Blanc, Cabernet Sauvignon, and Napa Gamay Blush.

BARENGO VINEYARDS

Long a source of distinctive Lodi-district reds, the name survives on Ruby Cabernet and dessert wines sold only at Dino Barengo's original cellar, now LOST HILLS WINERY.

BARGETTO'S SANTA CRUZ WINERY Santa Cruz
T, S, D $5–$17 A family-owned winery in Soquel offers a broad range of conventionally styled wines from grapes bought increasingly in the Santa Cruz Mountains, but also elsewhere. The label dates from the end of Prohibition; current production of grape wines is about 30,000 cases.

** Santa Cruz Mountains Chardonnay, Gewürztraminer, White Zinfandel, Napa Cabernet Sauvignon, Santa Cruz Mountains Cabernet Sauvignon, Pinot Noir, white and red table wine.

BARON & KOLB San Luis Obispo T $6–$7.50
Retired Los Angeles fire chiefs Thomas Baron and James Kolb built a winery in the Paso Robles AVA in time to make 86s. Production pushes 7,000 cases a year, all from local grapes.

NYR: Chardonnay, Muscat Canelli, Sauvignon Blanc, White Zinfandel, Cabernet Sauvignon, Firehouse Red and White.

BARREL-FERMENTED

A self-explanatory technique meant to induce early complexity in white wines, especially Chardonnay but also Sauvignon Blanc. In a few instances it is done with Chenin Blanc and French Colombard, and even more rarely with Rieslings and Traminers. Its use is sometimes noted on labels.

BATES WINERY, WILLIAM
A new-in-1989 label for $3.50–$4 Chardonnay, White Zinfandel, and White Grenache produced by The Wine Group at its Franzia winery. All are vintage-dated.

BAY CELLARS   Alameda   T $9–$18
One of Berkeley's ever-evolving roster of downtown wineries belongs to Carole and Richard Rotblatt, who buy most of their grapes in Napa, but some in San Luis Obispo. Production is at 2,000 cases; the first vintage was 82.
NYR: Napa Chardonnay, Napa Cabernet Sauvignon, Carneros Pinot Noir, and Paso Robles Syrah.

BEAULIEU VINEYARD   Napa   T,D $6–$26
One of Napa's grandest old names, dating from the turn of the century, has seldom been far from the front ranks in all that time, especially for its Cabernet Sauvignons. The winery and label were founded by Frenchman Georges de Latour and remained in his family's hands until 1969, when Heublein, Inc. bought both. The winery draws on Heublein-owned and controlled vineyards throughout the Napa Valley, supplementing these with grapes from independent growers under long-term contract. The company is shy about revealing volume of production, but educated guesses put the figure between 350,000 and 400,000 cases.
**** Cabernet Sauvignon–Georges de Latour (named for the founder, produced from one or both of two well-proven vineyards at the heart of the Rutherford Bench, hallmarked both by varietal and American oak flavors, among the very finest for aging in recent vintages) 79 81 82 83 84 85.
*** Rutherford Cabernet Sauvignon (in the same style as the de Latour, but not so firmly tannic or so deeply flavored as the senior partner) 81 82 84 85 86; Sauvignon Blanc (crisp, firm textures match with rich, ripe flavors of the grape in a wine deliberately kept away from oak; at its finest with white fish but versatile at the table) 84 85 87 88; Muscat de Frontignan (a dessert wine, perhaps a bit rough with youth, but sturdy and age-worthy).
→* Carneros Chardonnay (starts out understated to neutral, then gains richness and intensity with two to three years in bottle; Carneros Pinot Noir (sound, steady, beginning to show distinctive style).
** Cabernet Sauvignon–Beautour (simple, styled for early drinking); Chardonnay (plain, agreeable); Johannisberg Riesling; Chablis; Pinot Noir; Burgundy; Gamay.

BEL ARBORS
This good-value second label (originally Bel Arbres) of Fetzer Vineyards has served various purposes. In recent years it has been dedicated to a list of blush wines, but in 1988 was returning to a broader line of $3–$5 varietals including Chardonnay and Fumé Blanc.

BELLE CREEK RANCH   Butte   T $7.50–$15

Proprietor Jim Bowman thinks he has the smallest winery in California—and at 200 to 400 cases a year he could be right. He makes wine from his own tiny vineyard in the town of Paradise and unfermented juice bought from a winery at Lodi. His first vintage was 86.
NYR: Cabernet Sauvignon and Zinfandel.

BELLEROSE VINEYARD   Sonoma T $7–$16
Charles Richard has set himself to the task of producing quality copies of French wines using grapes from his plowed-by-horses, 52-acre vineyard in Dry Creek Valley just w. of Healdsburg. Richard started with a Cabernet Sauvignon 79 that may still be his most memorable wine. Current production: 6,000 cases.
** Cuvée Bellerose (a proprietary, Cabernet-based blend that has been changeable with the seasons); Merlot (softer echo of the flagship); Sauvignon Blanc (a bit rustic).
NYR: Workhorse Red (less pricey Cabernet-based blend from the home vineyard introduced with an 81).

BELVEDERE WINE CO.   Sonoma   T $3.15–$13
A partnership directed by Peter Friedman produces 250,000 cases of wine a year in two distinctly separate price ranges. The top-of-the-line Grapemaker series is all from designated vineyards in Sonoma and Napa, save for a Carneros Chardonnay; the less costly Discovery series is blended from made and bought wines from throughout the coast counties and is far the larger partner by volume.
** Alexander Valley Cabernet Sauvignon–Robert Young (a bit sturdier than most from its AVA); Russian River Valley Chardonnay–Bacigalupi (ripe, well-wooded, sometimes a bit heady); Carneros Chardonnay (new with 86 but lean, firm, if it follows its predecessor from Winery Lake vineyard); Pinot Noir–Bacigalupi (an exact echo of its white cousin from the same vineyard).
[**] Discovery Chardonnay (Sonoma); Sauvignon Blanc (Sonoma); Cabernet Sauvignon (Lake); White Zinfandel (California); white table wine and red table wine (both Sonoma). All sound, quite steady.

BENZIGER OF GLEN ELLEN   Sonoma   T $8–$17
Wines under the new-in-1988 Benziger label used to be the flagships for Glen Ellen Vineyards, but had to find a new identity when the latter label became synonymous with inexpensive commodity bottlings. The label began with 86s from Sonoma County, mostly Sonoma Valley grapes, the Cabernet estate-bottled from the Benziger's 40 acres at the winery in hills w. of the town of Glen Ellen. Rankings carry over from earlier vintages under the Glen Ellen name; the volume is a drop in the 3.8-million-case Glen Ellen bucket.
*** Fumé Blanc (richly varietal, balanced, polished) 86 87 88.
→* Estate Cabernet Sauvignon (supple, distinctly herbaceous) 85 86; Sonoma County Cabernet Sauvignon (not as richly flavored as the estate bottling, but close); and Chardonnay (polished, focused on fruit) 87.
NYR: Semillon, Muscat Canelli, Merlot, and Pinot Noir.

BERGFELD 1885   Napa   T $3–$13
The first wines under this still-developing premium label for best-of-the-house varietals from the Napa Valley Cooperative Winery are 85s. As of early 1989, about 7,000 cases of wine were in Bergfeld bottles, still being sold only at the winery. The plan is to work slowly into the national market. The co-op has been in existence since the end of Prohibition, but this is its first try at bottled wines for retail sale. The name, incidentally, comes from the first winery built on the s. St. Helena site now occupied by the co-op, and its founding date.
NYR: Chardonnay, Sauvignon Blanc, Semillon, Merlot, Pinot Noir, white table wine. Cabernet Sauvignon is a likely addition before 1990 runs its course.

BERINGER VINEYARD   Napa   T $5–$35
One of Napa's grand old names from pre-Prohibition times is almost certainly at the peak of its fame now. Founded in 1881 by a pair of brothers from Rhineland, the winery had a good run before 1914, and another one under the second generation's direction during the 1940s. However, it faded physically and in reputation throughout the 1950s and 1960s. The revival began in 1969 when Nestlé, Inc. took over. The company has developed more than 1,000 acres of prime vineyard in the Napa Valley, and another 500 in neighboring Knights Valley just across the Sonoma line n. of Calistoga. These properties supply nearly all of the grapes for Beringer's 250,000 cases of premium varietals; bought-in grapes go into almost 2 million cases of White Zinfandel and Chenin Blanc. NAPA RIDGE is a second label. Other Nestlé, Inc. wineries are CHÂTEAU SOUVERAIN and MERIDIAN.
***   Chardonnay–Private Reserve (dark gold and toasty until 86, now paler and more focused on fruit flavors) 81 84 85 86; Cabernet Sauvignon–Private Reserve (based in grapes from Lemmon Ranch and State Lane Vineyard, always dark, faintly cedary, built to last) 78 79 81 83 85.
→*   Chardonnay Estate (less rich than Reserve, but set the style for it); Cabernet Sauvignon–Lemmon Ranch (softer, more understated than Reserve); Cabernet Sauvignon–Knights Valley (wonderfully supple for early drinking, rich with Cabernet flavors); Napa Fumé Blanc (sturdy, age-worthy); Knights Valley Sauvignon Blanc (softer, quicker to mature than the Napa Fumé); Gewürztraminer (underrated . . . superior varietal after three years) 80 85 87 88.
**   Dry French Colombard; Chenin Blanc; Gamay Beaujolais; White Zinfandel.
NYR: Zinfandel.

BIANCHI VINEYARDS   Fresno   T $2.99–$4.99
From small beginnings in 1974, Joseph Bianchi and family have worked up to 75,000 cases of wine a year, most of it from Bianchi-owned vineyards in the adjoining counties of Fresno and Madera.
*→**   French Colombard, Chenin Blanc, Blanc de Blanc (blended white), Chablis, White Zinfandel, Rosé, Zinfandel, Burgundy, and Lambrusco (the latter made as a varietal

from a 20-acre planting of the Italian variety that goes into the wine of the same name there).

BLACK MONUKKA
A Muscat-related black grape used rarely to make dessert wine labeled as Angelica or as a varietal.

BLACK MOUNTAIN VINEYARD Sonoma T
$9–$18 Ken Toth, longtime grower, backed into the label for his prestige wines, even though Black Mountain had been the name of his 120-acre vineyard on hills near Healdsburg from the start. Toth bought the J. W. Morris winery in 1983 and used that label until 1987, when he added Black Mountain Vineyard only for estate wines, each named after a particular section of the property; the name goes on less than 20,000 cases a year. J. W. MORRIS continues as a larger-volume second label.
NYR: Chardonnay (deftly toasty 85), Sauvignon Blanc, Petite Sirah, and Zinfandel.

BLACK MUSCAT
In essence a varietal or semivarietal dessert wine from dark-skinned Muscats (there is actually no Black Muscat variety), most of them bottled young to capitalize on the pronounced fruit flavors of the grape.

BLACK SHEEP VINTNERS Calaveras T
$6.50–$12 Like many other 1,200-case wineries, Black Sheep is the product of a home winemaking hobby gone out of control. Dave Olson went commercial with an 84 Zinfandel and has not looked back. All of the wines are from bought-in Amador and Calaveras county grapes. Distribution is only in the Sierra foothills. The name, says Jan Olson, comes from their resolute refusal to accept a role model.
NYR: Zinfandel, Cabernet Sauvignon, Sauvignon Blanc, Muscat Canelli.

BLANC DE BLANC(S)
Literally white (wine) from white (grapes). The term is used mostly to identify sparkling wines made from Chardonnay or Chardonnay and Pinot Blanc, but it sometimes is a name for generic table wine or sparkling wine made from varieties not traditional to Champagne.

BLANC DE CABERNET SAUVIGNON, BLANC DE PINOT NOIR, ETC.
Varietal BLUSH wines.

BLANC DE NOIR(S)
White (wine) from black (grapes). Principal name for sparkling wines from Pinot Noir or Pinot Noir–based blends. Less often a euphemism for BLUSH on pale pink table wines.

BLANC VINEYARDS Mendocino T $8.50
This estate's Cabernet Sauvignon is labeled Robert Blanc after the owner of the 150-acre Redwood Valley vineyard that yields it. The family makes only 1,500 cases, selling all of it in California. They had made Chardonnay, Sauvignon Blanc, and Cabernet Blanc, but dropped all three after the 87s to concentrate on the red. The first vintage was 82.
NYR: Cabernet Sauvignon.

BLUE HERON LAKE VINEYARD Napa T $14
An established 24-acre vineyard in the newly designated Wild Horse Valley AVA began making estate wine in leased space with an 85 Chardonnay. The permanent cellar is under construction; annual volume approaches 3,000 cases. Owner David Mahaffey is his own winemaker.
NYR: Chardonnay. Pinot Noir joins the list with an 88.

BLUSH
The most accurate of several generic names for pale pink wines made from black grapes using white wine production techniques. Typical examples: Blanc de Noirs, Cabernet Sauvignon Blanc, Blanc de Pinot Noir, and White Zinfandel. Most are made off-dry to outright sweet, and bottled swiftly to capture all of their youthful fruit flavors. Drier, wood-aged alternatives exist, many under the name *vin gris*.

BOEGER WINERY El Dorado T $4.88–$12.50
From 35 acres of family-owned vineyard on Apple Hill (above Placerville) and another 20 leased acres 800 feet higher up the Sierra foothills, Greg Boeger makes 10,000 to 12,000 cases of mostly varietal wines each year; the exceptions are Hangtown Gold and Hangtown Red, proprietaries named after a Gold Rush mode of local justice that gave Placerville its original name. Boeger started in 1973 on a property first planted to vines in the 1860s.
** Merlot (husky to slightly rustic, full of Merlot flavors), Cabernet Sauvignon (also husky, flavorful), Zinfandel (same bold style as the other reds), White Zinfandel, Chardonnay, Sauvignon Blanc, Johannisberg Riesling, Hangtown Gold, Hangtown Red.

BOGLE VINEYARDS Yolo T $5–$8
From 650 acres of vines grown behind levees in the Sacramento River delta—in the Clarksburg AVA—a family-owned winery produces an ever-growing stream of wine. The total, a spokesman says, has so far surpassed the 18,000 cases of 1984 that the firm does not wish to reveal its current volume, but it could do 200,000 cases without sacrificing estate-bottled status. The first vintage: 79.
• Chardonnay, Chenin Blanc, Sauvignon Blanc, Semillon, Cabernet Sauvignon, Merlot, Petite Sirah, Zinfandel.

BOND
Shorthand for bonded winery or bonded wine cellar. A bond is a federal permit to make and store wine commercially.

BONNY DOON VINEYARD Santa Cruz Mountains T $6.25–$20 Self-confessed Rhônophile Randall Grahm has set up shop on an impressively chilly, foggy, seaward-facing slope not quite 4 miles from the Pacific Ocean and about twice that far n. of Santa Cruz. A 25-acre vineyard first planted to Chardonnay and Cabernet Sauvignon was being budded over in 1988–89 to Marsanne, Roussanne, Viognier, and a bit of Syrah as part of Grahm's desire to bring Rhône-like wines to the Americas. Meanwhile, he buys most of his grapes from warmish vineyards in southern Santa Clara and eastern Contra Costa counties. His first vintage was 81; production exceeds 8,000 cases.

*** Le Cigare Volant (French for flying saucer, in tribute to the heroic vignerons of Châteauneuf-du-Pape, who have forbidden the things to land among their vines; a bold, vital, heady Grenache-Syrah-Mourvedre blend) 82 83 84 85.
** Monterey Chardonnay (toasty).
NYR: Old Telegram (a Mourvedre named in honor of Le Vieux Télégraphe, a Rhône from the same grape; new with 87); Le Sophiste/Cuvée des Philosophes (a Marsanne-Roussanne blend still being made 40 cases to a vintage, but programmed to amplify itself); Grahm Crew (variable blend, most recently of Mourvedre); Vin Gris of Le Cigare Volant (a dry, wood-aged, partridge-eye type).

BORRA'S CELLAR   San Joaquin   T $?
Steven Borra has stopped making an annual 3,000 cases of White Barbera from his 30-acre vineyard on Lodi's s. side to bud over to Cabernet Sauvignon. He started with Barbera, White Barbera and Zinfandel in 79 and plans to resume with nothing but Cabernet in 89.

BOTRYTIS CINEREA
Often shortened to *Botrytis;* a curious mold that complicates but does not spoil the flavor of grapes while concentrating their qualities through dehydration. It is responsible for sweet (4% r.s.) to ultrasweet (35% r.s.) wines usually categorized as Late Harvest, Select Late Harvest, Individual Bunch Selected, Individual Berry Selected, or similar. Most are from White Riesling and Gewürztraminer; a steadily growing proportion come from Semillon, Sauvignon Blanc, or a blend of the two. A few come from Chardonnay and Chenin Blanc. The Sauternes and Coteaux du Layons of France and the Auslesen to Trockenbeerenauslesen of Germany are products of the same beneficent mold.

BOUCHAINE   Napa   T $11.50–$19
After various thoughts about its own name (Château Bouchaine and Bouchaine Vineyard have come and gone) and what it would make (Cabernet Sauvignon has disappeared), the 15,000-case winery has settled on the two great varieties from Burgundy, only from Carneros grapes. The winery began with 81s.
** Chardonnay (toasty, barrel-fermented school through 85); Pinot Noir (up and down as a Napa Valley wine, purely Carneros only from 86 on).
NYR: Chardonnay Reserve (starts with an 86, the first pure Carneros white); Pinot Noir Reserve (also starts with an 86).

BOYER
A winemaker label that belongs to Richard Boyer (Ventana Vineyards), who makes only $13 Monterey Chardonnay from his employer's vineyard using leased space. The debut 86 was impressively rich and complex in its fruit flavors. A separate winery is in the works near Greenfield; volume will remain at 1,200 to 1,500 cases.

BRANDER VINEYARD, THE   Santa Barbara   T $5.50–$13   An estate winery near the Santa Ynez Valley town of Los Olivos dates from 1981. Owner C. Frederic Brander makes 8,000 cases per year from his family's 40

acres. Brander's s.-sloping vineyard predates the winery by several years. The winery also makes good-value wines under a second label, ST. CARL; the roster changes year to year.
*** Sauvignon Blanc (lean, tart, complex, understated in a region that tends to overstate the variety) 84 85 86 87.
** Chardonnay (aromatic of ripe fruit); Cabernet Blanc (dry blush of distinct character).
NYR: Bouchet (recent, very promising Cabernet Franc–Merlot blend has been supple, polished, all fruit/no veggies through its first three vintages) 84 85 86.

BRAREN-PAULI WINERY   Sonoma   T $7.50–$11
Owning partners Larry Braren (the winemaker) and William Pauli started in Mendocino's Potter Valley in 1980, and slowly moved the winery to a Sonoma County site w. of Petaluma beginning in 1985. They select grapes from their own 100 acres in Potter Valley AVA and 35 acres in Redwood Valley, and also buy in Sonoma's Dry Creek Valley and Alexander Valley AVAs. From all these sources Larry Braren makes about 6,000 cases of wine a year. The plan is to stay at 10,000 cases or less.
** Potter Valley Chardonnay (well-wooded), Dry Creek Valley Cabernet Sauvignon, Alexander Valley Merlot, and Redwood Valley Zinfandel.

BRICELAND VINEYARDS   Humboldt   T $6–$14
A partnership has positioned itself as a pioneer in the nascent Willow Creek AVA near the Humboldt County town of Redway. While the vines get going, the winery is tuning up with grapes bought from Mendocino's Anderson Valley. The first vintage was 84; production is about 1,000 cases.
NYR: Chardonnay (rustic), Johannisberg Riesling, Gewürztraminer, Sauvignon Blanc, Cabernet Sauvignon (also rough-hewn), Pinot Noir, and champagne-method sparkling wine.

BRITTON CELLARS   Temecula   T $4.75–$10
A 1984 start-up named after the principal partner grows 22 acres of its own and buys grapes in Temecula and the Central Coast to round out the 8,000 cases of production.
NYR: Chardonnay, Sauvignon Blanc, White Riesling, Cabernet Sauvignon, Merlot, Zinfandel, and Zinfandel Pearl (a blush).

BRIX
A scale for measuring sugar and thus potential alcohol in grapes. It is very nearly but not exactly the percentage of sugar in the fruit. In California, most white wines are harvested at 21 to 22.5 degrees Brix, while a majority of reds are picked at 22 to 23.5 degrees. Grapes for sparkling wines are usually picked at 18 to 19 degrees. To determine the yield of alcohol in dry wines, winemakers multiply the degree of sugar by .55 to .6, depending on temperature, yeast strain, and other factors. Botrytised grapes for late-harvest wines have reached as much as 54 degrees Brix, but more commonly range from 28 to 34. In the case of late-harvest wines, concentrated sugar inhibits the formation of alcohol, so the usual multipliers do not function.

BRUCE WINERY, DAVID Santa Cruz Mountains T
$4.50–$18 At the beginning in 1964, physician/owner
David Bruce marched to a drummer no other winemaker
heard; his wines—from 25 estate acres and bought-in
grapes—were always huge and hugely individualistic, but
not always in the same way from year to year. In recent
vintages, the distance between Bruce wines and others has
narrowed markedly, though the wines remain distinctive,
and they have been less variable themselves. Production is
32,000 cases a year.
** Chardonnay-Estate, Sonoma-Mendocino Chardonnay;
Santa Cruz Mountains Cabernet Sauvignon; Pinot Noir–
Estate, red table wine, white table wine.
NYR: Côte de Shandon (under a distinctive label, an experimental blend of Syrah, Carignane, and Cabernet Pfeffer
first done in 86, attractive then). A white and a *vin gris* are
to come.

BRUT
See CHAMPAGNE.

BUEHLER VINEYARDS Napa T $6–$14.50
From 62 sharply sloping acres on hills above Lake Hennessy, e. of St. Helena, John Buehler makes 20,000 cases
of wine a year, all but a fraction of the White Zinfandel
estate grown. The first vintage: 78.
** Pinot Blanc (firm, aromatic of its variety); Cabernet Sauvignon (extremely dark, tannic, and heavy in the early going, but has lightened up and acquired some polish since);
Zinfandel (echoes the Cabernet); White Zinfandel.

BUENA VISTA Sonoma T,D $6–$18
A pioneer company has been transformed since 1979 by the
ownership of the German firm A. Racke, and since 1981 by
the winemaking of Jill Davis. The name goes back to
Agoston Haraszthy's ownership of a property just e. of
Sonoma town in the 1870s, but that laid idle from just
before Prohibition until the late 1940s. Then newspaperman Frank Bartholomew revived it as a small winery in
Haraszthy's original buildings. Now it is a 110,000-case
winery based in 700 acres of vines—soon to be 1,100—all
in one ranch straddling the Sonoma-Napa county line in
Carneros. Most of the wines are estate grown, though the
owner does buy Sauvignon Blanc in Lake and Sonoma counties, and Zinfandel from a Sonoma Valley neighbor.
*** Chardonnay (both the Estate and Private Reserve bottlings are full to bursting with the flavors of the variety, and
balanced to age well) 83 84 85 86 87; Lake County Sauvignon Blanc (pale, just off-dry, intense with the melonlike
flavors of Sauvignon, appealing early) 85 86 87 88; Alexander Valley Sauvignon Blanc (lean, dry herbaceous) 85 86
87; Dry Sherry (distinct FLOR, its base stock around for decades now, one of California's most impressive), and Cream
Sherry (the richer, sweeter, darker running mate has even
more depths of flavor than its pale cousin).
-→* Cabernet Sauvignon–Estate, Cabernet Sauvignon–Private Reserve (surprisingly ripe, almost jammy fruit
aromas pervade both in youth; otherwise, lean, tart, intrigu-

ing candidates for aging) 84 85; Pinot Noir (tart, even a bit hard, but the flavors promise much) 81 83 85; Johannisberg Riesling (off-dry, nicely scented), Gewürztraminer (understated).

NYR: Domaine Buena Vista proprietaries—Chaarblanc (blend based in Chardonnay), Spiceling (Riesling plus Gewürztraminer), and Steelhead Run (blanc de Pinot Noir). The early wines have been appealingly clean and fresh.

BULK

Any wine not yet packaged for retail sale. The term is misused in place of JUG (or increasingly, bag-in-a-box) to identify ordinary table wine sold in large containers.

BULK PROCESS

Synonym for CHARMAT PROCESS.

BURGER

White grape of dim flavors but useful acidity in warm regions; rarely if ever made as a varietal in recent years; almost half the 2,500 acres in the state grow in San Joaquin County, mostly for use in Charmat sparkling wines.

BURGESS CELLARS   Napa   T $8.95–$16.95

For the first decade after the winery's 1972 founding, it was a source of heavyweight reds and whites. Since 1981, the style has become more refined, though these wines are still closer to hearty than delicate. Tom and Linda Burgess own 20 acres of vineyard at the winery in hills e. of St. Helena, another 50 (called Triere) near Yountville. They buy Napa grapes to round out production at 30,000 cases per year.
→* Zinfandel (from upland vineyards at and near the winery, big but balanced and richly varietal) 81 83 84.
** Chardonnay–Triere Vineyard (recently slimmed down and less dependent on wood); Cabernet Sauvignon–Vintage Selection (distinctly perfumed by new wood and a shade weighty).

BURGUNDY

Once predominant, it is now a fading name for generic red wine.

BUTTERFLY CREEK WINERY   Mariposa   T

$6.50–$12   John Gerken helped extend the Sierra-foothill wine region a long way s. when he planted 20 acres of vineyard at the town of Mariposa, at the front door to Yosemite National Park. The first vintage for Butterfly Creek was 86; production is about 9,000 cases, all estate grown.
NYR: Pinot Blanc, White Riesling, Cabernet Sauvignon, Merlot.

BYNUM WINERY, DAVIS   Sonoma   T $5.50–$14

After wayward beginnings in an Albany (Alameda County) storefront and a feint toward Napa, onetime newspaperman Bynum moved to the Russian River Valley near Rio Nido in 1973. Slow but steady progress since has made the label a bit of a sleeper in recent vintages. Volume is near its peak at 28,000 cases, almost entirely from bought-in Sonoma grapes.

→*   Chardonnay–Artist Series (fine fruit plus a deft hint of oak; balanced) 84 85 87; Pinot Noir–Artist Series (dark, firm with tannins, ages well; good varietal flavors) 83 84 85; Gewürztraminer (off-dry, fine aromas of lichee) 85 87.

**   Chardonnay, Pinot Noir, Cabernet Sauvignon (sound); Cabernet Sauvignon–Artist Series (consistently agreeable); Fumé Blanc. Small lots of Merlot and Pinot Blanc may join the list by 1990.

BYRON VINEYARD   Santa Barbara   T $6–$16
Longtime Zaca Mesa winemaker Byron Kenneth Brown established his own winery and label in 1984 to focus on Santa Maria Valley Chardonnay and Pinot Noir, mostly from bought grapes. In 1988 he finished the plunge, acquiring most of his 175 acres of mature vineyard in two parcels. Production is at 15,000 cases.
NYR: Pinot Noir (distinctively regional, balanced, polished smooth) 84 85 86; Pinot Noir–Reserve (begun with outstanding, rich 86); Chardonnay (light, firm textures, toasty) 84 85 86; Chardonnay-Reserve (toastier, fuller than regular); Cabernet Sauvignon, and Sauvignon Blanc (has the regional vegetativeness; well-balanced).

CABERNET FRANC

A black grape variety closely related to Cabernet Sauvignon and increasingly, its varietal wine. Cabernet Franc has only recently begun to be planted in California; bearing acreage in 1988 was a modest 850 (365 of it in Napa, 240 in Sonoma). Though first planted as a variety to be blended with Cabernet Sauvignon—still an important role—its emergence as a varietal in its own right seems assured. Though the variety has done well in the North Coast, its greatest future may lie in the Central Coast, where wines from it have been considerably more appealing than Cabernet Sauvignons grown in the same areas.

CABERNET SAUVIGNON

For the past three decades, the premier black grape and varietal red wine of coastal California, especially the North Coast, and most especially the Napa Valley. The variety ripens more fully almost everywhere in California than it does in its original home, Bordeaux, yielding fleshier wines with higher average alcohols. However, in the North Coast, its flavors can remain so strikingly similar to the originals that skillful tasters regularly confuse the origins of wines from Cabernet in head-to-head blind comparisons. Contrarily, Cabernets from the Central Coast—Monterey and Santa Barbara especially—have tended thus far to have exaggerated herbaceous or vegetative flavors. Current bearing acreage is 24,390, the all-time high. Leading counties in plantings are Napa (6,805 acres), Sonoma (5,480), Monterey (2,705), San Luis Obispo (1,215), Lake (1,060), and Mendocino (975).

CABERNET SAUVIGNON BLANC

A BLUSH from Cabernet Sauvignon grapes. Variations on the name include Cabernet Blanc and White Cabernet.

CACHE CELLARS Solano T $6–$12
Full-time pilot, part-time winemaker Charles Lowe makes about 4,000 cases of varietals a year at a cellar just w. of the University of California–Davis campus. All of the grapes are bought-in, mostly from Napa. His first vintage was 78.
• Napa Valley Cabernet Sauvignon, Napa Valley or Sonoma Pinot Noir, Napa Valley Sauvignon Blanc, and Napa Valley Late Harvest Semillon.

CACHE CREEK Yolo T $5.95
Jay Barth, a home winemaker turned professional, grows all of the grapes for his annual 1,000 cases of wine. Two out of three of them come from University of California–developed varieties planted on his ranch n.w. of Woodland. Barth's first vintage was 85.
NYR: Sauvignon Blanc, Symphony, and Carmine.

CADENASSO WINERY Solano T,D $2–$3
A family-owned winery moved from its original, post-Prohibition location at Fairfield to smaller quarters in nearby Suisun City in 1987. Owner Frank Cadenasso mainly sells at the cellar door.
*→** Chardonnay, Chenin Blanc, Gray Riesling, Chablis, White Zinfandel, Cabernet Sauvignon, Pinot Noir, Zinfandel, Vino Rosso, and Passionata (a flavored proprietary).

CAFARO
Joe Cafaro (ex-Chappellet, ex–Robert Keenan, now Sinskey) started his winemaker label with an 86 Napa Valley Merlot and 86 Napa Valley Cabernet Sauvignon that are noticeably more restrained than many of the wines that have earned him his reputation. The first vintage yielded 600 cases; both wines are priced at $18.

CAIN CELLARS Napa T $8–$20
An architecturally ambitious winery owned by Jerry and Joyce Cain sits at one edge of a 110-acre-and-expanding vineyard well up Spring Mountain from St. Helena. All of the plantings are of Bordeaux varieties, which appear in various forms under a label begun with 81s. Current production is 30,000 cases, the whites entirely from grapes bought from Napa growers, the reds partly from bought-in Napa grapes.
NYR: Cabernet Sauvignon (intensely flavored, fleshy); Merlot (softer than the Cabernet but similar in style); Cain Five (an astute estate blend of Cabernet Sauvignon, Cabernet Franc, Malbec, Merlot, and Petit Verdot intensely flavored by both grapes and wood) 85; Carneros Chardonnay (firm, crisp, full of fruit and wood flavors); Napa Valley Chardonnay (fuller-bodied but similar); and Sauvignon Blanc (house style rules).

CAKEBREAD CELLARS Napa T $11–$35
Exuberant Jack Cakebread and his (comparatively) introspective son, Bruce, meet halfway on the style of their three well-received wines, which still leaves them bolder than most. The annual 40,000 cases come mostly from their own 67 acres, most of them adjoining the winery just n. of Oakville, the rest in hills just to the w. What the Cakebreads do not

grow they buy from nearby neighbors. The first vintage was 73.

*** Chardonnay (subtlest and silkiest of the wines but still big and rich in Chardonnay flavors) 84 87; Chardonnay-Reserve (leans more toward toasty flavors than the regular); Sauvignon Blanc (big, slightly rough, full of ripe Napa melon aromas) 83 84 85 86 87; Cabernet Sauvignon (toned back from early days, but still pungently flavored and sturdy) 81 83 84 85; and Cabernet Sauvignon–Reserve (the regular only more so).

CALAFIA CELLARS

Randle Johnson's is one of the first of a now fast-growing crop of winemaker's labels, having begun with 79s. Johnson (Hess Collection) makes 2,500 cases of $8–$18 wine a year in leased space pending construction of a cellar of his own. All of the grapes are bought from Napa growers, the Cabernet and Merlot from Mt. Veeder, the Sauvignon Blanc from Rutherford.

** Sauvignon Blanc (straightforward, reliable); Merlot (fine, weedy flavors, deft touch of wood); and Cabernet Sauvignon.

CALERA WINE CO. San Benito T $11.75–$40

The quest for a perfect California Pinot Noir landed proprietor Josh Jensen high in the w. hills of San Benito County with 24 acres of the great Burgundian red variety planted in limaceous soils, and a cellar built over the dramatic bones of an old limekiln. Since the first vintage, 75, Jensen's second focus has shifted slowly from Zinfandel toward Chardonnay so that the former is about to disappear. Annual production is 10,000 cases.

*** San Benito Pinot Noir (Jensen, Reed, and Selleck are separate blocks within the estate vineyard, all of them producers of big, ripe, slightly heavy Pinots); Santa Barbara Pinot Noir (from Santa Maria AVA grapes that give lighter, livelier textures but similar flavors to the estate wines).

** Chardonnay (thoroughly toasty).

CALIFORNIA SOLEIL

A grower-owned label for appealingly soft, reliably fruity $6 Napa Valley Johannisberg Riesling from Ray Mayeri's valley-floor vineyard at Oakville. The first vintage was 82.

CALIFORNIA WINE CORP.

The corporate name for a winery now operating primarily as BANDIERA WINERY, but also the owner of the Arroyo Sonoma, John B. Merritt, Potter Valley, and Sage Canyon labels.

CALLAWAY VINEYARDS AND WINERY Temecula

T $5.25–$9.75 The first and still by far the largest explorer of the Temecula district. Launched by Ely Callaway in 1974, and sold to Hiram Walker in 1981, the winery now produces only white wines from its own 720 acres (320 original acres plus another 400 purchased in 1987) and other vineyards at Temecula. Annual production is 150,000 cases and planned to expand slightly.

[**]Chardonnay-Callalees (soft, approachable, some complexity from time on the lees gets no aging in wood).

** Fumé Blanc (the drier of two wines from Sauvignon Blanc gets time in wood and ages quickly in bottle); Sauvignon Blanc (a bit sweet but livelier and fresher in taste than its running mate); Morning Harvest Chenin Blanc (pleasantly fruity); White Riesling (ditto); and Spring Wine (appealing sipper, hints at Gewürz). Sweet Nancy, a botrytised Chenin Blanc, appears in small lots when the noble mold strikes.

CAMBIASO

From the 1930s until recently Cambiaso was the name of a winery now called DOMAINE ST. GEORGE.

CAMBRIA VINEYARDS   Santa Barbara   T

$14–$25   A new, Chardonnay-dominated winery draws on 710 acres of what was planted as Tepusquet Vineyard in the Santa Maria Valley, but now belongs to Jess Jackson (also Kendall-Jackson). The first vintage, 88, yielded 18,000 cases.

NYR: Chardonnay, Chardonnay-Reserve, and Pinot Noir.

CANTERBURY

A second label for Napa's STRATFORD goes on small lots of price-worthy $5–$7 Chardonnay and Sauvignon Blanc.

CAPARONE VINEYARDS   San Luis Obispo   T

$7–$7.90   In every vintage since 79, owner/winemaker Dave Caparone has specialized in Cabernet Sauvignon and Merlot from the Central Coast, mostly the Santa Maria Valley AVA. But his goal all along has been to champion Nebbiolo and Brunello in California. His 7 acres n. of the town of Paso Robles yielded small lots of 88s due for release in 1991 or 1992. Total annual production is 3,000 cases. ** Cabernet Sauvignon (dark, tannic, strongly flavored by both its region and long aging in wood); Merlot (dark, well-wooded). Winter Mist, an episodic entry, is an eccentric but intriguing $10-per-half-bottle, late-harvest Gamay from the hills e. of Paso Robles.

CAPORALE   Napa   T $7.99–$11.99

Owner/winemaker Mark Caporale started in San Luis Obispo with 85s, but soon after bought vineyards in the Napa Valley and moved his winery there. Current annual production is 20,000 cases from his own Napa Chardonnay and San Luis Obispo Merlot, plus bought-in Napa Cabernet grapes.

NYR: Chardonnay, Cabernet Sauvignon, and Merlot.

CARBONIC MACERATION

The technique of fermenting whole clusters rather than crushed fruit to capture lively textures and curiously distinct bouquets something like banana oil. Originally developed in France's Beaujolais, it came to be much overused in California in the seventies for light reds subtitled Nouveau or some variation on that theme. A hardy and more skillful few still use carbonic maceration to produce Nouveaus from Gamay and other grapes, but it now is more often a tool used in small proportions to give extra dimension to Pinot Noirs.

CAREY CELLARS, J. Santa Barbara T $5.50–$14
Three doctors J—a father and two sons—started the winery
on 25 acres of Santa Ynez Valley AVA vineyard just in time
to make 78s. The founders sold in 1988 to Firestone Vineyards, which is now operating the winery and its vineyard as
a separate entity. Locally bought grapes boost annual production to 7,000 cases.
** Chardonnay, Sauvignon Blanc (rich, not so vegetative as
most in its region); Cabernet Sauvignon (beats regional vegetative flavors); Cabernet Sauvignon–LaQuesta Vineyard
(an estate bottling); Merlot; and Cabernet Blanc. Semillon
and Pinot Noir are irregularly on the roster.

CARIGNANE
In California, a relatively characterless black grape from the
s. of France and n. of Spain (where it is Cariñena), and from
a few producers, its varietal wine. Carignane's wines do
balance well, making them useful in blends. Slightly more
than half of the state's 14,345 acres are in the San Joaquin
Valley counties of Madera and San Joaquin. Of the coastal
counties, Mendocino has the most extensive plantings
(1,400 acres).

CARLO ROSSI
Lowest-priced label in E. & J. GALLO roster; primarily for
generic wines in big bottles.

CARMENET Sonoma T $4.95–$25
The winery was founded in 1982 as one of the Chalone, Inc.
group. It and its 50-acre vineyard are right at the top of Mt.
Pisgah in the Sonoma Valley. Most of the grapes for the
Carmenet label come from its own vines, but some come
from a Chalone-affiliated vineyard in San Luis Obispo
County's Edna Valley AVA. Total production is 27,000
cases.
NYR: Sonoma White Table Wine (based in Sauvignon Blanc,
thus far quite heavy in both flavor and texture); Edna Valley
White Table Wine (also Sauvignon-based, not quite so heavy
but no lightweight); and Red Table Wine (Cabernet-based
blend, dark, weighty, hinting at raisiny-ripe).

CARMINE
One of the grape varieties developed at the University of
California–Davis by Dr. H. P. Olmo to produce Cabernet-
like wines in regions too warm for Cabernet Sauvignon itself to perform well. Thus far it is only just at the trial stage.

CARNELIAN
With Carmine and Centurion, another of the varieties developed at the University of California–Davis by Dr. H. P.
Olmo to produce Cabernet-like wines in warm growing regions. Several producers have made varietal wines from it,
but their number has dwindled since 1984. Still, there are
1,340 acres planted, nearly all in Fresno, Kern, and San
Joaquin counties.

CARNEROS AVA (also Los Carneros AVA)
A long sweep of low, rolling hills cuts across the southerly

tips of both Napa and Sonoma counties, offering a multitude of exposures, but mostly southerly ones. Between the wind-driven fogs off San Francisco Bay and the moderating influence of the bay itself, Carneros has one of the coolest summer climates in either county. Even before the AVA was established in 1983, Chardonnay and Pinot Noir grapes from the region were much in demand for both still and sparkling wines. Merlot and Cabernet Sauvignon have yielded memorable wines from small plantings. Total acreage now exceeds 7,000; major new plantings are in the works for every year through 1991—probably beyond. The smaller Napa portion is also entitled to use the Napa Valley Appellation; most of the Sonoma side also qualifies as Sonoma Valley AVA. Napa has six wineries; four are on the Sonoma side. More are in the works.

CARNEROS CREEK   Napa   T $8.90–$20

After years of supplementing their Carneros Chardonnays and Pinot Noirs with other varietal wines from other places, winemaker Francis Mahoney and his partners have settled in as specialists in the two wines from their home region, with a bit of Carneros Cabernet Sauvignon kept for leavening. A fair portion of the Pinot Noir comes from 21 acres of winery-owned vineyards; the rest is bought-in from neighbors. Total annual production is 20,000 cases.
*** Pinot Noir (always distinct Pinot flavors, but also has smoke-and-mirrors tones from the winemaking) 84 85.
** Chardonnay (has been toasty), and Cabernet Sauvignon.
NYR: Fleur de Carneros Pinot Noir (a light style for early drinking begun with an 87); Carneros Signature Pinot Noir (the reserve bottling, also starts with an 87).

CARRIE VINEYARDS, MAURICE   Temecula   T

$5.50–$7.50   A family-owned winery based in a 34-acre vineyard had its first wine made in leased space in 1985, then opened its own cellars the following year. Production is 12,000 cases; owners Gordon and Maurice van Roekel plan to become an estate winery as another 84 acres is planted. Meanwhile, other Temecula growers and one in the Santa Maria AVA supplement the estate crop.
NYR: Chardonnay, Chenin Blanc, Johannisberg Riesling, Muscat Canelli, Sauvignon Blanc, White Zinfandel, Merlot, and Petite Sirah, plus a generic red named Cody's Crush and a generic white called Heather's Mist.

CARROUSEL CELLARS   Santa Clara   T

$7.50–$12   The weekend winery of John and Carol De Santis began with 81s. Annual production at their cellar in Gilroy hovers at 500 cases, with Cabernet Sauvignon from their own vines, other types from grapes bought in the neighborhood.
• Chardonnay, Cabernet Sauvignon, Zinfandel.

CARTLIDGE & BROWN

The prestige label of Napa's STRATFORD goes only on a small-lot, $12 Napa Valley Chardonnay that has been impressively polished and subtle since its first vintage, 81.

CASA DE FRUTA   San Benito   T $5.50–$12
A 14-acre vineyard supplies grapes for wines sold only at the owner's adjacent roadside tourist attraction e. of Hollister.

CASA NUESTRA   Napa   T $6.60–$11
Napa lawyer Gene Kirkham and his wife Cody make 1,500 cases a year from their 22 acres not far n. of St. Helena. Chenin Blanc has been a specialty from the first vintage, 80. Cabernet Franc is meant to become its red counterpart.
[**] Chenin Blanc (alternates between bone-dry and just off-dry, with 86 and 88 bone-dry, 85 and 87 off-dry at 0.5 r.s.). Also: Tinto, a generic red.
NYR: Cabernet Franc, Late Harvest Chenin Blanc.

CASTORO CELLARS
From the first vintage of his winemaker's label, 79, Niels Udsen has leased space from wineries in Paso Robles to make his wines, now up to an annual 10,000 cases. The $4.50–$8.50 list includes Chardonnay, Fumé Blanc, White Zinfandel, and Cabernet Sauvignon. Pinot Noir begins with 87. Udsen buys grapes in Paso Robles, the Santa Maria Valley, and Monterey.

CASWELL VINEYARDS   Sonoma   T $5–$15
Photographer-turned-winemaker Dwight Caswell, Jr., has an inquiring turn of mind that keeps his roster of wines fluid as he takes up and drops wine types year by year. Nearly all of the grapes for 4,000 cases are bought in Sonoma County; the winery is well w. in the Russian River Valley AVA near Sebastopol. The first vintage was 83.
• Chardonnay, Gewürztraminer, Sauvignon Blanc, Claret (a variable Cabernet-based blend), Pinot Noir, and Zinfandel.

CAYMUS VINEYARD   Napa   T $8–$35
The fame of the house rests on brawny Cabernet Sauvignons from the owning Charles Wagner family's 70 acres of vineyards e. of Rutherford, but the winery gets good marks from critics right across the board. Annual production has edged up to 35,000 cases since the first vintage, 70, not counting a good-value second label, LIBERTY SCHOOL.
→** Estate Cabernet Sauvignon (dark, firm, intense Cabernet flavors ever more heartily seasoned by new oak) 74 75 78 79 81 84 85; and Estate Cabernet Sauvignon–Special Selection (a larger-than-life echo of the regular bottling).
*** Cabernet Sauvignon–Napa Cuvée (from bought-in grapes, and a shade smaller in all dimensions than the estate bottling but still plenty rich in all respects; since 84); Zinfandel (from vineyards in the e. hills, hearty, woody); and Sauvignon Blanc (surprisingly delicate, lightsome).
** Chardonnay (steady); Estate Pinot Noir (soundly made, a hint soft, suggests the faintest raisining); Estate Pinot Noir–Special Selection (riper, more distinctly touched by new wood than the regular); and Pinot Noir Blanc (subtitled Oeil de Perdrix, dry, wood-aged blush).
NYR: Cabernet Franc (tiny lots from one acre to date).

CECHETTI-SEBASTIANI

A merchant label belonging to Don Sebastiani of Sebastiani Vineyards and his brother-in-law, used thus far for rather indistinct Chardonnay, Cabernet Sauvignon, and Pinot Noir.

CENTRAL COAST AVA

Central Coast is a blanket AVA encompassing all vineyards in the counties of Alameda, Monterey, San Benito, San Luis Obispo, Santa Barbara, Santa Clara, and Santa Cruz. In historic usage, Central Coast included the counties as such; as finally defined, the AVA excludes some parts of the region where grapes have not been or cannot be grown. In recent years growers in San Luis Obispo and Santa Barbara have been using Central Coast only in reference to vineyards within their two counties, especially in connection with their Central Coast Wine Growers Association.

CENTURION

With CARMINE and CARNELIAN, a black grape variety developed as a warm-climate replacement for Cabernet Sauvignon by Dr. H. P. Olmo at the University of California–Davis. The grape is just making its first appearances in varietal red wine. To date 590 acres are in bearing, 510 of those in Fresno County.

CHALK HILL AVA

A small district, Chalk Hill starts on flats between Healdsburg and Windsor and reaches eastward up the slopes that give it its name. It is sandwiched among the Russian River Valley AVA to the w., the Alexander Valley AVA to the n. and e., and the Knights Valley AVA to the e. and s. Close to 900 of its 1,000 planted acres are in Chardonnay and Sauvignon Blanc.

CHALK HILL WINERY   Sonoma   T $8–$12

Since the first plantings in 1974, owner Frederick C. Furth has developed a dramatic 310-acre vineyard on 710 acres of steeply rolling hills e. of Windsor. All of the 65,000 cases of wine made in his winery come from his own vines; the plan is to grow to 100,000 cases, remaining an estate all the while. The first vintages from the property (80 through 82) went under the name Donna Maria, while some bought-in grapes were bottled under the Chalk Hill name as a second label. Chalk Hill then became the primary name.
** Chardonnay (pleasing fruit flavors, sometimes a bit heady); Sauvignon Blanc (typical grassy Sonoman); Cabernet Sauvignon.
NYR: Merlot (debut is 87), and Late Harvest Sauvignon Blanc (when the opportunity arises).

CHALONE AVA

A tiny, one-winery AVA high in the Gavilan Mountains e. of the Salinas Valley town of Soledad. Its quartz-laden soils are given mostly to Chardonnay and Pinot Noir, less to Chenin Blanc, Pinot Blanc, and recently, Cabernet Sauvignon.

CHALONE VINEYARDS   Monterey   T $10–$28

Once a tiny, remote winery known only to a handful of initiates, Chalone has come to be a familiar name both as a corporation owning several wineries, and as a vineyard and winery in itself. Chalone, the winery, now has 174 acres of vineyards and produces 12,000 cases a year on the way to 25,000. From the early 1960s—when a few hundred cases were a lot of wine—until now, the ideals have remained Burgundian to the point of attempting to duplicate the damp, chill environment in the old walls at Beaune with humidified underground cellars.

*** Chardonnay (lean to outright austere, and marked by toasty flavors from oak barrels); Pinot Blanc (a bit more straightforwardly flavored by the grapes than the Chardonnay, and somehow less austere); Chenin Blanc (shows what dry, wood-aged wine can be from this grape variety).

** Pinot Noir (in recent vintages, especially 84, hard with tannins and heady).

CHAMISAL VINEYARDS San Luis Obispo T $13
Norman Goss and family's 57-acre vineyard and 3,000-case winery in Edna Valley are devoted almost entirely to Chardonnay, and have been from the initial vintage, 79. However, a patch of Cabernet Sauvignon sometimes is used for a bit of Cabernet Sauvignon Blanc.

** Chardonnay (dark, weighty, and well-wooded through 85; paler and more delicately balanced in 86 and since).

CHAMPAGNE
By California law, any sparkling wine made by the champagne method (*méthode champenoise*), Carstens transfer, or Charmat bulk process can be called Champagne if an appellation accompanies the word. Labels must also indicate which technique was used in production if the word Champagne appears on the package. Led by the several French-owned companies, many now forswear the name Champagne and just say *méthode champenoise* or a variation of that statement. Relative sweetness is indicated by Natural (dry, no dosage), Brut (usually .7 to 1.2% r.s. in champagne-method bottlings, 1.2 to 2% in Charmats), Extra Dry (usually +2%), or rarely, Demi-Sec (same as Extra Dry). White wines may be further identified as Blanc de Blanc (primarily white grapes) or Blanc de Noir (primarily black grapes). A rare few carry varietal labels (Champagne de Chardonnay). Pink types are called Champagne Rosé (Brut if from a prestige label) and Pink Champagne (sweet, usually Charmat); full-out reds are called Champagne Rouge or Sparkling Burgundy. Red sparklers are quite rare now even in the lowest-price echelon.

CHANDON
The label name of DOMAINE CHANDON.

CHAPPELLET VINEYARD Napa T $7.50–$18
The Donn Chappellet family has been quiet but persistent in establishing a loyal following since 1968. All of the wines are estate bottled from 110 acres of dramatic vineyards on n.-facing slopes that look down onto Lake Hennessey, a reservoir in steep hills e. of Rutherford. Peak production is

30,000 cases a year. The winery holds back older vintages for sale direct from the door.

→** Cabernet Sauvignon (early vintages austere, recent ones fleshier in support of textbook varietal flavors; favorite years labeled Signature from 80 onward) 80 84 85.
** Chardonnay (lean, understated, 86 best in some time); Chenin Blanc (truly dry, deftly marked by oak aging, lasts well).

CHARBONO
A little-grown northern Italian and/or southern French variety (the original spelling in California was Charbonneau) and its wine. Because of Inglenook's long tradition of making almost infinitely age-worthy Charbonos, it is the only varietal type with a fan club that holds black-tie dinners. Of 84 acres in the state, 74 grow in the Napa Valley.

CHARDONNAY
The white grape variety and its varietal wine. California's most talked-about, most age-worthy white wines come from the grape that long before had put white Burgundy at the pinnacle in France. The flavor association given by the University of California is applelike, but oak aging often revolutionizes the tastes to richer ones more reminiscent of peach, or even pineapple. Chardonnay has proven widely adaptable, yielding memorable wines throughout coastal California. Napa Valley has the edge historically, but Sonoma and Mendocino have yielded impressive examples in recent vintages. Santa Barbara is also doing exceptionally well with the grape, and the coolest parts of the Sierra foothills show promise. Current total bearing acreage in the state is 34,880 and climbing fast. Leading counties by acreage are Sonoma (8,330), Napa (7,715), Monterey (4,105), Santa Barbara (2,840), Mendocino (2,155) and San Luis Obispo (1,380).

CHARIS VINEYARDS
Dry Creek Valley grower Jack Florence makes 2,000 cases a year of $6.50–$7.50 Sauvignon Blanc and Cabernet Sauvignon (deft, supple) from a vineyard with considerably more capacity. He has leased cellar space since his first vintage, 81. The pronunciation, incidentally, is "ka-RISS."

CHARMAT PROCESS
A French-invented method of producing sparkling wines in which the secondary fermentation takes place in pressurized 2,000-to-5,000-gallon tanks. Newly bubbly wine is then filtered under pressure into bottles. The cost-cutting process is mostly used to make inexpensive sparkling wines that can be called Champagne but must carry on their labels the words "Charmat process" or "bulk process."

CHÂTEAU BOSWELL   Napa   T $18
From a cartoon of a stone castle n. of St. Helena come 1,000 to 1,500 cases of wine a year from bought-in Napa grapes. In 79 and for several vintages after, Cabernet Sauvignon was the only wine. Chardonnay joined the list in 86.
** Cabernet Sauvignon (reliably sound, well-balanced, distinctly varietal flavors) 79 81 84.
NYR: Chardonnay.

CHATEAU BOUCHAINE
The former name of a winery now called just BOUCHAINE.

CHATEAU CHEVALIER
One of Napa's pre-Prohibition wineries has stood idle since the Gil Nickel family (Far Niente) purchased it in 1984. The Nickels have been seeking a buyer to reopen it. Winery and vineyard are on Spring Mountain.

CHATEAU CHEVRE Napa T $8.50–$25
Retired airline pilot Gerald Hazen named his cellar after the Yountville property's former role as a dairy-goat farm. His first vintage was 79. Most of the grapes for an annual 3,000 to 3,500 cases come from 7 acres of Merlot at the winery and 11 acres of mixed plantings in the Big Ranch Road district.
** Merlot (rich, rough, calls for patience; early vintages are aging well); and Sauvignon Blanc (also hardy).
NYR: Cabernet Franc (tiny lots so far), and an unnamed blend based in Cabernet, to begin with an 86.

CHÂTEAU DE BAUN Sonoma T,S $6.50–$14
A one-grape, seven-wine winery meant to sing the praises of H. P. Olmo's splendidly aromatic Muscat of Alexandria x Grenache Gris cross, Symphony. The first vintage was 86; current volume is 18,000 cases, all from Kenneth and Grace de Baun's 116 acres in the Russian River Valley n.w. of Santa Rosa.
NYR: Overture (dry); Prelude (off-dry sipper, wonderfully scented of its grape variety); Theme (sweet); and Finale (dessert-sweet) are the still editions. Romance (dry) and Rhapsody (off-dry, superior sipper) are the champagne-method sparklers. Classical Jazz (off-dry, pale pink from a bit of Pinot Noir) rounds out the line.

CHÂTEAU DE LEU Solano T $4–$7
A family-owned, 5,000 case winery in the Solano–Green Valley AVA a short distance n. of Fairfield. Ben Volkhardt's first wines were 81s. All then and since have come from his 80 acres at the winery.
• Chardonnay, Sauvignon Blanc, and Pinot Noir.

CHÂTEAU DIANA Sonoma T $3.99–$6
Although there is an aging cellar in the Dry Creek Valley, Château Diana is basically a merchant label buying and blending wines from all parts of the state, primarily the Central Coast. A small percentage of an annual 200,000 to 300,000 cases sells under the Château Diana name; the rest sells under private labels.
NYR: Chardonnay, Chenin Blanc, Fumé Blanc, White Zinfandel, Cabernet Sauvignon Blanc, Cabernet Sauvignon, and Peaches (impressively peachy-flavored white).

CHÂTEAU DU LAC
A sometimes-label for special lots from KENDALL-JACKSON.

CHÂTEAU JULIEN Monterey T $5.75–$17
All of the emphasis is on Chardonnay and has been since some bought-in-bulk 81s prefigured the first crush in 82. The 40,000-case winery is at the mouth of Carmel Valley, at the edge of the town of Carmel; all of the grapes are bought

from growers in Monterey's Salinas Valley some miles e.
** Monterey Chardonnay, Chardonnay–Paraiso Springs
Vineyard, Chardonnay–Cobblestone Vineyard, and
Chardonnay–San Bernabe Vineyard (distinctly toasty); Sau-
vignon Blanc; Johannisberg Riesling; Cabernet Sauvignon;
and Merlot.

CHATEAU MONTELENA T $7.50–$20
A partnership of four revived a famous pre-Prohibition label
in 1969 and quickly put more luster on the name than it had
during its first heyday, largely with Chardonnays. The winery and 100 acres of vineyard are n. of Calistoga, hard
against the foot of Mt. St. Helena. Bo Barrett, son of the
principal partner, follows in the footsteps of Miljenko
Grgich (Grgich Hills) and Jerry Luper (Rutherford Hill) as
winemaker. Current production is 28,000 cases.
→** Napa Valley Chardonnay and Alexander Valley
Chardonnay (both crisp, subtle in well-married flavors of
fruit and wood; the Napa is a little firmer).
** Cabernet Sauvignon (dark, ultratannic, sometimes
marked by the farmyard aromas familiar in some French
wines); Zinfandel (small lots, also in the dark, tannic vein),
and Johannisberg Riesling (off-dry, appealing).

CHÂTEAU NAPA-BEAUCANON Napa T $6–$15
Owned by the French *négociant* firm Lebegue, the winery
and 65 acres of vines sit between Rutherford and St. Helena.
The owners have another 90 acres near the city of Napa and
in 1988 were beginning to develop 100 more n. of St. Helena. Current production by Bordelais winemaker Jean-
Marie Maureze is 20,000 cases; the plan is to expand to
50,000 as the vineyards mature. Maureze's first Napa wines
were 86s made in leased space; the winery went up in time
for the 88s.
NYR: Chardonnay, Chenin Blanc, Cabernet Sauvignon, and
Merlot.

CHÂTEAU POTELLE Napa T $8.50–$20
In 1989 Jean-Noel and Marketta Fourmeaux du Sartel
bought the former Vose Vineyard on Mt. Veeder as a home
for the label they had founded in 1983, and also acquired a
90-acre vineyard on the Silverado Trail as a source of grapes.
They will continue to make about 22,000 cases a year, less
of it from bought-in grapes as their own vines come into
play.
NYR: Napa Sauvignon Blanc, Napa Chardonnay, Alexander Valley Cabernet Sauvignon, and Alexander Valley Cabernet Sauvignon–Reserve (all stylish, often impressive in
vintages to date). A second label, Domaine Potelle, goes on
a $6 California Chardonnay.

CHATEAU ST. JEAN Sonoma T,S $4–$18
The winery broke in front of the pack when it was founded
in 1974 and has managed to stay among the leaders in
Chardonnay and especially Late Harvest Johannisberg
Rieslings ever since. In 1981, the founding partners added
champagne-method sparkling wine as a semi-independent
venture. In 1984, they sold all of St. Jean to Suntory, the

Japanese wine and spirits producer. The new owner has kept Richard Arrowood, the original winemaker, at his post. The 175,000-case still wine cellars and 77 acres of vineyard are at Kenwood; another vineyard called Petite Étoile is in the Russian River Valley. The sparkling wines are made at a separate Russian River Valley winery at Graton; volume is about 25,000 cases.

→* Late Harvest Johannisberg Riesling, Select Late Harvest Johannisberg Riesling, and Special Select Late Harvest Johannisberg Riesling (durable nectars).

→* Chardonnay–Robert Young, Chardonnay–Belle Terre, Chardonnay–McCrea, and Chardonnay–St. Jean (understated, hard young); Pinot Blanc–Robert Young (tart, spare); Fumé Blanc–Petite Étoile (pungent Sonoma grassy flavors); Sonoma County Johannisberg Riesling (off-dry, overflowing with berrylike to apricotty Riesling flavors).

** Chardonnay, Fumé Blanc, Vin Blanc. Brut, Blanc de Blanc.

NYR: Pinot Noir, Cabernet Sauvignon; sparkling Grande Cuvée.

CHÂTEAU SOUVERAIN Sonoma T $4–$12

This winery has crowded a lot of history into its early years. It began in 1972 as Villa Fontaine under the ownership of Pillsbury, the flour-products people. Several owners and three name changes later, it belongs to Nestlé, Inc. and appears set on a steady course of making quality Sonoma wines. Annual production two years after the 1985 purchase was 150,000 cases, with room to grow to 300,000. NYR: Chardonnay (good value), Carneros Chardonnay–Reserve (outstanding varietal flavors and fine balance in 85 and 86), Gewürztraminer, Johannisberg Riesling, Chenin Blanc, Colombard Blanc, White Zinfandel, Cabernet Sauvignon (supple, polished in 85), Merlot (ditto to Cabernet) 85 86, and Dry Creek Zinfandel (almost too understated in 86).

CHÂTEAU WOLTNER Napa T $24–$54

The ex-owners of Ch. La Mission–Haut Brion learned something about pricing before they sold their Bordeaux property and developed a 55-acre Chardonnay vineyard in hills e. of St. Helena. The vineyard's and the label's first vintage was 86.

NYR: Estate Reserve, St. Thomas Vineyard, and Titus Vineyard (the latter two separately identified blocks; first wines conventional Napa Chardonnays).

CHENIN BLANC

A white grape and its varietal wine. Chenin Blanc's ancestral home is the Loire, which provided the off-dry to sweet models that govern the style of most California Chenins. At 40,100 bearing acres, the variety is second only to French Colombard in total plantings, though only a small portion of the total crop goes into varietals. Extensive plantings in the San Joaquin Valley produce bland but agreeable grapes that go mostly into generic whites. The leading counties in acreage there are Madera (6,060), Kern (5,350), Fresno (4,505), San Joaquin (4,050), and Merced (3,305). In the coastal counties that produce most of the varietal wines, the fruit flavors are pleasant if somewhat simple—perhaps all the more agreeable for casual drinking because of that. The major coastal plantings are in Monterey (4,600) and Napa (2,370). Yolo's 575 acres in the Clarksburg AVA are among the most prized.

CHIANTI
An increasingly rare generic name for red wines in recent years. The name was borrowed from Tuscany in Italy.

CHILES VALLEY
A subregion of Napa that rises several hundred feet higher than the main valley in hills to the e. of St. Helena and Calistoga. Though highly defined topographically, it is not a separate AVA, but rather included in the Napa Valley AVA.

CHIMNEY ROCK   Napa   T $10.50–$15
Owners Hack and Stella Wilson abandoned the cola business for a 75-acre vineyard and 12,000-case winery in the Stag's Leap district of southern Napa. When the vineyard is mature, production is planned to level out at 20,000 cases. The first wines were 84s made in temporary quarters; the permanent winery was ready well ahead of the 89s.
NYR: Sauvignon Blanc, Chardonnay, and Cabernet Sauvignon.

CHRISTIAN BROTHERS WINERY, THE   Napa/Fresno   T,S,D $3.89–$16   In 1989, Heublein, Inc. bought the winery from the Catholic teaching order that founded it in 1888. The properties include 1,200 acres of vines and two substantial cellars in the Napa Valley for table and sparkling wines, plus another 1,200 acres and two big cellars in the San Joaquin Valley for dessert wines and brandies. The Brothers also bought substantial tonnage in both regions to round out an annual volume close to one million cases. The original owners had mounted an aggressive campaign in recent years to upgrade an image that had faded somewhat because they stayed too long with nonvintage blending of their foremost varietals. The new look included Reserve bottlings as well as vintage dates. Heublein has not announced any change of course.
** Chardonnay (reliably appealing), Special Reserve Chardonnay (distinctly perfumed by new oak), Fumé Blanc, Chenin Blanc (well off-dry), Johannisberg Riesling, White Zinfandel, Estate Cabernet Sauvignon (big jump in quality, character with 85), Merlot, and Zinfandel all come under The Christian Brothers label, as do Napa Classic Red, White, and Blush. The Christian Brothers dessert wines are Dry Sherry, Golden Sherry, Cream Sherry, Meloso Cream, Ruby Port, Tawny Port, and Vintage Tawny Port.
* Mont LaSalle Chablis, Burgundy, Napa Rosé, and a blush are relatively dry generics. Blanc, Blush, Le Peach, and Wild Berry are generic and flavored sweet wines labeled Château La Salle.

CHRISTINE WOODS   Mendocino   T $4–$10
Not named for the owner (Vernon Rose) or one of his old flames, but rather for a logging hamlet in an old Anderson Valley forest where Rose had his first, tiny cellar. All 1,000

cases come from a small vineyard near Navarro, since late 1988 the site of Rose's permanent cellar. His first wine was an 83 Cabernet.

NYR: Chardonnay, White Riesling, Sauvignon Blanc, Cabernet Sauvignon, and Merlot.

CHRISTOPHE VINEYARDS

A growing merchant brand owned by France's Jean-Claude Boisset, S.A. offers well-made, good-value $3.50–$10 wines from North Coast and Central Coast sources. The roster: Joliesse (white), Mauve (blush), Sauvignon Blanc, Chardonnay, Chardonnay-Reserve, and Cabernet Sauvignon–Reserve.

CIENEGA VALLEY AVA

Developed by Almaden Vineyards before it pulled out of the region, the area runs along the w. side of a small river valley s. of Hollister. A sub-AVA, Lime Kiln Valley, lies within its southern tip. Three small wineries, two of them with vineyards of their own, are within its boundaries. Much of the Almaden vineyard that defined the AVA has been abandoned.

CILURZO VINEYARD AND WINERY Temecula T
$6–$12   Vincenzo Cilurzo's main lighting job is in television; his moonlighting job since 1978 has been running a winery that slowly got too big to be a hobby. In 1987–88 he and his wife, Audrey, dropped the last of such offbeat, quasi-homemades as Vincheno and Chenite, and hired a full-time winemaker to run the 10,000-case cellar. A small part of that volume comes from their own 9 acres, the rest from locally bought grapes.

*→·** Chardonnay, Sauvignon Blanc, Chenin Blanc, White Zinfandel, Nouveau Petite Sirah, Petite Sirah, Pinot Noir, and Cabernet Sauvignon. Late Harvest Johannisberg comes when a vintage permits.

CLAIBORNE & CHURCHILL San Luis Obispo T
$5–$8   What Claiborne (Clay) Thompson really wants to do is make dry whites in the Alsatian style. In one of the neater twists in the age of Chardonnay, he makes a bit of Chardonnay to help underwrite his nobler cause. The winery at San Luis Obispo town draws entirely on Central Coast grapes, most of them from the Santa Maria Valley AVA. Thompson's first vintage was 83; current annual production is 3,000 cases.

• Gewürztraminer, Dry Riesling (barely off-dry), Dry Muscat (as a counterpart to Tokay d'Alsace), and Proprietor's Blend (subtitled Edelzwicker after the Alsatian model).

CLARET

A generic term for red wine, long out of vogue, is coming back on the labels of dry reds. Some are costly blends of the traditional varieties of Bordeaux (Cabernet Sauvignon, Cabernet Franc, Malbec, Merlot, and Petit Verdot).

CLARKSBURG AVA

A deep-soiled district in Sacramento and Yolo counties, it is entirely behind the levees that form man-made islands all through the Sacramento River delta. The AVA reaches from a point w. of Sacramento almost to Fairfield. Merritt Island is a sub-AVA within it. Both have won particular notice for fragrant Chenin Blancs, but the more than 1,000 acres of vineyards grow a wide spectrum of varieties.

CLINE CELLARS   Contra Costa   T $4–$18
Owner/winemaker Fred Cline started his cellars in eastern Contra Costa County in an effort to revive a flagging district where he had made wine as a boy at his Italian grandfather's side. His first vintage was 83. Within two years varieties with origins in the Rhône had caught his fancy. Cline is making 5,000 cases, all from 200 acres of graybeard vineyards he manages near the town of Oakley.
NYR: Mourvedre,   Oakley   Cuvée   (Mourvedre-Zinfandel-Carignane proprietary blend), Zinfandel, Late Harvest Zinfandel, and—lone white—Semillon.

CLOS DU BOIS   Sonoma   T $8–$22.50
A well-established Healdsburg winery with 540 acres of vineyards in the Alexander Valley and Dry Creek Valley AVAs. Changed hands in 1988, but not direction. Frank Woods founded the label with 74s and quickly moved to produce layers of each major varietal from regular through reserve to vineyard-designated. New owner Hiram Walker–Allied Lyons is continuing with that program. Annual production is 205,000 cases.
*** Chardonnay-Calcaire (big but has finesse) 81 83 84 85 86; Chardonnay-Flintwood (also big but finessey) 81 84 85 86 87; Marlstone (a proprietary based in Merlot and named after its Alexander Valley vineyard, always deftly balanced, and distinctive for its combination of varietal, regional, and oak flavors) 78 79 81 83.
→* Cabernet Sauvignon-Briarcrest (herbaceous and marked by American oaklike flavors); Cabernet Sauvignon–Proprietor's Reserve; Merlot; Alexander Valley Chardonnay–Barrel Fermented and Chardonnay–Proprietor's Reserve (deftly toasty), Sauvignon Blanc (Sonoma-grassy, reliable).
** Gewürztraminer; Pinot Noir; Early Harvest Johannisberg Riesling.

CLOS DU VAL WINE CO.   Napa   T $9–$30
The property of a French-American family was an overnight success with its first two vintages, 72 and 73. Bordeaux-born and -trained manager/partner/winemaker Bernard Portet has gone from strength to strength with Cabernet Sauvignon and Merlot made to the tastes of his ancestors, and he has thought original thoughts about Zinfandel. This, the original roster of wines, has been augmented by several others. Annual volume is now 55,000 cases, nearly all from owned and bought Napa grapes. Clos du Val's primary owned vineyards are 135 acres (mostly Cabernet and Merlot) at the winery, and 120 acres (mainly Chardonnay and Pinot Noir) in Carneros.
**** Cabernet Sauvignon (always silky and gracefully balanced, ever more complex and intriguing through at least a dozen years) 73 74 75 78 79 81 83 84 85; Cabernet Sauvignon–Reserve (an extra depth, a few extra layers of

flavor, separate it from the regular); and Merlot (softer textures and more straightforward flavors than the Cabernet, but still considerable wine) 81 83 84 85.

*** Semillon (ripe, richly flavored, and yet all polish and restraint, great with white-fleshed fish) 83 84 85; and Zinfandel (powerful in flavor, big, yet somehow honed to something approaching elegance) 80 81 83 85.

→* Chardonnay (lean, crisp, understated, fine in youth); Pinot Noir (round, velvety, distinctive in flavors).

CLOS PEGASE Napa T $8.50–$17
Meant from the outset to be as much a showplace of architecture and art as a working winery, Clos Pegase is just down-valley from Calistoga. The first wines were 84s made in leased space; the cellar was up in time for the 85s. All of the 40,000 cases are made from bought-in Napa grapes. NYR: Sauvignon Blanc (middle-of-the-road); Napa Valley Chardonnay (also sound, conventional); Carneros Chardonnay (new with 86); Cabernet Sauvignon; Merlot (new with 86); and Cabernet Franc (also first made in 86).

COCKTAIL SHERRY
See SHERRY.

COHN WINERY, B.R. Sonoma T $12–$18
Bruce Cohn's first and still primary career is managing rock groups (Doobie Brothers and others). His 5,000-case winery in the Sonoma Valley dates from 84. All of the grapes come from the owner's Olive Hill Vineyard near Glen Ellen. NYR: Chardonnay (big, toasty in the early going), and Cabernet Sauvignon (perfumed more by new oak than Cabernet in the debut 84). A Barrel Reserve Chardonnay begins with an 86.

COLD DUCK
Red sparkling wine type typically containing some Concord, though there is no legal requirement. A sweet sipper, it has faded steadily from favor after a brief heyday in the 1960s.

COLE RANCH AVA
A one-vineyard, no-winery AVA in hilly country s.e. of Ukiah in Mendocino County. The AVA is 150 acres, of which 61 are planted. The vineyard name has appeared on Fetzer Cabernet Sauvignons, but not in the past several vintages.

CONCANNON VINEYARD Alameda T
$3.60–$13.67 One of the Livermore Valley's finest names before and after Prohibition continues as a well-regarded label under its second owner since the founding family sold in 1982. Distiller's Company, Ltd. bought the property then and hired winemaker Sergio Traverso to refurbish both the old cellars and the adjoining 180 acres of vineyard. Distiller's sold in 1988 to a partnership of Traverso and the owners of Germany's Deinhard. The annual production of 85,000 cases comes from the home property plus purchased grapes, most from San Luis Obispo and Santa Barbara counties.

→* Estate Sauvignon Blanc (surprisingly full-bodied among Sauvignons, and complex in flavor) 85 86. Selected Vineyards Chardonnay (lean, crisp, a bit toasty); Estate Petite Sirah (fat, ripe).
** Estate Cabernet Sauvignon; White Zinfandel; Fumé Blanc; Petite Sirah.
* Vintage White, Burgundy.

CONGRESS SPRINGS VINEYARD Santa Clara T $5–$30 Partner and winemaker Dan Gehrs began making his mark with barrel-fermented whites from old vineyards in the Santa Cruz Mountains in his first vintage, 76. More recently he has developed an itch to make barrel-fermented, champagne-method sparklers. The winery and 11 acres of Chardonnay and Zinfandel are in steep country w. of Saratoga. The rest of the grapes for 30,000 cases come mostly from the Santa Cruz Mountain AVA and the San Ysidro vineyard in southern Santa Clara County, which Gehrs prizes.
*** Pinot Blanc (lean, tart, refreshing); Semillon (splendid, but dropping from the list for want of an audience); Estate Chardonnay, Santa Clara Chardonnay–barrel-fermented, and Santa Clara Chardonnay (all subtle, seamless marriages of fruit, oak flavors in light, crisp wines) 81 83 84 85.
• Estate Zinfandel, Santa Cruz Mountains Cabernet Franc, and Pinot Noir.
NYR: Brut (new with 86).

CONN CREEK Napa T $9.50–$13.50
The Rutherford winery was bought in 1986 by Stimson Lane, a company more familiar to wine connoisseurs as Washington's Château Ste.-Michelle. The new owners added two wines to a short roster, but have minimized changes in the direction set by Bill and Kathy Collins, who launched the label with a 73 Cabernet. About a quarter of the annual 30,000 cases come from long-affiliated vineyards called Tres Niños (mostly Chardonnay e. of Yountville) and Collins (Zinfandel n. of St. Helena); the rest is from bought Napa grapes.
** Cabernet Sauvignon (ripe, fleshy, flavorful of Cabernet); Chardonnay (big, almost tropically ripe fruit); and Zinfandel (sturdy, from old vines).
NYR: Merlot (first try in 85), and Sauvignon Blanc (86 debut).

CONROTTO WINERY, A. Santa Clara T $2.95–$8.95 In the Hecker Pass district w. of Gilroy, Jim Burr continues with a 5,000-case winery long owned and run by his late father-in-law, Anselmo Conrotto. Burr supplements grapes from his own 13.5 acres at the winery with others bought from the area and also Monterey.
* Burgundy, Chablis, Vin Rosé, Chardonnay, Chenin Blanc, Symphony, White Zinfandel, Cabernet Sauvignon, Grenache, Carignane, Petite Sirah, Cream Sherry, and others.

COOK WINERY, R & J Yolo T $3.99–$8.99
In the Clarksburg AVA, behind levees on the n. bank of the Sacramento River, the 50,000-case winery of Roger and Joanne Cook first crushed in 79. Most of the grapes come

from the Cooks' own 130 acres of vines next to the cellars, but they supplement that crop with grapes from a rented ranch plus bought-in Chardonnay.

• Chardonnay, Fumé Blanc, Chenin Blanc, White Merlot, Cabernet Sauvignon, Petite Sirah, Merlot (ripe, soft, a bit woody), Delta Red, Delta White, and Delta Blush. There is also a proprietary from Orange Muscat called Moonlight Mist.

COOK'S AMERICAN CHAMPAGNE San Joaquin S $3.99–$5.99 A brand of Charmat Champagne owned by Guild and made at a Guild cellar in Lodi. Volume is 1.1 million cases.

[*] Brut (particularly good value, well made), Extra Dry, Blush (agreeably fruity), Blanc de Noir and Grand Reserve Champagnes, and a sparkling White Zinfandel.

CORBETT CANYON San Luis Obispo T $4.49–$8 A substantial winery in the Edna Valley has had three owners since 1983. The Wine Group purchased it from Glenmore Distillers in 1988 to be the prestige label in a stable that includes Franzia and Mogen David. The new owners then purchased the 200-acre Los Alamos Vineyard in Santa Barbara County as the basic source for the annual production, now well past 100,000 cases and climbing. The winery also buys grapes from both Santa Barbara and San Luis Obispo counties. All of the wines except White Zinfandel are Central Coast, or a more specific appellation within that region.

** Reserve Chardonnay; Reserve Pinot Noir (impressive 86 from Santa Barbara); Select Chardonnay (subtly toasty, well-balanced); Sauvignon Blanc; and Cabernet Sauvignon. [*→**] Coastal Classic Chardonnay (reliably pleasing, focused on fruit); Fumé Blanc (distinctly regional, well made); White Zinfandel; and Cabernet Sauvignon.

COSENTINO WINE CO. Stanislaus/Napa T,S $10–$22 A winery in transition. Owner Mitchell Cosentino started in 1980 at a base in Modesto using mostly San Joaquin and Sacramento Valley grapes, and selling his wine under the now disappearing Crystal Valley label. He has slowly shifted toward North Coast grapes since and broke ground in 1989 for a winery just n. of Yountville, to be closer to the Mendocino and Napa vineyards from which he buys grapes. Production is at 12,000 cases on the way to a planned maximum of 20,000.

NYR: Cabernet Sauvignon (sturdy, rich with fruit, noticeably marked by new oak flavors); Cabernet Franc (lots of tannic spine, plenty of fruit); Merlot; The Poet (Cabernet-based proprietary in same vein as other reds); The Sculptor Chardonnay; and North Coast Chardonnay. A sparkler sells under the Robins Glow label. Sonoma Pinot Noir and Francesca d'Amore (an off-dry, lightly fortified, Muscat-based proprietary).

COTURRI & SONS, H. Sonoma T $8.50–$13.75 A family-owned winery near Glen Ellen in the Sonoma Valley AVA makes 3,000 cases a year of wines to which neither

SO_2 nor any other preservative is added, and which see little or no filtration. Part of the production comes from the family's 25-acre vineyard; the rest is from grapes bought in Sonoma Valley. The first vintage was 79.

• Cabernet Sauvignon, Pinot Noir, Zinfandel (all tending toward thick textures and plummy to raisiny flavors).

CREAM SHERRY
See SHERRY.

CREMANT
A term originally from Champagne for wines made by the champagne method, but with about one-third the CO_2 found in Champagnes. Californian versions thus far have been dessert sweet. Schramsberg pioneered the type; others are now following.

CRESCINI   Santa Cruz   T $6.50–$10
Located in Soquel, the part-time winery of Richard and Paule Crescini yields about 1,500 cases a year of wines from grapes bought as far n. as Napa, as far s. as Monterey. The Crescinis started with 80s. Most of what they make sells directly from the winery or by mail order.

• Napa Sauvignon Blanc (the only white), Monterey Cabernet Franc (from Ventana), Napa Cabernet Sauvignon (Rutherford), Santa Clara Petite Sirah, and Santa Clara Zinfandel.

CRESTA BLANCA
A historic California name with roots in Livermore, owned by Guild Winery; since 1987 it has been used only in the Asian export market. It was attached for some years to a Ukiah winery now known as Mendocino Vineyard.

CRESTON MANOR   San Luis Obispo   T
$6–$17.50   In 1982 a small partnership launched a 95-acre vineyard and 7,500-case winery in the remote s.e. quarter of the Paso Robles AVA. By 1988 the partnership had reconfigured, the vineyard holdings had expanded to 140 acres (the added acreage w. of Paso Robles town), and production approached 25,000 cases. In recent vintages all or virtually all of the grapes have come from the home AVA, most of the bought-in ones from near neighbors.

** Sauvignon Blanc (lean, refreshing early but has been quick to fade); Chardonnay (pleasing fruit flavors, well-balanced); White Zinfandel; Cabernet Sauvignon, Cabernet Sauvignon–Winemaker's Selection (some regional herbaceousness, but well-made, well-balanced); Petite de Noir (a Pinot Noir produced using carbonic maceration).

CRIBARI   San Joaquin/Fresno   T $3.29
Now the principal label for Guild Wineries, Cribari has been established as a table wine label focused on inexpensive varietals, mostly from San Joaquin Valley grapes. Production is at 2 million cases.

* Chardonnay, Fumé Blanc (just off-dry at 0.5% r.s.), Sauvignon Blanc (1.5% r.s.), French Colombard, Chenin Blanc, White Zinfandel, White Cabernet, Cabernet Sauvignon, and Zinfandel. California Red, White, and Blush are available only in 1.5-liter bottles.

CRICHTON HALL Napa T $16
The whole game is Chardonnay from Richard and Judith Crichton's 17 acres on the w. side of the valley just n. of the town of Napa. The first vintage was 85; production has peaked at 4,000 cases.
NYR: Chardonnay (toasty but retains intriguing facets of fruit, well-balanced).

CRONIN VINEYARDS Santa Clara T $12–$25
Of 1,200 cases a year, 800 are Chardonnay in four separate lots . . . just to keep people confused, according to owner/winemaker Duane Cronin. The first vintage at his winery in the Santa Cruz Mountains was 80.
• Napa Valley Chardonnay, Alexander Valley Chardonnay, Monterey Chardonnay–Ventana, and Estate Chardonnay. Also: Pinot Noir (Santa Cruz Mountains as often as possible), Napa Valley Cabernet Sauvignon, San Mateo County Cabernet-Merlot.

CRYSTAL CREEK
A brand owned by the proprietors of SAN MARTIN and operated through San Martin's cellars in southern Santa Clara County. Most but not all of the grapes are bought in Monterey County for $4–$7 Chardonnay, Sauvignon Blanc, White Zinfandel, and Cabernet Sauvignon. Early production is 70,000 cases a year; the plan is to grow rapidly.

CRYSTAL VALLEY
A fading second label for COSENTINO WINE COMPANY.

CUCAMONGA
A historic district in San Bernardino County just e. of the Los Angeles County line. Cucamonga spreads from the town of Ontario e. as far as Mira Loma, but only as tatters of its former self. Industrial and urban developments have reduced local vineyards from a peak of 12,000 acres to no more than 1,000, most of those under pressure. Dry, always hot, and on sandy soils, the district has been at its best with dessert types. The two most-planted varieties are Zinfandel and Mission.

CULBERTSON WINERY, JOHN Riverside S
$10.80–$17.50   A specialist in Champagne-method sparklers started amid the avocado groves of Fallbrook in San Diego County in 1980, and has since moved most of the operation northward to Temecula, from whence a majority of the grapes have come all along. Production has shot from 8,000 cases in 84 to 40,000 in 88.
** Brut (almost perfumey overtones from ripe fruit are its hallmark); Natural (drier than the Brut, otherwise similar).
NYR: Blanc de Noir, Cuvée Frontignan, Cuvée Rouge, and Brut Rosé.

THE CUTLER CELLAR
The winemaker label of Lance Cutler (Gundlach-Bundschu) goes on a Sonoma Valley Cabernet Sauvignon from Batto Ranch. Cutler's first vintage was 85.

CUVAISON, INC. Napa T $9.95–$19.50
The winery maundered along from its founding in 1970 until it was bought in 1979 by a Swiss banking family named

Schmidheiny. They installed their own management and winemaking teams and bought a 400-acre vineyard property in Carneros, the opposite end of the valley from their 65,000-case cellar near Calistoga. Cuvaison caught fire with its Chardonnay as soon as that vineyard came into play. The reds are now beginning to follow its lead.

→* Chardonnay (packed with fruit through 84; subtle, layered with flavors, beautifully balanced since) 85 86 87.

** Cabernet Sauvignon (steely hard with tannins until 84 began a turn toward greater approachability at no loss of intensity in flavor) 84; and Zinfandel.

NYR: Merlot (recent addition reinforces new style in reds).

CUVÉE
A blended lot of any sort . . . of vineyards, grape varieties, vintages, or all three. The word comes from Champagne and is most commonly used to identify specific bottlings of sparkling wines. It does, however, appear on still wines.

CYGNET CELLARS   San Benito   T $8.50
Since its first crush, 78, a weekend winery in the w. hills of the Paicines River Valley has specialized in big, ripe, heady, sometimes sweet reds. All of the grapes are bought, mostly from vineyards in the home county, but also from the Shandon area in San Luis Obispo's Paso Robles AVA. Owner/winemaker Jim Johnson produces about 2,000 cases a year.
• Zinfandel, Petite Sirah, Carignane, and Pinot St. George.

DALLA VALLE VINEYARD   Napa   T $15
The Dalla Valle family makes only Cabernet Sauvignon from its 24-acre vineyard on w.-facing slopes above the Silverado Trail at Oakville. The debut vintage, 86, yielded 700 cases; the goal is 2,000 as the vines mature. Dalla Valle's first wine was scheduled for release in late 1989.

DANIEL SOCIETY, JOHN
The company name behind DOMINUS and also a second label used for varietal Cabernet Sauvignons from the same vineyard source as the flagship, but deemed not quite up to the prestige label. An 84 was the first one.

DAUME WINERY   Ventura   T $7.50–$9
Owner/winemaker John Daume buys Central Coast grapes to make some 2,000 cases of wine a year, all of it sold in southern California. His first vintage was 82.
• Fumé Blanc, Chardonnay, Cabernet Sauvignon, and Zinfandel.

DEER PARK WINERY   Napa   T $4.50–$10
The family winery of Dave Clark draws grapes from its own and other vineyards on Howell Mountain to produce nearly all of its 5,000 cases a year, but gets a bit of Chardonnay from another vineyard it owns in San Diego County, of all places. Clark has been in his own cellars since 1979 after apprenticing at Clos du Val and Cuvaison.

[**] Zinfandel (recently Howell Mountain AVA, always sound, sturdy red); Petite Sirah (ditto to Zinfandel).

** Chardonnay (sometimes Napa, sometimes San Diego); Sauvignon Blanc (recently has become estate bottled from vines at the winery on Howell Mountain).

DEER VALLEY
A second label for SMITH & HOOK, giving way in 1989 to another second label, LONE OAK.

DEHLINGER WINERY Sonoma   T $9–$13
Owner/winemaker Tom Dehlinger has shown a sure sense of style in all his wines since the beginning 75s at his 9,000-case cellar and 31-acre vineyard in the Russian River Valley s.e. of Forestville. His particular bent seems to be for big, age-worthy reds. All of the wines except Merlot are now estate grown.
→* Pinot Noir (uncommonly dark, richly aromatic of well-married fruit, wood; not at peak form until eight years old in favorable vintages) 79 80 82 84 85 87.
*** Chardonnay (lean, tart, focused on slow-to-open varietal flavors) 85 87. A fine Zinfandel disappears after the 83.
** Cabernet Sauvignon (modestly herbaceous, well-ripened, fleshy—a rarity in the lower Russian River Valley). NYR: Merlot (begun with 84; thus far an echo of the Cabernet); Cabernet Franc (first tiny lot from 86).

DELICATO VINEYARDS San Joaquin Monterey
T,S $1.79–$9.95   Definitely a winery on the move both literally and figuratively. The owning Indelicato family began building the San Joaquin Valley cellar near Manteca in the thirties and sold only in bulk for years. They turned to bottled ordinary wines only with the seventies. Since then the trend has been upward and westward. In 1988 the family firm acquired 13,000 acres of Monterey County vineyard near King City (dwarfing its 265-acre property at the town of Clements) and quickly built a fermenting winery on the Monterey property. The Indelicatos already were bottling about 750,000 cases under various labels including Delicato, and selling still more in bulk.
** Spumante, Zinfandel, Petite Sirah.
* Moselle Blanc, Green Hungarian, Chablis, Sauterne, Vin Rosé, Burgundy.

DELOACH VINEYARDS Sonoma   T $6.75–$25
A still-rising star in the Russian River Valley, the winery has made its fame thus far for Chardonnay, but does well right across the board. Cecil DeLoach and family have seen sales grow from 10,000 to 70,000 cases since 1979, more than 20,000 of the current total Chardonnay. The family owns and leases 150 acres on several ranches between Santa Rosa and Forestville. Bought-in grapes come from the same neighborhood.
**** Chardonnay (manages to be firm, fat at same time, vibrates with aromas of ripe Chardonnay, the ultimate boiled-lobster-and-drawn-butter wine) 81 82 84 85 87; and Chardonnay-OFS (a slightly leaner, woodier, costlier running mate).
*** Pinot Noir (dark, tannic for type, richly scented with berries; slow to evolve) 79 81 82 84 86; Pinot Noir–OFS (the equivalent to the select Chardonnay); Zinfandel (dark, intensely varietal, sometimes a bit heady; a tomato sauce special) 79 84 85 87; White Zinfandel (superfruity, off-dry, yet cleansing) most recent.

** Gewürztraminer (pneumatic); Sauvignon Blanc (almost tropical ripe flavors in a wine that sees very little wood); Fumé Blanc (wood-aged, something of a poor man's Chardonnay).
NYR: Cabernet Sauvignon–OFS (in chosen vintages; next up, 86).

DELORIMIER Sonoma   T $8.50–$16
The DeLorimier family's estate winery, based in 65 acres of Alexander Valley vineyard e. of Geyserville, began with the vintage of 86. All the wines go by proprietary names, three because they are blends based in traditions of Bordeaux, the fourth to stay in step. Initial production is 5,000 cases; the plan is to grow to the capacity of the vineyard.
NYR: Spectrum (Sauvignon Blanc + Semillon); Lace (late-harvest Sauvignon Blanc); Mosaic (Cabernet Sauvignon + Merlot + Cabernet Franc); Prism (100% Chardonnay). All were attractive in their debut vintage.

DEMI-SEC
See CHAMPAGNE.

DEMOOR Napa   T $6.25–$14
The winery started in the midseventies as Napa Cellars and retains that name as a second label for modestly priced varietals. The DeMoor identity came in 1987 when new owners of that name took over the winery just n. of Yountville. They buy Napa grapes to make 14,000 cases of wine a year, with all the emphasis on Cabernet and Chardonnay.
*→** Chardonnay (ripe, quickly mature); Sauvignon Blanc (has also matured quickly); Cabernet Sauvignon (dark, ultratannic, with some farmyard aromas); and Zinfandel.

DE NATALE Sonoma   T $4.75–$6.50
Ron De Natale grew up making wine at his father's side, kept on as a home winemaker, and finally bonded a small, weekend winery in time to make 85s. Most of his grapes come from his 10-acre ranch in the Napa Valley and 5 acres nearer the winery in the Russian River Valley, but he buys Dry Creek Valley Zinfandel. Volume edges toward 1,000 cases.
NYR: Chardonnay, Sauvignon Blanc, Cabernet Sauvignon, Pinot Noir, and Zinfandel.

DESSERT WINE
For federal taxation purposes, this class includes all wines with brandy added to bring total alcohol between 17 and 21%: Angelicas, Ports, Muscatels, Sherries (no matter how dry), and Tokays. In normal English usage the term would also include such wines as Rieslings, Traminers, and Semillons, with 4% or more of sugar and 12% or less of alcohol, but these are usually categorized as LATE HARVEST by producers and consumers, and defined as table wines for tax purposes.

DEVLIN WINE CELLARS Santa Cruz   T
$4.50–$9.50   Chuck Devlin's Soquel winery is known for

sometimes-striking reds, less famous for whites. Devlin buys nearly all of his grapes for whites in the Central Coast and gets most of his reds from the same region but does reach n. to Sonoma. Production is about 10,000 cases a year, all sold at the cellar door or by mail order.

→* Sonoma Cabernet Sauvignon (lean, supple, understated for flavor); Santa Cruz Mountains Cabernet Sauvignon (firmer and rather more herbaceous than its running mate).

** Monterey Chardonnay–La Reina Vineyard; Santa Cruz Mountains Chardonnay; Gewürztraminer; Sauvignon Blanc; Muscat Canelli; White Riesling; White Zinfandel; Merlot; Pinot Noir.

DIAMOND CREEK VINEYARDS Napa T $30
At the outset, in 1972, Al Brounstein divided his 20-acre Cabernet Sauvignon vineyard in hills above Calistoga into three blocks: Volcanic Hill, Red Rock Terrace, Gravelly Meadow. Ever since, he has made separate lots of wine under those names, leaving a fanatically loyal clientele to endless debate of the relative merits. Total production is 3,000 cases, with Volcanic Hill about half of that.

*** Volcanic Hill, Red Rock Terrace, Gravelly Meadow (all three dark, tannic, intensely varietal) 79 81 83 ̇84.

DIAMOND OAKS VINEYARDS Sonoma T
$4.50–$11 Dinesh Maniar owns 350 acres of bearing vineyard, part in the Russian River Valley at Windsor, the rest in the Napa Valley at Calistoga and in Wild Horse Canyon e. of Napa city. He has been taking enough fruit to squeeze 30,000 cases of varietal wine a year through a hopelessly small, outmoded winery near Cloverdale. In 1988 Maniar cut production back in preparation for building a new winery that will allow him to expand to 60,000 cases a year. He offers Diamond Oaks as a reserve line and Thomas Knight Signature as a regular one.

• Diamond Oaks Cabernet Sauvignon, Chardonnay, and Sauvignon Blanc; Thomas Knight Signature Cabernet Sauvignon, Chardonnay, and Sauvignon Blanc.

DOLAN VINEYARDS Mendocino T $15
In Redwood Valley, the 1,200-case busman's holiday winery of Fetzer Vineyards' winemaker Paul Dolan uses bought-in local fruit to produce wines explicitly designed to Dolan's taste. His first vintage was 80.

** Cabernet Sauvignon (ripe, firm, well-wooded); Chardonnay (dark, woody, toasty).

DOMAINE BUENA VISTA
Separate label of BUENA VISTA VINEYARDS for its trio of attractive proprietaries.

DOMAINE CARNEROS Napa S $20
The new-in-1987 sparkling wine venture of France's Taittinger, U.S.'s Kobrand, and some private investors has an imposing cellar (styled after La Marqueterie at Reims) in Napa's half of Carneros amid its own 110 acres of vines. Debut of the estate-grown 87 Brut (Pinot Noir, Chardonnay, Pinot Blanc, Pinot Meunier) is scheduled for 1990.

Initial volume is 4,000 cases, with plans to grow to 40,000 within five years.

DOMAINE CHANDON   Napa   S $13.95–$18.95
Moët et Hennessey's Napa sparkling wine venture celebrated its tenth birthday in 1982 by hitting an annual sales mark of 250,000 cases. It is now edging past 500,000. Chandon's own vineyards (200 acres around the Yountville winery, 100 high in the Mayacamas range, 500 in Carneros and room to plant more there) dominate the cuvées, but bought-in grapes from the same areas add depth and stability. The company also owns the SHADOW CREEK label, bought in 1988.
→* Reserve (complex toasty notes, understated fruit flavors, lovely creamy texture).
*** Brut (a slightly paler echo of the Reserve); Blanc de Noirs (much the fullest-bodied, fullest-flavored of the three, and perhaps the best-suited with dinner).

DOMAINE FELIPE
A second label of MONT ST. JOHN for Napa varietals.

DOMAINE KARAKASH   Napa   T $8–$12·
Owner Miles Karakasevich's heart is with alambic brandies and liqueurs, but he does make table wine. The earliest vintages are from Mendocino grapes (he worked there); more recent wines have come from Sonoma and Napa fruit. His first vintage under the Karakash label was 83.
NYR: Chardonnay; Sauvignon Blanc; Charbay (a proprietary dessert wine of barrel-fermented Chardonnay and a brandy liqueur, with 18% alcohol and 10% r.s.).

DOMAINE LAURIER   Sonoma   T $7–$14.50
Jacob and Barbara Shilo launched the Sonoma–Green Valley cellar and vineyard in 1978. In 1989, after Jacob's death, Barbara sold the property to the same local investment group that owns Lyeth Vineyards. Production has edged past 17,000 cases. The estate vineyard n.w. of Forestville stays at 17 acres; all of the bought-in grapes come from growers in the tiny Sonoma–Green Valley AVA.
*** Sauvignon Blanc (fine Sauvignon flavors plus enticing extras gotten with blue smoke and mirrors) 84 85 86; Chardonnay (fine varietal flavors, well-balanced) 84 85 86.
** Pinot Noir (very pale yet wants years in bottle to develop pleasing bouquets); Cabernet Sauvignon (sound, steady).

DOMAINE MICHEL   Sonoma   T $16–$19
Swiss banker Jean-Jacques Michel owns 60 acres of Cabernet Sauvignon and Chardonnay on Dry Creek Valley benchlands, and a 25,000-case cellar set amid the vines. The label started with an 84 Cabernet Sauvignon and an 85 Chardonnay.
NYR: Cabernet Sauvignon (thoroughly ripe, a bit weighty in its first outings); Chardonnay (full to heavy, heavily scented by new wood in both of its first two vintages).

DOMAINE MONTREAUX   Napa   S $32
The owner of MONTICELLO CELLARS separated a part of his vineyards from the main block and built a separate winery

in which to produce tiny lots of distinctively styled sparkling wine. Production is about 600 cases, and planned to grow very slowly. The first vintage was 83; it will be succeeded by the 85.

NYR: Brut (powerfully flavored; style still resolving).

DOMAINE MUMM   Napa   S $15–$20

The joint-venture sparkling wine firm of G. H. Mumm and Seagrams, Inc. began making elements of the cuvées for nonvintage Napa Brut in 1983, with Guy DeVaux (longtime Gold Seal) as the resident champagnemaster and Michel Budin of Mumm as the French connection. The nonvintage wine has been joined by a vintage Brut produced only in selected years and a vineyard-designated vintage Brut from Winery Lake Vineyard in the Carneros AVA. The nonvintage comes from a broad range of Napa vineyards, the vintage from properties focused in Carneros and the Big Ranch Road district n. of Napa city. Current production at a new-in-1988 winery e. of Rutherford is 40,000 cases; the midterm goal is 125,000.

NYR: Brut–Cuvée Prestige (lean, crisp, delicately flavored); Brut–Vintage Reserve (richer flavors, creamier textures than the nonvintage, but still underplayed) 85; Brut–Winery Lake (some genuinely exotic overtones from the fruit separate it clearly—and intriguingly—from the vintage Brut in its first outing) 86.

DOMAINE NAPA   Napa   T $7.50–$15

This truly international venture is owned by Frenchman Michel Perret and has New Zealander Grant Taylor as winemaker. Vineyardist Perret's 10,000-case winery draws on his 10 acres at Rutherford and 200 that he manages in the Napa Valley. The first vintage was 83; the plan is to grow to 20,000 cases.

NYR: Cabernet Sauvignon (began to show some style with 85); Chardonnay (delicately toasty, underplayed all around).

DOMAINE ST. GEORGE   Sonoma   T $3.29–$5.99

The much-enlarged successor at Healdsburg of an old country winery called Cambiaso. Owned by an Asian company called Four Seas Investment, the 300,000-case Domaine St. George uses all bought grapes, most from Sonoma, some from Napa, and some from Clarksburg AVA.

*→** Chardonnay, Sauvignon Blanc, White Zinfandel, Cabernet Sauvignon, Proprietor Red, and Proprietor White.

DOMINUS   Napa   T $40

A Cabernet Sauvignon–based proprietary wine by the French-American collaboration of *bordelais* wine guru Christian Moeuix and Napa natives Robin Lail and Marcia Smith, daughters of longtime Inglenook owner John Daniel and owners of the great Napanook vineyard at Yountville, from whence the grapes. In 1988 the partners released their 84 ahead of the ultrafirm debut 83. Production is about 4,000 cases in leased space pending construction of a permanent cellar.

NYR: Dominus (firmly tannic, beautifully proportioned,

showing some signs of Bordeaux-like farmyard aromas but still closed up tight in early 1989) 84.

DONATONI WINERY   Los Angeles   T $9.50
In a warehouse just past the end of LAX runway 25R, airline pilot Hank Donatoni makes about 1,000 cases of wine a year. When he retires, he plans to pack up and move to Paso Robles, the region where he has bought most of his grapes since the start-up vintage, 79.
• Cabernet Sauvignon, Chardonnay.

DONNA MARIA VINEYARDS
Original name of winery now operating as CHALK HILL.

DORÉ, J. PATRICK
A merchant brand owned by Coastal Wines and named after its president, who buys and blends 200,000 cases of $4.49–$5.99 wine a year, most of the total from coastal counties. The good-value list: Chardonnay, Fumé Blanc, Chablis, White Zinfandel, Cabernet Sauvignon, and a Charmat Champagne.

DRY
Correctly, a wine with no fermentable sugar. As a tasting term, it describes just such a wine, one with no sweetness. To the public's confusion "dry" is often used on labels of wines with 1% r.s. and more (0.5% is the average human threshold for sweetness). Chenin Blancs are the notorious example.

DRY CREEK VALLEY AVA
This short, narrow valley running n.w. from Healdsburg has been a traditional source of rich Zinfandel and underrated Petite Sirah since the 1880s. In recent times Cabernet Sauvignon and Sauvignon Blanc have been added to the roster of successes. Current plantings exceed 5,500 acres; more than a dozen wineries lie within its boundaries.

DRY CREEK VINEYARD   Sonoma   T $6.25–$12
Ebullient David Stare got in on the ground floor of Sonoma's drive toward fine varietal wines in 1972 and has cut a swath since. Current sales of his (usually) all-Sonoma wines approach 80,000 cases a year. Small proportions of that total come from Stare's 60 acres of vineyard at the winery and another 35 acres in Alexander Valley.
*** Sauvignon Blanc (light, smoothly polished; early, distinctively flavored with the grassy notes typical of much Sonoma Sauvignon; later, intriguingly scented with aromas reminiscent of a good Italian deli) 84 85 86 87 88.
→* Cabernet Sauvignon (needs three or four years in bottle, then flavorful of Cabernet and agreeably smooth) 84 85; Chardonnay (agreeably varietal, sometimes a bit heady) 84 85 87; Zinfandel (robust); and Chenin Blanc (robust, dry).
NYR: Cabernet Franc (the first vintage was 85).

DRY SHERRY
See SHERRY.

DUCKHORN VINEYARDS   Napa   T $9.50–$20
Most of the fame belongs to the winery's three Merlots, but

the roster of Dan and Margaret Duckhorn's 18,000-case cellar has expanded to include two other types based in Bordeaux varieties. The label was founded in 1978. The Duckhorns have 7 acres of mature vines at the winery on the Silverado Trail n. of St. Helena, another 5 on Howell Mountain, and acquired another 15 acres (5 planted) just n. of the winery in 1988.
*** Merlot–Napa Valley (atypically tannic, well marked by oak); Merlot–Three Palms Vineyard (from vines near Calistoga, more intense than the Napa Valley bottling); Merlot–Vine Hill Ranch (the middle ground between the other two).
** Sauvignon Blanc (conventional); Cabernet Sauvignon (in the dark, tannic style set by the Merlots).

DUNN VINEYARDS Napa T $20–$30
Randall Dunn, the winemaker who first brought fame to Caymus Vineyards for Cabernet Sauvignon, now has his own one-varietal, 4,000-case cellar high in Napa's Howell Mountain sub-AVA. Dunn owns 5 acres of Cabernet, manages a similar property, and buys from neighbors for his Howell Mountain bottling; the Napa Valley edition is all from bought-in grapes, some from the mountain. His first vintage: 79.
*** Howell Mountain Cabernet Sauvignon (dark, tannic, intense in the way of Napa hillside Cabernets; the oldest vintage is still a pup) 79 81 82 83 84 85; Napa Valley Cabernet Sauvignon (a shade smaller and gentler all around than the Howell Mountain, which leaves plenty of room for it to be a firm, age-worthy red).

DUNNEWOOD
The most ambitious attempt yet by Guild Wineries to enter the premium wine market began in 1988 with 40,000 cases of $3.59–$9.49 Napa Valley Chardonnay, Sauvignon Blanc, and Cabernet Sauvignon, North Coast Chardonnay, and California Cabernet Sauvignon, Sauvignon Blanc, and White Zinfandel, plus a generic red and white. The wines will be made at Guild's Mendocino Vineyards winery in Ukiah until they catch hold or fall by the wayside. If they catch hold, the owners plan to build a Napa winery for the label. The reds made the better case in the first round.

DURNEY VINEYARDS Monterey T $5.50–$25
William Durney became the pioneer grower in Carmel Valley in 1968 when he began to plant what has become 130 acres of organically grown vineyard. His is now that hilly AVA's leading as well as largest winery at a shade less than 15,000 cases, all estate-grown. Durney is focusing increasingly on Chardonnay, Cabernet Sauvignon, and Pinot Noir.
** Cabernet Sauvignon (dark, firmly tannic; increasingly blended with Merlot and Malbec).
• Pinot Noir and Chardonnay. Also: Johannisberg Riesling, Chenin Blanc, Gamay Beaujolais in diminishing quantities.
NYR: Cabernet Sauvignon–Reserve.

DUXOUP WINE WORKS Sonoma T $7–$12
Andy Cutter really did grow up watching Marx Brothers movies; the winery's name condenses "easy as duck soup."

Cutter and his winemaker wife, Deborah, built their low-tech, high-standards Dry Creek Valley cellar to hold exactly 1,200 cases—as much as they can produce by themselves. Every drop is red, all from bought grapes. The first vintage: 81.

[**→***] Dry Creek Valley Napa Gamay (real red wine bottled just after its first birthday to catch the grape flavors) 85 86 87; Napa Valley Charbono (from Calistoga, big, round, drinkable early but balanced to permit aging) 83 84 85; Dry Creek Valley Syrah (as true to its grape as all the others, and the firmest for texture) 83 84 85; Dry Creek Valley Zinfandel (echoes the Syrah in substance and style) 83 84 85.

EAGLE RIDGE WINERY   Sonoma   T $6.50–$12
A small partnership established the winery in Petaluma in time to make 85s. Current production from grapes bought as far afield as Amador County is 3,000 cases, but the proprietors plan to grow well beyond that level.
NYR: Alexander Valley Sauvignon Blanc, Alexander Valley Fumé Blanc (wood-aged; the Sauvignon is not), Napa Valley Chardonnay, and Amador Zinfandel. To come: Ehrenfelser from California's only two acres planted to that German variety.

EAGLEPOINT VINEYARD
A label used by sparkling wine specialist SCHARFFENBERGER CELLARS for still wines, especially a lean, tart, long-lived Chardonnay. Both the label and the still wines it covers are to be phased out by 1990.

EARLY BURGUNDY
A standby black grape variety before Prohibition, it is little-grown now, but still does make rare appearances in pleasant though modest varietal red table wines. Of 210 acres, all but 70 in Monterey are in the North Coast counties.

EAST-SIDE WINERY
The legal name of a grower-cooperative cellar in Lodi that sells varietal table wines as OAK RIDGE WINERY, dessert wines as HANDEL & METTLER, and generic table wines as Royal Host.

EBERLE WINERY   San Luis Obispo   T $7–$12
Gary Eberle, the founding winemaker of Estrella River Vineyards, established his own 12,000-case winery in 1983 because he wished to get back to hands-on cellar work. The label began with a 79 Cabernet Sauvignon made in leased space. All of the wines have come from bought-in Paso Robles grapes, but Eberle planted his first 35 acres of Cabernet Sauvignon and Chardonnay in 1988.
→* Cabernet Sauvignon (accessible early, specifically varietal); Muscat Canelli (soft, as fresh as grapes straight off the vine, sold only at the winery).
** Chardonnay (fat, toasty, peaks early).

EDMUNDS ST. JOHN   Alameda   T $10–$15
Proprietor Steve Edmunds is one of California's burgeoning school of enthusiasts for grape varieties of the Rhône. His small cellar in Berkeley dates from the vintage of 85. Pro-

duction is at 1,500 cases a year and growing slowly, mostly using grapes purchased from an ancient vineyard on the slopes of Napa's Mt. Veeder.
NYR: Côtes Sauvage (blend of Grenache, Mourvedre, Syrah), Mourvedre, Syrah, Zinfandel, and a onetimer called Les Fleurs du Chapparal (blend of Carignane, Cabernet Sauvignon).

EDNA VALLEY AVA
One of the smallest AVAs in area encompasses 800 acres of vines in a shallow bowl just s. of the town of San Luis Obispo. Marine air off nearby San Luis Obispo Bay makes it one of the Central Coast's coolest regions. The principal planting is Chardonnay, which has earned the region its first fame and loftiest praise; Pinot Noir, Gewürztraminer, and a bit of Sauvignon Blanc also grow there.

EDNA VALLEY VINEYARDS San Luis Obispo T $6–$14.50 A joint venture of the Edna Valley's major grower, Paragon Vineyard, and Chalone, Inc. follows the winemaking style of its winemaking partner in every particular, even to include a humidified underground aging cellar, but is substantially larger at 47,000 cases on the way to 50,000.
*** Chardonnay (ample toasty notes from barrel fermentation and malolactic, but still enticingly perfumed by the grape variety from start to finish; well-balanced to age).
** Pinot Noir (vegetative regional flavors plus distinct charred taste from barrels; quick to go bricky, then brown); Vin Gris of Pinot Noir (dry, wood-aged, characterful).

EL DORADO AVA
Sprawling territory covering most of El Dorado County, certainly all of the Sierra-foothills terrain where grapes might be expected to grow. The heart of it is Apple Hill on the n.e. outskirts of Placerville; a long, skinny tail of vineyards stretches s. to join Amador County's SHENANDOAH VALLEY AVA. The tendency of growers is to avoid Zinfandel in favor of Cabernet Sauvignon, Chardonnay, and Sauvignon Blanc. Total acreage is about 450.

EL PASO DE ROBLES
Original name of a winery now operating as LA CASCADA.

ELIZABETH VINEYARDS
The grower label of Elizabeth Foster, who has small lots of Chardonnay and Sauvignon Blanc (attractive in its first outing) made from her vineyard in Mendocino's Redwood Valley. The first vintage was 87.

ELLISTON VINEYARDS Alameda T $5–$14
In Sunol, at the western edge of the Livermore Valley, the winery draws on two estate vineyards—a tiny one at the winery, a larger one a mile away, both just outside the Livermore AVA—to make 3,000 cases of wine a year. The first vintage for owners Ramon and Amy Awtrey was 85.
NYR: Chardonnay, Pinot Blanc, Pinot Gris (whites all strongly toasty), Merlot, Cabernet Sauvignon, Rosé of Ruby Cabernet.

EMERALD RIESLING
One of H. P. Olmo's early crosses (White Riesling x Muscat) at U.C.–Davis still has 2,600 acres planted to it, but has faded in recent years as a varietal wine. Current varietal wines come from small plantings in Temecula and the Central Coast; most of the acreage is in the San Joaquin Valley. The grape was bred to yield tart, fresh wines from warm to hot climate zones in the San Joaquin Valley; it performed well throughout the 1970s, but the wines failed to find an audience.

EMILE'S
Label of GUGLIELMO WINERY in Santa Clara County.

ENZ VINEYARDS   San Benito   T $5–$20
The owners of a small, rustic family winery buried deep in rural San Benito County favor the husky, heady style that comes easily in their one-winery AVA, Lime Kiln Valley. Robert and Susan Enz began with the vintage of 73; they currently produce about 10,000 cases a year, most of it from their own 40 acres.
*→** Pinot St. George, Zinfandel, White Zinfandel, Chardonnay, Orange Muscat, Mendocino Sauvignon Blanc, and Limestone (a proprietary, flavored wine at about 17% alcohol).

ESTANCIA
The label used by FRANCISCAN VINEYARDS for Alexander Valley Cabernet Sauvignons from the 220 acres located there, and Chardonnays originally from Alexander Valley, but beginning with 88, from a recently acquired 500-acre vineyard in Monterey County.

ESTATE BOTTLED
A nearly meaningless term applicable to wines assembled from any number of vineyards within any single AVA, so long as the vineyards are "owned or controlled" by the producing winery, and the winery is in the same AVA. A few use the tightest definition—a single, owned property—but their names must be learned one at a time.

ESTATE WILLIAM BACCALA/STEPHEN ZELLERBACH VINEYARDS   The labels have their origins in two independent wineries, but are now joined in a merchant firm based in Sonoma. The first vintage, 88, yielded 17,500 cases of $7–$10 Chardonnay and Sauvignon Blanc. The owners plan to add Merlot.

ESTRELLA RIVER   San Luis Obispo   T $5–$8
The firm now leases space in the winery it built in 1977 and buys grapes from the vineyard it began planting three years earlier, having sold the property to Wine World, Inc. (Beringer Vineyards) in 1988. After reaching a peak of 160,000 cases, the owners are retrenching toward 50,000.
** Cabernet Sauvignon, Syrah, Zinfandel (all three reds pleasant, soft, forward), Muscat Canelli (excellent Muscat flavors in a well-balanced sweet wine).
*→** Chardonnay, Chenin Blanc, Johannisberg Riesling, Sauvignon Blanc, White Zinfandel (all soft, understated, and quite quick to mature).

ÉTUDE

The winemaker label of consulting enologist Tony Soter covers technically impeccable $16 Carneros Pinot Noirs (textbook varietal, flawless balance) and Napa Valley Cabernet Sauvignons (all understatement and polish) made in leased space. Soter's label started with 84s; production is nearing 4,000 cases split evenly between the wines.

EVENSEN WINERY   Napa   T $6.50–$10

The Richard Evensen family planted Gewürztraminer in their 7 acres near Oakville in time to make a 79. The Evensens have been pleased with how the grape has grown ever since, but added a bought-in Chardonnay to their list with the vintage of 86 so as to have one egg for a second, more-easily-salable basket. Annual production is about 1,300 cases.

*** Gewürztraminer (dry, redolent of the licheelike aromas of the variety; in top form at 3 to 4 years) 85 86.
NYR: Chardonnay (well made, attractive in debut vintage).

EXTRA DRY
See CHAMPAGNE.

FAIRMONT   Napa   T $6.50–$8.50

Yugoslav-born George Kolarovich got to Napa by way of Australia's Barossa Valley in time to make 78s. He has been making small lots of wine in leased space ever since, but now has 22 acres of vineyards and a small cellar at St. Helena. Kolarovich produces about 10,000 cases a year from his own vines plus bought Napa wines.

** Cabernet Sauvignon, Chardonnay, Sauvignon Blanc, and Garnett's Blush.

FALCON CREST

A second label for SPRING MOUNTAIN VINEYARDS, after a TV soap opera set in part at the winery, goes on conventional $7.50–$9.60 Chardonnay, Sauvignon Blanc, and Cabernet Sauvignon.

FALLENLEAF VINEYARDS

The grower label of Frank Taylor goes on $10.50 Chardonnay and $8.50 Sauvignon Blanc from his 7.5-acre vineyard right on the line that sometimes divides, sometimes unites the Carneros and Sonoma AVAs. The first vintage was 86.

FAR NIENTE   Napa   T $26–$27.50

Gil Nickel's spare-nothing rehabilitation of a pre-Prohibition stone cellar at Oakville has become a particular darling of San Francisco socialites since the first crush in 1979. So has the label. Most of the wine comes from the affiliated and adjacent 100-acre Stelling vineyard.The Cabernet is estate bottled; the Chardonnay will be, but through 88 the winery was reaching out to other Napa growers to achieve its current total production of 36,000 cases.

**Chardonnay (ripe, soft, unmistakably toasty in style); Cabernet Sauvignon (fat, forward, well marked by oak).

FARRELL WINES, GARY

The winemaker label of Gary Farrell (Davis Bynum) dates from 82 and goes on an annual 3,000 cases of consistently well-made, vineyard-designated $8.75–$15 wines, all from Sonoma grapes. The roster is Alexander Valley Chardonnay–Hafner Vineyard, Russian River Chardonnay–Aquarius Ranch (both rich in fruit, deftly touched by wood), Russian River Valley Sauvignon Blanc–Laurel Grande Vineyard, and Russian River Valley Pinot Noir; and Sonoma Pinot Noir–Howard Allen Vineyard (textbook Pinot flavors, sturdy textures).

FARVIEW FARM
A grower-owned label has covered Paso Robles Merlots under earlier owners; a new owner is just resuming the label after a hiatus. The 51-acre vineyard is south of Paso Robles town.

FELTON-EMPIRE
Between 1976 and 1986, the winery called Felton-Empire occupied what had been before and now is again Hallcrest Vineyards in the Santa Cruz Mountains. One of the partners in the winery, William Gibb, is now operating Felton-Empire as a merchant label from a base in San Francisco.

FENESTRA WINERY Alameda T $5–$12
Lanny Replogle balances academics and winemaking as simultaneous careers. His wines come from bought-in grapes, most from Monterey, some from Livermore and Santa Clara County. Annual production at his rustic barn of a winery near Livermore has edged past 3,000 cases. Replogle first crushed in 1976 under the name Ventana; he changed names two years later to avoid confusion with the winery of Ventana Vineyards in Monterey County.
** Chardonnay–LaReina Vineyard (lightly toasty but fine fruit flavors), Pinot Blanc, White Riesling, Muscat Canelli, White Zinfandel, Cabernet Sauvignon–Smith & Hook Vineyard.

FERRARA WINERY San Diego T,D $3–$6
An old-line producer of jug wines from local grapes.

FERRARI-CARANO Sonoma T $9–$15
Ambitious newcomers in 1985, Reno hoteliers Don and Rhonda Carano feed a showcase winery in Dry Creek Valley with grapes from their own 1,000 acres of vines. One vineyard flanks the winery, a second is nearby, four others are in Alexander Valley, and the seventh (still to be planted as of early 1989) straddles the boundary between the Knights Valley and Alexander Valley AVAs. The plan is to reach 50,000 cases within five years of the first vintage, 85. NYR: Chardonnay (pleasing fruit flavors with a noticeable overlay from new oak in 85, 86); Sauvignon Blanc (fine balance, typical Sonoma Sauvignon flavors in the first two). Cabernet Sauvignon 86 and Merlot 86 will be the beginning of red wines; both are scheduled for release during 1989. A reserve Chardonnay is also in the cards.

FERRER, GLORIA Sonoma S $12–$15
The winery and 360 acres of vineyards are s.w. of Schellville, in the Sonoma half of the Carneros AVA. The owners of the Spanish sparkling wine houses of Freixenet and Segura Viudas, José Ferrer and family, launched the label in 1983 with a nonvintage Brut blended from bought wines.

After the company produced two vintages in leased space, Gloria Ferrer's permanent cellars were ready for the vintage of 86. Current production is 40,000 cases and designed to reach 65,000 by 1990. The longest-range plan calls for a maximum of 300,000 cases, always from Sonoma grapes. The name pays tribute to Ferrer's wife.

NYR: Vintage Brut (crisp, even lean) Blanc de Noirs, Brut–Cuvée Royale (richest flavors, textures of the trio).

FETZER VINEYARD Mendocino T $3.80–$11

It was only yesterday that Fetzer was a brand-new, small, family-owned winery with one patch of replanted vineyard in Redwood Valley. In fact the starting year was 1968, but nonetheless, the strides from 110 to 1,000 planted acres and from 10,000 to 1.7 million cases have been longer and swifter than the mind can easily grasp. All of the family acreage is in Mendocino: the Home Ranch in Redwood Valley, Sun Dial Vineyard n. of Hopland, and Valley Oaks Ranch e. of that. The Fetzers also buy grapes in Lake, Sonoma, Monterey, and Amador counties. The most amazing aspect is that the wines have improved all along the way under the remarkable direction of nine brothers and sisters, plus winemaker Paul Dolan. Fetzer wines come at three levels: vintage varietals in volumes ranging upward from 100,000 cases, Barrel Select wines at 20,000 to 40,000 cases, and Reserve wines at 3,000 to 4,000 cases. The family is developing its second label, BEL ARBORS, to fit one step down the price ladder from the vintage series.

[***] Cabernet Sauvignon–Barrel Select (splendid Cabernet flavors, fine balance) 84 85; Cabernet Sauvignon–Reserve (more definite flavors of new oak than Barrel Select) 85.

[**] Cabernet Sauvignon–Lake County (fine Cabernet flavors, nice touch of oak, well-balanced for current consumption; Chardonnay–Barrel Select (pleasant, reliable); Fumé Blanc–Valley Oaks (distinct Sauvignon); Gewürztraminer (clean, fresh flavors, sweet enough for sipping); Johannisberg Riesling (fresh, sweet); Zinfandel (regular, Reserve, and Ricetti Vineyard all flavorful, bold).

** Chardonnay–Sun Dial (agreeably fruity).

[*] Premium White, Red.

FICKLIN VINEYARD Madera D $7.75–$18

California's premier producer of Port types since 1948 uses only Tinta Madeira, Touriga, Tinta Cao, and Souzao—all varieties brought from Port's original home in the Douro River valley of Portugal—to make Tinta, usually as nonvintage, increasingly as vintage Special Bottling. The family's 40 acres, not far from the town of Madera, yield all of the grapes for an annual 10,000 cases.

*** Tinta, nonvintage (richly flavorful; hovers between vintage-character Port and Ruby in style, but closer to the former; though easy to drink young and slow to age in bottle, it does mature in memorable ways); Vintage (current release, 1980 Special Bottling #5, restores a long-idle earlier program of wines made to comply with all the standards of Vintage Ports as they are made in Portugal; its last predecessor, #4, from 58, continues in fine fettle).

FIDDLETOWN AVA
A tiny Sierra-foothills AVA flanks the larger Shenandoah Valley at its upper, eastern end; Zinfandel monopolizes plantings that go back, some of them, to Gold Rush times.

FIELD STONE WINERY Sonoma T $6.50–$20
The winery started out in 1976 as a sort of field experiment station for the late Wallace Johnson, the inventor of the first practical mechanical harvester and an innovator in field crushing systems. Now owned by the John Staton family (Johnson's daughter and son-in-law), it has matured into a sturdily independent, nearly estate property at the heart of the Alexander Valley. The Statons own 50 acres of vineyard at the winery and are partners with other family members in another 100 nearby. Production is at 12,000 cases.
** Petite Sirah (richly flavored, sturdy); Cabernet Sauvignon (ditto ... and abandoning vineyard-designated bottlings for one solid performer); Gewürztraminer (just off-dry and going drier); Sauvignon Blanc; Rosé of Petite Sirah (surprisingly lighthearted, fresh flavors).
NYR: Chardonnay (added with 87, mostly from bought-in grapes).

FIELDBROOK VALLEY WINERY Humboldt T
$6–$10.50 The oldest operating winery in the county dates from 1976. Owner/winemaker Robert Hodgson moonlights from teaching at California State University–Humboldt to turn out 1,000 to 1,500 cases a year, every drop sold in and around Eureka and Arcata. Most of the grapes are bought in Humboldt, Mendocino, and Napa Counties.
• Chardonnay, Dry Chenin Blanc, Cabernet Sauvignon, Pinot Noir, Zinfandel.

FILIPPI VINTAGE CO., J. Cucamonga T,S,D
$1.85–$5 The major winery in its much-shrunken district sells most of its annual production as altar wine under the Guasti Altar label, but does offer a wide range of table and dessert types under the Château Filippi, Joseph Filippi, and Thomas Vineyards labels, almost all through its own five retail outlets in southern California. The Filippis farm more than 100 acres of vineyard in Cucamonga, most of them planted to Zinfandel. Annual production capacity is about 75,000 cases.
* Zinfandel, Chianti, Burgundy, Cabernet Sauvignon, Vin Rosé, Chablis, Rhine, Haute Sauterne, Chardonnay, Chenin Blanc, Light Sweet Muscat, Ruby Port, Tawny Port, Golden Muscatel, Tokay, Pale Dry Sherry, Golden Angelica, and others.

FILSINGER VINEYARDS & WINERY Temecula
T,S $2.50–$10 A family-owned, 26-acre vineyard and 5,000-case estate winery sit toward the s. edge of the Temecula AVA. The label began with the 80 vintage; sparklers are a recent venture. Owner William Filsinger and son Eric are the winemakers.
** Chardonnay (pleasantly soft, straightforwardly fruity 85). Also: Fumé Blanc (oak-aged); Sauvignon Blanc (no

oak); Emerald Riesling (one of few varietals from H. P. Olmo's Riesling-based cross); Gewürztraminer (added in 85); Gamay Beaujolais, Cabernet Sauvignon, Gamay Blush, White Zinfandel.
NYR: Brut, Pink Champagne.

FIRESTONE VINEYARD   Santa Barbara   T
$3.75–$20   Brooks Firestone and family were early leaders in developing the Santa Ynez Valley as a wine district, beginning in 1975, and remain among the foremost producers there. Winemaker Allison Green draws on 265 acres of mesa-top vineyards north of the town of Los Olivos to produce 75,000 cases of estate wine a year.
[**] Chardonnay (winning fruit flavors dominate); Merlot (supple, polished, leaned toward the fruity side of the variety); Johannisberg Riesling (soft, altogether appealing); Gewürztraminer (shows the way in its region); Late Harvest Johannisberg Riesling (can be outstanding).
** Cabernet Sauvignon (beats the vegetal character of its region better than most); Cabernet Sauvignon–Reserve (a more intense, much more expensive companion to the regular bottling); Pinot Noir; Sauvignon Blanc; Rosé of Cabernet Sauvignon; red table wine; white table wine.

FISHER VINEYARDS   Sonoma   T $11–$24
Owner Fred Fisher makes nothing but Chardonnay and Cabernet Sauvignon at his winery in the high hills between Santa Rosa and St. Helena, but takes endless pleasure in elaborating the details within them. To achieve complexity, he blends bought-in grapes with Cabernet Sauvignon from his 46 acres at Calistoga, but less than he did before. Fisher also blends his Chardonnays, but keeps one block from 19 acres at the winery separate. He uses the Coach-Insignia designation (yes, he is a "body by Fisher," Fisher) to identify his top wines. His winery dates from the vintage of 79 and is now at 10,000 cases annual production.
→·* Chardonnay–Coach Insignia (understated flavors, firm textures); Cabernet Sauvignon–Coach Insignia (ditto).
** Napa-Sonoma Chardonnay.
NYR: Chardonnay–Whitney's Vineyard (a slow-aging wine from the favored block at the winery).

FITZPATRICK WINERY   El Dorado   T $5–$9
Since 1980, a small producer of big Sierra-foothills wines that draw mainly on vineyards in the home county though some bottlings carry Amador, Calaveras, and Nevada county appellations. Annual production is 2,000 cases, almost all of it sold from the cellar door.
*→·*** Cabernet Sauvignon, Cabernet Franc, Zinfandel, Chardonnay, Sauvignon Blanc, Chenin Blanc, White Zinfandel, and White Cabernet (all husky, the reds sometimes heady).

FLAX
A grower label based in 50 acres in the Russian River Valley goes only on 3,600 cases of $14 Chardonnay (splendid varietal flavors, lush textures in each of its first four outings).

The first vintage was 83. Art-supply dealer Philip Flax has the wine made next door at Mark West Vineyards.

FLOR
The filmy yeast that gives Fino Sherries their characteristic earthy taste is also used in a few California sherry types, sometimes as a surface film in the Spanish way, sometimes as a stirred-in culture. The latter technique, called submerged flor, is more common. Buena Vista Dry Sherry and Weibel Dry Sherry show the flavor most fully.

FLORA
A white grape, and rarely, its varietal wines. Developed at U.C.–Davis by Dr. H. P. Olmo, Flora crosses Gewürztraminer with Semillon. As its name hints, the result bears considerable aromatic similarity to Gewürztraminer, the Muscats, and other perfumey grapes without being identical to any. This is more true in cooler regions; in the warmest districts it tends to taste more like Semillon. Mendocino County has 26 acres, Napa 75, and Kern 182. The variety has struggled to find a place of its own, although several wines made from it have been attractive off-dry sippers.

FLORA SPRINGS WINE CO. Napa T
$8.50–$30 Several branches of the Komes family own this label and are major Napa growers with 400 acres. Their winery selects sparingly from four principal properties (two at St. Helena, one at Oakville, one in Chiles Valley) to make 18,000 cases of wine a year at a fine old stone cellar on one of the vineyards just s. of St. Helena. The first vintage was 78.
*** Sauvignon Blanc (delicate, almost wispy, yet possessed of enough spine to age well for as long as five years) 84 85 86 87.
** Chardonnay (definite varietal tinged by oak, sometimes a bit rough); Chardonnay–Barrel Fermented (a bit richer and oakier than the regular); Cabernet Sauvignon (dark, richly flavored by both grapes and wood); and Merlot (dark, firm).
NYR: Trilogy (equal blend of Cabernet, Merlot, and Cabernet Franc first made in 84 hews to the dark, firm style).

FOGARTY WINERY, THOMAS Santa Cruz
Mountains T $8–$15 Like most cellars in the vineyard-shy Santa Cruz Mountains AVA, Fogarty looks outside the region for a large part of its grapes. The 7,500-case winery had its first vintage in 81.
** Santa Cruz Mountains Chardonnay, Edna Valley Chardonnay, Monterey Chardonnay–Ventana Vineyard, and Carneros Chardonnay; Napa Cabernet Sauvignon–Steltzner Vineyard; Carneros Pinot Noir; and Santa Cruz Mountains Gewürztraminer.

FOLIE A DEUX Napa T $7–$14.50
The winery just n. of St. Helena dates from 1981. The name is a cheerful admission by owners Dr. Larry and Evie Dizmang that they started long after everybody knew that a small winery is no place to make a fortune. The label is a visual pun on the Rorschach test. (Both are mental health

professionals.) They own 14.5 acres of Cabernet at the winery and have family ties to 27 acres of Chardonnay near Yountville. With bought-in Napa grapes, annual production is 8,000 cases and ready to grow another 2,000.

*** Chardonnay (splendid Chardonnay flavors deftly complicated by oak; crisp, firm) 81 83 84 85; Dry Chenin Blanc (much in the style of the Chardonnay); Dry Muscat.

NYR: Cabernet Sauvignon (to be estate bottled beginning with a debut 86); Fantasy (a 90% Chardonnay/10% Muscat, champagne-method sparkler launched with 300 cases of 87).

FOLLE BLANCHE
Little-grown white grape originally from Cognac region, and its varietal wine. Only Louis M. Martini produces a California version. Of 82 acres, 55 are in Napa and 23 in Sonoma. As made by Martini, it is America's closest counterpart to the leanest, crispest Soaves.

FOPPIANO WINE CO., LOUIS J. Sonoma T
$7.50–$9.50 This old-line family firm in the Russian River Valley at the w. side of Healdsburg began marketing varietals under its own label in 1970 after a long career in the bulk trade. Some of the reds come entirely from 200 family-owned acres at the winery; most of the wines depend partly on grapes bought from independent growers in Sonoma; a few come from farther afield in the North Coast. The Foppianos bottle two prestige varietals under their $14–$18 Fox Mountain label. They also sell $3.50–$4.50 generics and varietals under their Riverside Farms label.

[**] Foppiano Petite Sirah (dark, sturdy, willing to age); Cabernet Sauvignon (herbaceous Cabernet plus agreeable bouquets, nicely understated); Riverside Farms Zinfandel (used to be under the main label, still a solid accompaniment to tomato-sauced entrées).

*→** Foppiano Chardonnay, Foppiano Sauvignon Blanc (well marked by dry, papery bouquets from oak); Riverside Farms Fumé Blanc (ditto to the main label Sauvignon); Riverside Farms White Zinfandel; Riverside Farms Chenin Blanc (pleasant off-dry type).

NYR: Fox Mountain Cabernet Sauvignon (stylish in 85 after ultratannic 84), and Fox Mountain Chardonnay (complex, well-balanced in first outings).

FORMAN WINERY Napa T $18
After an illustrious career at Sterling, and when he is not on duty as consulting winemaker to Charles F. Shaw and others, Ric Forman also makes small lots of wine to his distinct sense of style in his own 1,500-to-2,000-case cellar in the first rank of hills e. of St. Helena. He grows most of his own grapes on 6 acres on Howell Mountain and another 41 in which he is a partner at Rutherford. His first vintage of Forman Cabernet was 83, of Chardonnay, 84.

NYR: Chardonnay (ripe, well-wooded); Cabernet Sauvignon (also ripe, marked by new wood; has all the Bordelais grapes save Malbec in the blend).

FORTINO WINERY Santa Clara T $4.75–$10.50
From not much stainless steel, no centrifuge, and no pre-

tensions come straightforward wines in the best Italianate tradition of Hecker Pass. The main source of grapes for 30,000 cases of a 26-wine roster come from Ernest Fortino's own 75 acres at the winery and in nearby San Martin. Fortino started in the mid-1970s, in a cellar owned by the Cassa Brothers before him.

*→** Gamay Beaujolais, Pinot Noir, Ruby Cabernet, Petit Syrah, Charbono, Cabernet Sauvignon, Burgundy Reserve (all plummy-ripe, even faintly raisiny, but sound and reliable); Chardonnay, Chenin Blanc, Chablis, White Burgundy, Malvasia Bianca, Grand Noir Rosé, Vin Rosé.

FOUNTAINGROVE
One of California's grand names before Prohibition, when the winery was part of a utopian commune near Santa Rosa, in Sonoma County. The name now belongs to MARTINI & PRATI.

FOX MOUNTAIN
The prestige label of LOUIS J. FOPPIANO.

FOXEN VINEYARD   Santa Barbara   T $14–$16
A pair of partners made 1,100 cases of wine in 1988 and look to grow to 3,000 very slowly. They buy all of their grapes, mostly in the Santa Maria Valley AVA, but also in Santa Ynez Valley AVA. The announced goal is old-fashioned, hand-crafted French styles. Their first wine was an 87 Cabernet.
NYR: Chardonnay, Cabernet Sauvignon, and Pinot Noir.

FRANCISCAN VINEYARDS   Napa   T $6–$15
Founded in 1972, it was bought in 1979 by the German firm of Peter Eckes, which took current winery president Agustin Huneeus as a 50/50 partner in 1985. The company sells wines from its 250 acres of Napa vineyards under its own name, wines from its 220-acre vineyard in Alexander Valley and its 500-acre property in Monterey County (bought in 1988) under the Estancia label. Current production is around 100,000 cases and planned to double as the Monterey vineyard comes into full bearing. The winemaking has been on the upswing since Huneeus installed Greg Upton in the cellars.

[**]Franciscan Cabernet Sauvignon, Cabernet Sauvignon–Reserve, Merlot (all three reds subtle, supple); Chardonnay; Chardonnay–Reserve (focus is on varietal flavors but wood is a note); Johannisberg Riesling–Select Late Harvest (episodically).

NYR: Franciscan Zinfandel (coming back into the fold with 88), and Franciscan Cabernet-based proprietary, called Meritage.

[**] Estancia Alexander Valley Chardonnay (roundly fruity, nicely tinted by oak; being replaced by Monterey appellation beginning with 88).

** Estancia Alexander Valley Sauvignon Blanc (bouquetish from wood); Alexander Valley Cabernet Sauvignon (soft, herby).

FRANKEN RIESLING
Seldom-used alternative name for SYLVANER.

FRANZIA San Joaquin Valley T,S,D $2–$3
Owned by a corporation called The Wine Group, the Ripon winery has become king of the bag-in-a-box market in recent years under both the Franzia and Summit labels. Franzia wines continue to be sold in bottles as well. Most of the grapes are bought within the San Joaquin Valley. Late in 1988, The Wine Group launched a $3.50–$4 group of varietal wines made at Franzia under the name of William Bates Winery; these have some Central Coast grapes in them. Franzia's owner also owns CORBETT CANYON WINERY. The company has grown shy about production figures, but in 1984 the number was on the order of 5 million cases.
* Chablis, Rhine, Chardonnay, Chenin Blanc, French Colombard, Sauvignon Blanc, Rosé, Blush, Blush Red, White Zinfandel, White Grenache, Burgundy, Cabernet Sauvignon; Extra Dry Champagne, Spumante, Dutch Almond Sparkling Wine.

FRED'S FRIENDS
This patridge-eye still wine is a whimsical tribute to Count Frederic Chandon, made from cuvée rejects and press wines at DOMAINE CHANDON and sold at the cellar door or in Chandon's restaurant at the winery.

FREEMARK ABBEY Napa T $7.75–$20
No other winery comes to mind so readily for placing every one of its wine types so high so often on the lists of connoisseurs. The cellar just n. of St. Helena dates from 1967 under its present ownership by a small group of partners (the name goes back to 1939, the oldest winery building to 1886). All of the grapes for 33,000 cases come from partner-owned Napa Valley vineyards, with the single exception of Cabernet Bosché. All of the vineyards lie between St. Helena and the Big Ranch Road district on Napa city's n. side.
[****]Chardonnay (more focused on fruit, crisper in texture than riper, woodier pre-80 vintages) 80 81 82 84 85 87.
****Cabernet Bosché (from the 14-acre vineyard of an independent grower at Rutherford; lean, hard early, then supply, rich, complex with age) 73 74 78 79 81 83 85; Edelwein Gold (deliciously honeyed, late-harvest wine from Johannisberg Riesling, ages five years easily, sometimes many more).
*** Cabernet Sauvignon (lean, hard early; long, delicately scented, supple after a decade) 78 79 80 81 83 85.
** Johannisberg Riesling (soft, off-dry, best young).
NYR: Cabernet Sauvignon–Sycamore Vineyard (most accessibly fruity of the Cabernets, to judge by the debut 84).

FREMONT CREEK
The grower-owned label of Andrew Beckstoffer is used for wines from his extensive holdings in the Napa Valley and in the Ukiah district of Mendocino County. The debut wines are a Cabernet Sauvignon 85, a Chardonnay 86, and a Sauvignon Blanc 86, all made in leased space in Napa. The price range is $7–$9.50; initial production is modest in volume.

FRENCH COLOMBARD
A singularly aromatic white grape and its flowery-smelling

wine. Most of the successful producers ferment the wine cold and leave it perceptibly sweet for summer sipping. The variety hits its peak in Mendocino's Ukiah district (1,000 acres) and northern Sonoma County (1,250 acres), but has enough acidity to grow well in the San Joaquin Valley where 53,500 of the state's 69,700 acres yield the backbone of many generic whites.

FRENCH VALLEY VINEYARDS Temecula T $5–$8.50 This family-owned winery is producing 2,000 cases of wine a year from Temecula grapes, most of them bought-in. The first wine was a Chenin Blanc 82 made in leased space; the winery began operating on its own in 86. NYR: Chardonnay, Chenin Blanc, Johannisberg Riesling, Sauvignon Blanc, Cabernet Blanc, Cabernet Sauvignon.

FREY VINEYARDS, LTD. Mendocino T $6–$10 The farming is as organic as the winemaking at this family-owned, 6,000- to 8,000-case cellar in Redwood Valley. Most of the grapes are grown by the Freys, but they buy from two neighbors who are also certified organic growers. The first vintage was 80.
** Cabernet Sauvignon, Zinfandel, Syrah, Sauvignon Blanc, Gewürztraminer.

FRICK WINERY Sonoma T $6–$12 William Frick started out in Santa Cruz in 1977 with a purist's dedication to the perfect Pinot Noir. In 1988, after his interest turned to other varieties, he moved to the ridge between the Alexander and Dry Creek valleys. He still makes a Pinot Noir from outside Sonoma, but the direction is toward varieties that grow well in the appellations closest to the cellar door. Production is 2,000 cases a year.
** Petite Sirah, Zinfandel, Grenache, Pinot Noir.

FRITZ CELLARS Sonoma T $7–$12 Donald Fritz's 15,000-case winery is in Dry Creek Valley, along with three of four vineyards that total 95 acres. The fourth is in the Russian River Valley. Fritz also buys Alexander Valley Cabernet Sauvignon. The hallmark wine of the house is Chardonnay. The label dates from 79; the cellar was built in 1981.
*** Russian River Valley Chardonnay (ample, attractive fruit, well-balanced for keeping) 85 86 87; Dry Creek Valley Chardonnay (fuller, more straightforward flavors) 85 86.
** Dry Creek Valley Sauvignon Blanc, Dry Creek Valley Zinfandel, Alexander Valley Cabernet Sauvignon. Late Harvest Sauvignon Blanc and Late Harvest Zinfandel are episodic and sold only at the winery.

FROG'S LEAP WINE CELLARS Napa T $9–$14 The name pays lighthearted—and the label design exquisite—tribute to the creekside property's past life as a frog farm for San Francisco French restaurants. Co-owned by Larry Turley and John Williams and located n. of St. Helena, Frog's Leap was launched with 81s; current production is at 16,000 cases and aimed toward 20,000. Some of the grapes come from Williams's 10 acres of Cabernet at Rutherford, most from bought-in Napa grapes.

*** Sauvignon Blanc (rich with the melony note of ripe Napa Sauvignon) 85 86 87 88; Zinfandel (intermittent due to the loss of the original source of grapes, but firm of texture, rich of berrylike flavors when it has appeared) 81 85 87.

NYR: Cabernet Sauvignon (a chameleon, but impressively balanced between firm and delicate at its best) 82 84; Chardonnay (of the ultratoasty school).

FUMÉ BLANC
An alternative name for SAUVIGNON BLANC often used on labels.

GAINEY VINEYARD, THE   Santa Barbara   T
$7–$14.50   The privately owned winery is anchored in 54 acres of estate vineyard in the Santa Ynez Valley AVA just e. of Solvang, but buys from local growers to round out production of 12,000 cases. The label began with an 82 Chardonnay from purchased wines; the first wines made on newly built premises were 84s; in 1985 Rich Longoria (ex–J. Carey) came aboard as winemaker. The focus, as at most cellars, is on Cabernet and Chardonnay.

NYR: Chardonnay, Chardonnay–Limited Selection; Sauvignon Blanc (blended with a bit of Semillon); Johannisberg Riesling; Cabernet Sauvignon; Cabernet Sauvignon–Limited Selection. Merlot, Pinot Noir, and Select Late Harvest Johannisberg Rieslings make irregular appearances on the roster.

GALLEANO WINERY   Cucamonga   T,D $2.75–$6
Zinfandel is the primary production from 550 acres of owned and leased vineyard. Most of the wine made at the old-line family winery near Mira Loma is sold in bulk, but the Galleanos offer a broad range of wines only at their winery.

* Zinfandel, Chianti, Burgundy, White Zinfandel, Vin Rosé, Pink Chablis, Muscat, and others.

GALLO WINERY, E. & J.   ubiquitous   T,S,D
$2.99–$9   The brothers Ernest and Julio Gallo command the American market, command the respect of the industry, and increasingly, command the attention of critics. The scale of their winery cannot be grasped: annual sales are in the 40- to 50-million-case range; the firm owns or controls fermenting facilities throughout the San Joaquin Valley and in Sonoma, which, together with the bottling winery at Modesto, hold 300 million gallons of cooperage; included in that total is an underground oak-aging cellar equal in size to seven football fields . . . all of this operated by a winemaking staff with more Ph.D.'s on it than the University of California at Davis has in its Department of Viticulture and Enology. The Gallos started in 1934 with about 50,000 gallons of redwood tanks in an old railroad warehouse at Modesto. The Reserve Cellars of Ernest and Julio Gallo and E. & J. Gallo are the primary labels, but the company also makes Spumante Ballatore, Tott's, and Carlo Rossi, plus Boone's Farm fruit and flavored wines.

[***] Spumante Ballatore (perfectly captures the flavor of fresh Muscat grapes in a well-balanced Charmat sparkler styled on Asti Spumantes but cleaner tasting than they).

[**] Reserve Cellars of Ernest and Julio Gallo North Coast Chablis (affable fruit flavors, unshakably reliable; Burgundy (a youthful-tasting red counterpart); E. & J. Gallo Livingston Cream (a complex sweet sherry-type).

** Sauvignon Blanc (light-bodied, grassy); Cabernet Sauvignon (fat, ripe, marked by oak); Zinfandel (same vein as Cabernet but less woody); Gewürztraminer (just off-dry, well perfumed by its grapes).

[*] E. & J. Gallo Chablis, Pink Chablis, Hearty Burgundy, Rhine, Reserve Cellars of Ernest & Julio Gallo Johannisberg Riesling, Blush Chablis, André Champagnes (Brut, Extra Dry, and Rosé, all well off-dry to sweet).

NYR: E. & J. Gallo Chardonnay (thus far has tended to be hard, and strongly scented by oak); White Grenache; Tott's (sparkler first released in 1988; first try impressive as a typically soft, roundly fruity Charmat bubbly).

GAMAY   (also: Napa Gamay)
A black grape and its varietal wine. Nearly all of 2,200 acres are in the coast counties, especially Napa (637), Sonoma (287), and Monterey (305); the acreage dropped by half between 1980 and 1986. The grape variety does not appear to be that used in Beaujolais today, but most of the wines made from it in the 1980s follow that lead: sound, readily accessible, dependent on their fruit flavors and thus sold early. After a flurry of "Nouveaux" made purely by CAR-BONIC MACERATION during the 1970s, most of a small band of producers have drifted back to cool but otherwise conventional fermentation for most of the wine, macerating a small proportion of their total production—if any—for blending back into conventionally fermented red. A very few continue to produce Nouveau by carbonic maceration.

GAMAY BEAUJOLAIS
A black grape and its varietal wine. The grape is now widely believed to be a particularly feeble clone of PINOT NOIR; the varietal wine from it is a steadily dwindling presence in the market. There are 2,175 acres of vineyard identified as Gamay Beaujolais still in the state; Mendocino (575), Monterey (417), Sonoma (295), and Napa (289) are the leading districts. Like the darker, sturdier Gamays, most Gamay Beaujolais are made to be drunk up early for their youthful fruit.

GAN EDEN   Sonoma   T $7.50–$18
Gan Eden is one of a growing number of wineries that are completely revamping the image of kosher wine by turning away from Concord grapes and to the classic vinifera varieties. Using only bought-in Sonoma grapes, the winery has grown to 25,000 cases a year since its first vintage, 85, winning substantial critical praise in the process.

NYR: Chardonnay (splendid varietal flavors in each of its first three vintages); Cabernet Sauvignon (the debut 85 shows finesse and balance); Gamay Beaujolais (the fresh-fruity member of the roster). Dry Chenin Blanc and dry and sweet Gewürztraminers were still available in 1989, but were to disappear from the list as existing stocks ran out.

GAUER ESTATE VINEYARD Sonoma T $15

Wines under the label are also showcases for grapes from a 500-acre vineyard on lofty slopes at the eastern edge of the Alexander Valley. The label is growing toward the 10,000-case range. The wines are made at the owner's big Vinwood Cellars, a custom-crush winery used by a number of independent labels. The first vintage was 87. A Cabernet-based proprietary blend is to join Chardonnay with 88.

NYR: Chardonnay (deftly marked by oak, nicely balanced in 87).

GAVILAN

An increasingly active second label within the Chalone family originally used for a Napa French Colombard, now expanded to cover Carneros Chardonnay and others. A majority of the wines are made at Carmenet.

GEMELLO WINERY

For four decades it was a small cellar on a commercial street in Mountain View. The label now goes on red wines of OBESTER WINERY. Sandy Obester, a granddaughter of founder John Gemello, produces about 1,000 cases of Gemello a year, using grapes from a wide variety of sources.

** Alexander Valley Cabernet Sauvignon; Santa Clara Zinfandel.

GENERIC

Wine types named simply for their color (rosé, claret) or for real or fancied resemblances to the wines of another region (Burgundy, Rhine, Champagne, Port). U.S. law imposes no requirements on grape varieties permitted to be used, nor on technique or style.

GEORIS WINERY Monterey T $20

Walter Georis grows Merlot and small patches of Cabernet Franc, Petit Verdot, and Cabernet Sauvignon on 20 acres in Carmel Valley, and makes about 700 cases of estate Merlot from his grapes. Georis's debut 85 was made in leased space; his own winery went up in time to make the 88. The plan is to peak at about 1,000 cases when all 28 plantable acres are bearing.

NYR: Merlot.

GERWER WINERY El Dorado T $4.50–$8.75

In the Sierra foothills south of Placerville, Vernon Gerwer's cellar produces about 5,000 cases a year, all from El Dorado grapes, partly from the proprietor's own 11 acres. Gerwer began making wine in 1981 under the Stony Creek label; he changed to his own name in 1983 because there were so many Stonys around.

*→** Chardonnay; Sauvignon Blanc (estate); Petite Sirah; Ruby Cabernet (estate); and red table wine.

GEWÜRZTRAMINER

A pink-skinned grape variety and its varietal white wine. The variety originated in the Italo-Austrian town of Tramin (though currently grown mainly in Alsace); some speaker of

German added *gewürz,* meaning spicy, to explain its pungent aroma. In California, spicy is a minority report; most examples are flowery to licheelike. Most of the 3,660 acres are in the coast counties, where Mendocino (319 acres) and Sonoma (1,083 acres) appear to be best adapted to growing the variety for age-worthy dry wines in the Alsatian tradition, especially in the Anderson Valley and Russian River Valley AVAs. Napa (333 acres) also grows the grape well for dry wines. Monterey (890 acres) and Santa Barbara (887 acres) seem better suited to off-dry styles than to the dry. The American market appears to prefer the wine with 1.0% to 2.5% r.s., a style that a majority of producers in all districts follow. A few wines from Gewürztraminer are made as *Botrytis*-affected late-harvest types with 4% to 30% r.s.

GEYSER PEAK Sonoma T,S $5.50–$18
Geyser Peak is now the brand of the Trione Winery. Sonoma grower Henry Trione put his name on the company and left the label intact when he purchased the winery from the Jos. Schlitz Brewing Co. in 1982. The named stayed when Australian wine giant Penfolds bought half-interest in 1989. The winery began to take its current, 500,000-case form in 1974, when Schlitz bought a small, pre-Prohibition cellar from a wine-vinegar producer and built a modern cellar around it. The Trione family also owns 850 acres of vines, with six ranches in Alexander Valley, three in the Russian River Valley, and one in Carneros. The family acquired an as-yet-unplanted 1,000-acre ranch in Lake County in 1988.
** Chardonnay, Fumé Blanc, Chenin Blanc, Johannisberg Riesling, Gewürztraminer, vintage white, Cabernet Sauvignon, Pinot Noir, Zinfandel, vintage red, Pinot Noir Blanc, Rosé of Cabernet, Brut and Blanc de Noirs Champagne-method sparklers.
NYR: Reserve Alexandre (a Cabernet-based proprietary that has shown well in its first outings), Reserve Cabernet Sauvignon, Reserve Chardonnay, and Opulence (a sweet, somewhat heady proprietary based in Gewürztraminer).

GIBSON VINEYARDS Fresno T,D $1.90
The focus of this grower co-op winery anchored at Fresno is generic table and dessert wines offered to the price conscious in bottles under the Gibson label, and in bag-in-a-box packages under the name Silverstone. Gibson, also prominent in fruit wines, dates from the end of Prohibition.
* French Colombard, Chablis, Rhine, Blush, Vin Rosé, Vino Robusto, Burgundy, Cream Sherry, Muscatel, Port, White Port, Vermouth (sweet and dry), Kentucky Cabin, and others.

GIRARD WINERY Napa T $6.50–$20
A family-owned winery e. of Oakville draws nearly all of its grapes from 50 acres adjacent to the cellars and another 30 in the hills w. of Yountville. As it matures, the latter vineyard will expand production, which is currently at 15,000 cases. The first vintage was 81.
** Cabernet Sauvignon (dark, tannic, well-wooded); Cab-

ernet Sauvignon–Reserve (a more intense edition of the regular); Chardonnay (lean, sometimes even a bit hard, and well-wooded); Chenin Blanc (roundly fruity, the only non-estate wine); and—only at the winery—small lots of Semillon and Zinfandel. An Oregon Pinot Noir is temporarily labeled Girard; it is to acquire a separate identity.

GIUMARRA VINEYARDS Kern T $2.89–$5.99
The winery and a substantial vineyard are located e. of Bakersfield, toward the southern limit of grapes in the San Joaquin Valley. The owning family has been making a concerted effort in recent years to capture a share of the bag-in-a-box market, but still offers all of its wines in bottles as well. All of the generics are made with San Joaquin Valley fruit; some of the varietals are part or whole from Central Coast grapes. The firm dates from 1946; the family does not release production figures, but does say volume exceeds 500,000 cases.
* Burgundy, Chablis, Rhine, Vin Rosé.
NYR: Cabernet Sauvignon (oak-aged), Chardonnay (sees oak), Chenin-Blanc, Johannisberg Riesling, and Gewürztraminer (as a blush).

GLEN ELLEN WINERY Sonoma T $3.49–$12
Glen Ellen is the California wine business's latest Topsy, a winery that just growed. Bruno Benziger and family started in 1980 as a Sonoma Valley winery with 55 acres of vineyard and the prospects of selling 40,000 cases within a couple of years. Then they hit upon the notion of selling a "Proprietor's Reserve" series of varietals at very modest prices, using bought-in wines from every corner of the state. In 1988 they did 2.4 million cases and are projecting 3.8 million for 1989. Along the way the Benzigers became one of the latest to discover that selling cheap and expensive wine under the same label is a near impossible act; in 1988, they repackaged the Sonoma Valley wines that got them started under the new BENZIGER OF GLEN ELLEN label.
[*] Proprietor's Reserve series: Cabernet Sauvignon, Merlot, Table Red, White Zinfandel, Chardonnay, Sauvignon Blanc, Select Dry White, Table White (all California appellation, all sound, the reds more attractive than the whites of late).
NYR: Imagery Series: Cabernet Sauvignon–Sonoma Valley; Chardonnay–Sonoma Valley (introduced in 1988 only at the winery; scheduled to enter general distribution during 1989).

GLEN OAKS
A second label of Louis M. Martini for good-value, $3.50 California White, Rosetta (rosé), Red, and Chianti.

GOLD HILL VINEYARD El Dorado T $2.50–$10
As a name, Gold Hill has been around for some years, but current owner Henry Battjes started anew in 1988 at Coloma, with wines going back to 83. All of the grapes for an annual 2,000 cases come from his 35 acres near Placerville.
NYR: Cabernet Sauvignon, Chardonnay, Chenin Blanc, Johannisberg Riesling.

GOLDEN CHASSELAS   (also: Palomino)
A white grape variety, and rarely, its varietal wine. The primary grape of Spanish Sherries goes principally into sherry types in California, but occasionally makes varietal table wines under its alternative name. The 2,370 acres are widely scattered throughout the state; Fresno County leads with 785.

GOLDEN CREEK   Sonoma   T $4.50–$7.50
Ladi Danielik grows 12 acres of grapes toward the top end of the Sonoma Valley and makes about 2,000 cases of wine a year from his vineyard. His first vintage was 83.
NYR: Cabernet Sauvignon; Merlot; Caberlot (a no-surprise blend); Sauvignon Blanc, and Gewürztraminer.

GOOSECROSS CELLARS   Napa   T $13
Ray Gorsuch could not resist the name. Gorsuch is an old Celtic word for a place where geese cross; his vineyard is an annual haven for a flight of Canadian geese. And so. The only wine is Chardonnay, all from his 11 acres e. of Yountville from 85 through 87; the volume jumped from 3,000 to 6,000 cases in 88 when he added grapes bought from a neighbor to his own.
NYR: Chardonnay (toasty thus far).

GRACE FAMILY CELLAR   Napa   T $50
For some years Richard Grace and family sold the grapes from their sloping acre n. of St. Helena to Caymus Vineyards, which produced a vineyard-designated Cabernet from them. When the Graces planted the second acre, they also built a small cellar and took over production under the watchful eye of Charley Wagner. Volume is 500 cases a year, all sold to a mailing list.
*** Cabernet Sauvignon (dark, firm, well-wooded in the Caymus fashion) 81 82 84 85.

GRAESER WINERY, RICHARD L.   Napa   T
$7.50–$15.50   The owner abandoned the lettuce business in Los Angeles for grape-growing and winemaking in Napa in time to make red 85s from his 8-acre vineyard in the hills w. of Calistoga, and whites from bought-in Napa Valley grapes.
NYR: Chardonnay, Semillon, Cabernet Sauvignon, Cabernet Franc, Merlot.

GRAND CRU   Sonoma   T $5.50–$18
Most of the grapes for this steadily expanding winery come from the home county, but it does go outside to Clarksburg for Chenin Blanc, Carneros for Chardonnay, and more broadly still for White Zinfandel and its lowest-priced Cabernet and Sauvignon Blanc. The label dates from 1972; the winery was bought in 1981 by current owners Walt and Bettina Dreyer; Robert Magnani has been the winemaker from the first day. Current production is 60,000 cases.
***Gewürztraminer (sipping-sweet at 2% r.s., but flavorful and firm enough to do well at the dinner table) 85 87 88; Sauvignon Blanc (shows the melony side of Sauvignon, smooth, balanced); Clarksburg Chenin Blanc (reliably pleasing sipper); California White Zinfandel (soft, fruity).

** Sonoma Cabernet Sauvignon; Alexander Valley Cabernet Sauvignon–Collector's Reserve (firm in youth, deftly touched by new oak).
[*] California Cabernet Sauvignon and Sauvignon Blanc. NYR: Chardonnay (added to roster with 87).

GRAND NOIR
A black grape with fewer than 100 acres planted in the state, and rarely, its varietal wine.

GRANITE SPRINGS   El Dorado   T,D $4.25–$9.50
Lynne and Les Russell make 10,000 cases of wine a year from their own 25 acres s. of Placerville and other Sierra-foothill grapes, nearly all of them from the home county. The first wines were 80s made in leased space; the Russells built their own cellar in time for the 81s.
** Zinfandel, Zinfandel–Winemaker Reserve, Zinfandel–Higgins Vineyard; Cabernet Sauvignon–Estate Bottled; Petite Sirah; White Zinfandel; Chenin Blanc; Sauvignon Blanc; Sierra Reserve White (sturdy, straightforward, every one). NYR: Vintage Port (blends Petite Sirah and Zinfandel; introduced with 85).

GRAY RIESLING   (also: Grey Riesling)
A faintly pink grape and its white varietal wines. No Riesling, but the surprisingly bright offshoot of a French grape, the Trousseau. Simple but pleasant fruit flavors make for modest but well-balanced wines, a few of which may show a hint of color from the grapes' rosy skins. The University of California does not recommend planting Gray Riesling in the state, but the wine's followers lap up everything that can be coaxed out of 1,760 acres, almost half of that in Monterey. Alameda and Napa counties have more than 300 acres each. The wines are almost inevitably off-dry, at 0.6% to 1.5% r.s.

GREEN & RED VINEYARD   Napa   T $6–$11.75
Jay Heminway has patiently carved 17 acres of vineyard out of the steep hills at the upper end of Chiles Valley, from which he makes a bit more than 2,000 cases of estate Zinfandel and Chardonnay; production tops 3,000 with the help of bought-in grapes that augment his supply of White Zinfandel. Heminway started with a 79 Zinfandel. The name, incidentally, takes notice of the colors of two vastly differing soil series.
[**]Zinfandel (dry, lean, subdued in fruit flavors . . . almost an Italianate style); Chardonnay (straightforward flavors, also dry and lean); White Zinfandel.

GREEN HUNGARIAN
A dull white grape of uncertain origin, and its varietal wines. Though the University of California recommends against planting it, the bland wines from it enjoy a certain vogue. The 312 acres planted to it yield apparently inexhaustible crops to judge from the floods of off-dry to outright sweet wine on the market. Mendocino has 239 acres; five coastal and two San Joaquin Valley counties divide the rest evenly.

GREENSTONE WINERY Amador T,S,D $4–$10
Two southern California couples began to leave their careers in teaching in 1981 when they opened their winery near Ione, just where the Sierra foothills begin to curl up from the San Joaquin Valley floor. They buy Amador grapes to supplement their own 23 acres; production is currently at 10,000 cases.
*→** French Colombard, Chenin Blanc, Muscat Canelli, White Zinfandel, Rosé of Zinfandel, and Zin-Syrah.
NYR: Crystal Blush (a fortified dessert wine blended of Orange Muscat and Black Muscat). There are tiny lots of Cabernet Sauvignon and Barbera.

GREENWOOD RIDGE Mendocino T $7.50–$10.75   Allan Green's 8-acre vineyard and 3,000-case winery sit high on a ridge above the Anderson Valley's prevailing fogs, which has allowed him to plant White Riesling in the shaded spots and Cabernet Sauvignon on the exposed ones. Green also buys grapes in Lake and Mendocino counties for other varietal types. The winery dates from 1980.
*** White Riesling–Estate (tart, understated fruit somehow lingers longer than most; seems less sweet than 1.6% r.s. suggests); Lake County White Riesling (sweeter than the Estate at 4% r.s.)
** Cabernet Sauvignon–Estate (pungent with the herby side of Cabernet; nicely balanced, supple).
NYR: Sauvignon Blanc; Muscat Canelli.

GRENACHE
A red grape and its varietal red and rosé wines. A Rhône variety that acquired a post-Prohibition reputation for ripening very poorly in the coast counties, it has 12,000 of its 14,670 acres in the San Joaquin Valley, where it performs well as a base for rosés, port types, and as a flavoring component in generic red blends. The recent surge of popularity in Rhône grapes has reawakened the interest of growers in the coastal regions, but few practical results are yet in hand.

GRGICH HILLS Napa T $7.75–$22
The partnership of winemaker Miljenko (Mike) Grgich and grower Austin Hills dates from 1977. Before they joined forces, Hills had been a grower for some years, and Grgich a winemaker at several Napa wineries, most notably Robert Mondavi and Château Montelena. Production currently stands at 40,000 cases, the planned maximum, much of it from 250 acres owned individually by Hills and by the winery. Hills's properties are e. of Rutherford, and e. of Napa city. The winery owns small ranches at the cellars just n. of Rutherford and at Yountville, plus 110 acres in Carneros, bought in 1988 and just beginning to be planted.
→* Chardonnay (lean, even hard early, and slow to evolve but often worth the wait); Fumé Blanc (leans slightly to the grassy side of the variety); Zinfandel (big, dark, well-wooded, usually from Sonoma but sometimes from Napa); Johannisberg Riesling (deft, delicate); Late Harvest Johannisberg Riesling (not a sticky, but closer in style to a Spätlese, and thus all delicacy).
NYR: Cabernet Sauvignon (supple, polished 85).

GRIGNOLINO
A rarely planted black grape with origins in Italy's Piedmont, and its varietal red wine. Napa has 16 acres; Santa Clara has had as many as 34. Only HEITZ CELLARS currently produces substantial amounts of Grignolino in California, exclusively from its own planting at the winery.

GROTH VINEYARDS & WINERY Napa T
$7.50–$16 Two estate vineyards, 121 acres at Oakville and 43 s. of Yountville, supply a family-owned, 30,000-case winery. Owners Dennis and Elizabeth Groth plan, in 1989, to unite the previously scattered parts of their cellars on the Oakville property in preparation for growing to the planned maximum size of 40,000 cases. The label began with 82s.
NYR: Cabernet Sauvignon (polished, subtle in 84, 85); Cabernet Sauvignon–Reserve (aimed at a bigger style); and Chardonnay (big, marked by perfumes from new wood).

GROVER GULCH WINERY Santa Cruz T
$5.50–$9.50 Longtime winemakers Dennis Bassano and Reinhold Banek launched their 750-case winery at Soquel in 1979 to make sturdy, ripe, old-fashioned reds, originally from Hecker Pass grapes. More recently they have turned to Santa Cruz Mountains vineyards.
• Cabernet Sauvignon, Carignane, Petite Sirah, and Zinfandel.

GUENOC VALLEY AVA
A one-winery AVA in upland Lake County—just n. of Napa's Pope Valley—cradles 225 acres of vineyard within the boundaries of a single 13,000-acre ranch.

GUENOC WINERY Lake T $5.50–$17.50
Once the property of nineteenth-century actress Lillie Langtry, it now belongs to Orville and William Magoon, who use her likeness on their primary label. Several of the wines are estate bottled from 225 acres on the site where Lillie first planted vines (the Magoons won AVA status for the Guenoc Valley in 1982); they supplement their own crops of Sauvignon Blanc, Petite Sirah, and Zinfandel with bought-in Lake County and other North Coast fruit. The first vintage was 81; production is now about 75,000 cases.
[**] Sauvignon Blanc (melony, full-bodied); Chardonnay (steady, leans to fruit flavors); Zinfandel (rich in berrylike fruit, firmly structured); Petite Sirah (firm structures, berrylike fruit flavors).
NYR: Cabernet Sauvignon–Premier Cuvée, Chardonnay–Premier Cuvée (both estate bottled); Merlot (also estate bottled).

GUGLIELMO WINERY, EMILIO Santa Clara T,D
$2.95–$20 An old-line family winery not far s. of San Jose grows 115 acres of vines on the spot and buys grapes—primarily in Monterey and San Luis Obispo—to make about 50,000 cases of wine in three separate price categories under three related labels. The top of the line are varietals under the Guglielmo Reserve; Mt. Madonna covers regular varietals; Emile's is the label for the generics.
** Guglielmo Cabernet Sauvignon–Reserve, Petite Sirah, and Chardonnay.

** Mt. Madonna Chardonnay, Sauvignon Blanc, Chenin Blanc, Johannisberg Riesling, White Zinfandel, Cabernet Sauvignon, Merlot, Zinfandel, Claret (an estate-bottled blend of Petite Sirah and Zinfandel), Cream Sherry, and others.
*→** Emile's Premium White, Blanc Sec (the drier white), and Red.

GUILD WINERIES
Lodi-based Guild has disappeared from labels and become, instead, the umbrella name for a far-flung group of grower cooperative labels and wineries, principally COOK'S AMERICAN CHAMPAGNE, CRIBARI, DUNNEWOOD, and MENDOCINO VINEYARD.

GUNDLACH-BUNDSCHU VINEYARD CO. Sonoma
T $4–$20 Owner/grower Jim Bundschu, whose family goes back to the beginnings of Sonoma wine, and winemaker Lance Cutler go their merry way whether the trendies are with them or not. In the late 1980s, while others chase after delicacy, they resolutely pursue big, full-flavored, outright robust wines. With the single exception of Chardonnay from Sangiacomo, Gundlach-Bundschu now uses only estate grapes from the 130-year-old, always-in-the-family Rhinefarm Vineyard s.e. of Sonoma town, a second property nearby, and a more-recently-acquired third ranch on the w. side of Sonoma Valley. Combined acreage of the three is 375; total production is 50,000 cases. The winery had been buying from other Sonoma Valley growers in recent years.
→* Cabernet Sauvignon–Rhinefarm (dark, intensely herbaceous); Gewürztraminer (fine varietal flavors, dry).
** Sonoma Valley Chardonnay, Sonoma Valley Chardonnay–Sangiacomo (both understated for fruit, and tending to be a bit heady); Pinot Noir (berryish fruit, soft tannins); Merlot; Sonoma Riesling; and only at the winery, Kleinberger.

HACIENDA WINE CELLARS Sonoma T $6–$18
Hacienda is one of those wineries that has turned out a number of outstanding wines without ever making a huge splash. Located on part of Agoston Haraszthy's old property at the s.e. corner of Sonoma town, it was begun in 1973 by Frank Bartholomew, then bought from him in 1977 by current owner Crawford Cooley. The 25,000-case annual production is anchored in grapes from the owner's 110 acres of vineyards (40 at the winery, 70 near Cloverdale in the Alexander Valley), but there are some bought-in grapes.
*** Chardonnay (was lean, even hard, and slow to evolve; recent vintages fuller flavored and rounder in texture) 81 85 86; Gewürztraminer (redolent of its variety, just off-dry, a sure bet to repay two year's aging in bottle) 85 86 88.
→* Pinot Noir (ripe, soft, sometimes heady, old-fashioned California Pinot from old vines at the winery) 79 81 84 85; Sauvignon Blanc (an 83 addition, thus far enticing with ripe varietal flavors); Chenin Blanc (just off-dry but firm, with fresh, regional flavors from CLARKSBURG AVA grapes, the only non-Sonomans).

** Cabernet Sauvignon (splendid in 77, fine in 79, then uncertain in more recent vintages, but seemed to be regaining its footing with 84, 85).
NYR: Cabernet Sauvignon–Réserve; Antares (proprietary blend of Cabernet family; debut 86 scheduled for 1989 release).

HAFNER VINEYARD   Sonoma   T $12–$16
In the heart of the Alexander Valley AVA, Hafner was designed by the owning family to sell most of an annual 10,000 cases direct to mail order clients, the rest to restaurants. Founded with the vintage of 82, it draws on 100 estate acres for all of its grapes.
• Chardonnay and Cabernet Sauvignon.
NYR: Reserve Chardonnay (begun with 84), Late Harvest Riesling (occasional, as development of *Botrytis* permits).

HAGAFEN
The pioneer maker of dry, varietal kosher wines dates from 1980, or 5471—the label gives the vintages using both calendars. Ernie Weir, a Domaine Chandon vineyard manager by day, and his wife buy Napa grapes and lease Napa cellar space to make 6,000 cases of $5.75–$8.75 wine a year.
** Johannisberg Riesling (well off-dry, pleasingly fruity, the pioneering varietal type).
NYR: Chardonnay (added in 83, thus far toasty), Cabernet Sauvignon (since 82), Pinot Noir Blanc (an 84 entrant in the list). Reserve Chardonnay 88 and Reserve Cabernet Sauvignon 87 were due for release in 1989.

HALLCREST VINEYARDS   Santa Cruz Mountains   T $6.50–$16.50   One of the earliest of the small, prestige wine labels of California disappeared for 21 vintages after the death of founder Chaffee Hall, only to be revived at the original site in 1988 by a young couple named Schumacher. In Hall's day, the only two wines were Johannisberg Riesling and Cabernet Sauvignon grown on 5 estate acres. The modern revival takes a broader view, beginning with 85 and 86 wines the new owners made elsewhere under the name of Schumacher-Davis. The early volume is 3,000 cases, with a plan to go to 7,000.
NYR: Napa Sauvignon Blanc, Napa Cabernet Sauvignon, El Dorado Cabernet Sauvignon, Mendocino Chardonnay, Napa-Sonoma Chardonnay, Monterey White Riesling, and Santa Cruz Mountains Estate Johannisberg Riesling. A Sierra Foothills Zinfandel remains under the Schumacher label.

HANDEL & METTLER   San Joaquin   D $7–$11
In 1986 a revitalized East-Side winery in Lodi set up Handel & Mettler as a separate label to produce fine dessert wines (its table wine side is under the OAK RIDGE label). East-Side dates from 1934 and has some of California's oldest stocks of sherry- and port-types with which to work. It also has somebody with a sense of humor in the name department.
NYR: Dry Dock Sherry, Vintage Port, Spinnaker Tawny Port, and Victoria Cream.

HANDLEY CELLARS Mendocino T,S
$5.50–$16.75 Owner/winemaker Milla Handley honed her craft at Château St. Jean before launching her Anderson Valley cellar with about 3,000 cases of 82. She buys grapes from near neighbors for her sparklers, Gewürztraminer and one Chardonnay; Dry Creek Valley grapes from her family's vineyard go into the Sauvignon Blanc and a second Chardonnay. Production nears 12,000 cases on the way to a planned peak of 15,000.
NYR: Dry Creek Valley Chardonnay (ripe, full of fruit, but deftly complicated by toasty notes; has earned its basketful of fair medals) 85 86 87; Anderson Valley Chardonnay (leaner, harder, slower to evolve than its running mate) 83 85; Sauvignon Blanc (typical Sonoma-grassy); Gewürztraminer (spot-on example from one of California's outstanding regions for the variety) 86 87; Brightlighter (winsome, Traminer-based blended wine; the name is local dialect for city slicker). Brut (has all the earmarks of becoming a stylish Champagne-method sparkler) 84; Rosé (ditto to Brut) 84.

HANNA VINEYARD Sonoma T $8.75–$15
San Francisco heart surgeon Dr. Elias Hanna dipped cautiously into the wine business in 1985, with 11 acres of vines and a 5,000-case winery in the Russian River Valley between Santa Rosa and Sebastopol. By 1988 he had taken a plunge, with an added 100 acres in Alexander Valley and a winery at 13,000 cases on the way to 30,000.
→* Chardonnay (good varietal subtly kissed by oak); Sauvignon Blanc (lean, firm, full of Sonoma grass flavors). NYR: Cabernet Sauvignon (debut 85 ripe, full, well-wooded).

HANZELL VINEYARD Sonoma T $17–$22
On a slope n.w. of Sonoma town, in a winery designed for the purpose, James D. Zellerbach set California Chardonnay and Pinot Noir on new courses in the midfifties through judicious use of new French oak barrels as a source of added complexity. Dozens of subsequent imitators have matched and improved upon his early results while scores have committed horrible excesses. Since she bought it in 1968, London-based Barbara deBrye and winemaker Bob Sessions have pursued Zellerbach's goal of equalling the quality of good Burgundy. (The winery went idle after Zellerbach's death in 1963. The current owner bought it from the estate of Douglas Day, who had first revived it in 1965.)
*** Pinot Noir (ultraripe, distinctly marked by wood, quite apt to age into something spectacular and altogether Californian) 79 81 84 85.
→* Chardonnay (also ultraripe and well marked by wood; often fine, sometimes a bit heavy and heady). NYR: Cabernet Sauvignon (a newcomer to the lists with an 81).

HARBOR WINERY Sacramento T,D $6.50–$9
Full-time English professor and part-time winemaker Charles Myers likes old-fashioned techniques and old-fashioned wines. He buys grapes from Napa and Sierra foot-

hills to produce exactly what he wants at his 1,000-case winery on the riverbank at Sacramento—midway between his two sources of grapes and only a little more than a walk from campus. Much of Harbor's production sells in the East and Southeast.

*** Amador Mission del Sol (one of a few contemporary varietals from the grape the Franciscan fathers brought; lifted to 17% alcohol with brandy; well aged in wood but even more intriguing if given time in bottle).

→* Napa Cabernet Sauvignon (ripe, full-bodied, well kissed by oak; able to age well) 78 79; Napa Semillon (deep-hued, ripe in the old style); Napa Chardonnay (follows same pattern as Semillon); Amador Zinfandel (ripe, hearty).

HART VINEYARDS Temecula T $6–$9.50
Ex-teacher Travis Hart grows 11 acres of Cabernet Sauvignon, Merlot, and Sauvignon Blanc and buys the rest of his grapes locally to make 3,500 cases of wine a year. Hart is not quite a pioneer in Temecula, having begun with the vintage of 80, but his is one of the region's oldest, steadiest cellars all the same.

• Chardonnay, Dry Chenin Blanc, Sauvignon Blanc, White Riesling, Cabernet Sauvignon–Blanc, Merlot, and Cabernet Sauvignon.

HAVENS WINE CELLARS
Teaching literature finally was not half as much fun as making wine for Michael Havens, so he ended a peripatetic career as a home-winemaking academic (Washington State, SUNY–Stony Brook, UCLA, U.C.–Davis) to devote himself full-time to his $8–$14 wines, which, since 84, have been made in leased space from vineyards in Calistoga and Carneros.
NYR: Chardonnay, Sauvignon Blanc, Merlot (85 firm in texture, complex in flavor), Merlot-Reserve.

HAWK CREST
Good-value second label of STAG'S LEAP WINE CELLARS, especially for accessible $7.50 Chardonnay and Cabernet Sauvignon.

HAYWOOD WINERY Sonoma T $4.50–$14.50
Peter Haywood's 84 acres of vines and 34,000-case winery occupy some of the steep slope looming above the Sonoma town plaza in Sonoma Valley. The first crush was 80; the label won quick respect for a Chardonnay 81, but has gone on to greater fame for its reds.

*** Zinfandel (dark, packed with flavor, sometimes quite heady) 81 83 85 86.

** Chardonnay (full-bodied, full-flavored, often peaks early); Fumé Blanc, White Riesling; Gewürztraminer; Cabernet Sauvignon.

[*] Linguini White, Spaghetti Red.

HECKER PASS
An old-time region for Italianate country jug wines in Santa Clara County well s. of San Jose, just w. of Gilroy. Vineyards are rapidly giving way to housing tracts and shopping centers, but nearly a dozen wineries continue to operate there, most of them turned toward upscale varietals.

HECKER PASS WINERY   Santa Clara   T,D
$3.95–$7.95   Of several family wineries strung along the Hecker Pass Highway w. of Gilroy in southern Santa Clara County, Mario Fortino's has the edge for subtlety and style in its reds. From Fortino's own 14 acres at the winery come all of his annual 1,800 cases. His first vintage was 72.
[*→**] Zinfandel, Petite Sirah, Grenache (all lean, dry, understated for fruit flavors).
* Grenache Rosé, Carignane Rosé, Zinfandel Ruby (off-dry), Petite Sirah Select (off-dry), Cream Sherry, Ruby Port, Burgundy, and Chablis.

HEITZ CELLARS   Napa   T,D $4.95–$37.50
Joe Heitz first won fame for Chardonnay, but has turned his attention ever more toward Cabernet Sauvignon—predictably, given the renown of his Martha's Vineyard bottlings. The cellars date from 1965, when a two-car garage could hold them; since then the Heitzs have built a 40,000-case winery and accumulated 115 acres of vineyards at four sites, all near St. Helena. They now buy only the grapes for their two individual-vineyard Cabernet Sauvignons. Heitz makes a practice of keeping older vintages of his reds available for sale at the winery.
**** Cabernet Sauvignon–Martha's Vineyard (ultraripe, spicy; rich in flavors and textures alike, ages reliably) 68 69 70 74 75 78 79 81 83 84; Cabernet Sauvignon–Bella Oaks (similar to but slightly scaled down from Martha's) 78 82 83 84.
*** Cabernet Sauvignon (follows the style) 79 81.
[**] Grignolino (intensely aromatic of something not distant from orange liqueurs, slow to age); Grignolino Rosé (characterful flavors, bone-dry); Joe's White (flavorful generic white); Ryan's Red (flavorful generic red). Also: Chardonnay.

HERITAGE CELLARS   Fresno   T $4.25–$8.50
The winery of Bobbie and Marvin Riding is interwoven with their restaurant and gift shop at the southern outskirt of the city of Fresno. It dates from 84; all of the grapes are bought from local, Central Coast, and North Coast vineyards. Annual volume is 10,000 cases; the goal is 40,000.
NYR: Chardonnay, Sauvignon Blanc, White Zinfandel, Cabernet Sauvignon, Zinfandel, and Muscat de Frontignan.

HESS COLLECTION   Napa $13.50–$22.50
Swiss owner Donald Hess is a collector of art, hence the "collection" in the name. His winery occupies the old Mont La Salle cellars of The Christian Brothers, right across Redwood Road from his hilly 280-acre vineyard. The first vintage for Hess was 83; annual production is 15,000 cases on the way to 50,000, all of it always to be estate bottled.
NYR: Chardonnay (sturdily built, noticeably tinted by new wood in the early vintages); Cabernet Sauvignon (ripe, full-bodied, straightforward); and Cabernet Sauvignon–Reserve.

HIDDEN CELLARS   Mendocino   T $7–$12
Anybody can find the winery now that it is not far from U.S. 101 s. of Ukiah, but in 1981—when it got its name—it truly was hidden in steep hills behind Talmage. Dennis Patton

and company buy grapes throughout Mendocino County to make 12,000 cases of wine a year. Patton seems to have a particular touch with botrytised late-harvest styles.

*** Late Harvest Johannisberg Riesling (unctuous textures, apricotlike intensity of fruit); Chanson d'Or (proprietary blend of botrytised Sauvignon Blanc, Semillon).

** Chardonnay (always noticeably varietal, sometimes a bit overwhelmed by perfumes of new wood); Sauvignon Blanc (steady); Johannisberg Riesling; Gewürztraminer; Cabernet Sauvignon; Zinfandel.

HILL WINERY, WILLIAM Napa T $11–$22
A onetime money wiz, William Hill looked at wine in the mid-1970s and decided that the way to get started was with prime vineyard land. He has bought and sold industriously ever since; his current bearing vineyards include 100 acres next to the Silverado Country Club just n.e. of the town of Napa, and 70 on Mt. Veeder; a recently acquired 255 acres for Chardonnay is in Carneros, and another ranch at the s.e. corner of Napa town is about to receive its first Cabernet vines. Meanwhile, he has gotten his annual production up to 70,000 cases since the inaugural 78s.

→* Chardonnay-Reserve (ripe heavyweight); Chardonnay–Silver Label (well-wooded); Cabernet Sauvignon Reserve (weighty, woody); and Cabernet Sauvignon–Silver Label (straightforward).

HONIG CELLARS, LOUIS Napa T $8.25
The winery has made its name on Sauvignon Blanc from the owning family's 54-acre vineyard at Rutherford. The first vintage was 81, originally as HNW from the initials of the three original partners. The name shift came with the 83.

[**] Sauvignon Blanc (light texture, specific of Sauvignon).
NYR: Cabernet Sauvignon (debut 86 to be released in 1990); Chardonnay (likely candidate to join the roster if an 87 still in barrel continues to hold form).

HOP KILN WINERY AT GRIFFIN VINEYARDS Sonoma T,S $4.50–$12 Physician/owner Dr. Martin Griffin likes wines that have something to say. From 1975 onward, his wines have lived up to that ideal. The winery really is an old hop kiln in the Russian River Valley—where most of its grapes are grown—but the owner buys some of his reds in Alexander Valley. Current annual production is 10,000 cases.

*** Gewürztraminer (dry, wonderfully intense of the variety).
[**] Marty's Big Red (Petite Sirah–based, uncompromisingly sturdy proprietary).
** Zinfandel (hearty stuff). Also: Chardonnay, Cabernet Sauvignon, Thousand Flowers (off-dry proprietary white).

HOUTZ VINEYARDS Santa Barbara T $5.50–$12 A family-owned, 16-acre vineyard threaded among houses at Los Olivos produces nearly all the grapes for 4,500 cases of mostly white wine; the rest comes from a neighbor. The first vintage for Dave and Margy Houtz was 84.

NYR: Chardonnay, Chenin Blanc, Sauvignon Blanc, Cabernet Blanc, and Cabernet Sauvignon.

HOWELL MOUNTAIN AVA

An upland (1,400-foot elevation and higher) sub-AVA in hills e. of the main Napa Valley owes nearly all of its recent reputation to Cabernet Sauvignon; its pre-Prohibition fame owed some to Cabernet, more to Zinfandel. Fewer than a dozen growers have an aggregate of fewer than 500 acres planted, most of it in gently sloped terrain. Four wineries are within the boundary. The revival began in the late seventies.

HUNTER ASHBY

Essentially a grower's label belonging to Napa's William Jaeger (Freemark Abbey, Jaeger-Inglewood, Rutherford Hill), it began with 84s and covers a variable annual volume of $9.60–$10 Chardonnay, Merlot, and Pinot Noir. The peak to date has been about 40,000 cases, mostly of Chardonnay.

HUNTER VINEYARD, ROBERT

Sonoma Valley grower Robert Hunter and Napa's Duckhorn Vineyards set out in 81 to make a Champagne-method sparkling wine to the highest standards, using only Hunter's grapes and taking three years as minimum time on the yeast. The rewards of the wine they called Brut de Noirs were considerable, but the costs were greater. They gave up the project with their 84, just going to market in 1989. All four vintages were made under contract at Chateau St. Jean's Graton cellars. In 1989 Hunter was considering a grower's label still Chardonnay under his name.

HUSCH VINEYARDS Mendocino T $5.50–$15

A surprisingly overlooked winery has one foot in the Anderson Valley and the other at Ukiah. The name and 21 acres of Anderson Valley vineyard (Pinot Noir, Chardonnay, Gewürztraminer) date from 1971, when Tony and Gretchen Husch were among the early growers and winemakers in a reviving district. Expansion into Ukiah began in 1979 when Hugo Oswald and family bought the Husch property and added to the fold their existing 110-acre La Ribera Ranch (Sauvignon Blanc, Cabernet Sauvignon, Chardonnay, Chenin Blanc). Not long after, the Oswalds enlarged the Anderson Valley property to 54 acres. They now have a winery in each valley.

*** Reserve Chardonnay (all Anderson Valley; firm, intensely perfumed by the grapes; sold only at the winery) 84 85 86 87; Gewürztraminer (intense of its variety, barely off-dry).

[**] Chardonnay (blends both valleys; full of applelike fruit flavors, fairly firm structure); Pinot Noir (dark, lively; benefits from bottle age to six or seven years, perhaps longer); Cabernet Sauvignon (focuses on ripe fruit; forward, accessible in most seasons).

** Sauvignon Blanc (pleasing melonlike fruit, sometimes accompanied by an earthy note); Chenin Blanc (straightforwardly varietal; well off-dry).

INGLENOOK–NAPA VALLEY Napa T
$6.50–$35 One of the grand old houses of Napa is being restored to the eminence it enjoyed between 1881 and Prohibition, and again from repeal until the late 1960s. The winery was family owned until 1964; Heublein, Inc. has been the sole proprietor since 1978. Under Heublein, owned and leased vineyards have been winnowed until—in 1989— only two levels of Napa wine remain under the label: Estate and Reserve. Three years earlier there were three, but the lowest tier is now bottled under a second label, RUTHERFORD ESTATE. Production is currently at 136,000 cases of Inglenook–Napa Valley, 100,000 cases of the second label.
*** Cabernet Sauvignon–Reserve (full-bodied, full-flavored, consistently age-worthy) 78 79 81 82 83.
[**] Chardonnay-Reserve (deftly touched by oak); Sauvignon Blanc–Reserve (Napa grassy); Charbono (husky, needs time in bottle); and Cabernet Sauvignon (delicate next to Reserve).
** Chardonnay (pleasing fruit, some wood tones) and Pinot Noir (firm, understated).
NYR: Reunion (big, firm, intensely flavored); Niebaum Claret (soft, fleshy textures, understated flavors); Merlot Reserve (fleshy, pleasantly fruity); and Gravion (subtle, polished Sauvignon-Semillon blend).

INGLENOOK-NAVALLE San Joaquin T
$3.49–$4.49 Once linked to Inglenook–Napa Valley, Navalle is now an entirely separate operation. The wines are produced at the Heublein Wines plant near Madera; sales are managed from Heublein, Inc. headquarters in Connecticut. The wines come primarily from San Joaquin Valley grapes; volume exceeds 3 million cases, mostly in 1.5-liter bottles. The Madera winery also is responsible for ALMADEN, CHARLES LEFRANC, and SYLVAN SPRINGS.
[*] Sauvignon Blanc, Chenin Blanc, French Colombard, Chablis, Rhine, White Zinfandel, White Cabernet, White Barbera, Blush, Rosé, Gamay Beaujolais, Zinfandel, Burgundy.`

INNISFREE
A 16,000-case winemaker label in which Joseph Phelps and some of his employees at Joseph Phelps Vineyards are partners. The $9.50, well-made, consistently attractive Cabernet Sauvignon and Chardonnay give excellent value.

IRON HORSE RANCH & VINEYARDS Sonoma T,S $10–$20 The 150-acre Iron Horse vineyard near Forestville started out in the hands of Sonoma Vineyards as one of the great hopes for Pinot Noir. Audrey and Barry Sterling acquired the ranch in time to make 79s, still with Pinot Noir in mind. Since then the property has evolved into one of the most prestigious of California's sparkling wine houses, though still Pinot Noir remains on the lists along with Chardonnay. The vineyard manager who developed the original vineyard, Forrest Tancer, continues as winemaker, partner, and grower of 11 acres in the Alexander Valley from whence the grapes for the Cabernet Sauvignon and Sauvignon Blancs. Production is now at 37,000 cases.

→**Brut (light to the point of being ethereal, and crisp); Blanc de Noirs–Wedding Cuvée (full, even fleshy, and subtly but deeply flavored by Pinot Noir); Blanc de Blancs (all Chardonnay, sturdy, slow to evolve).
*** Chardonnay (as lean, crisp, even tart as one would expect from a sparkling wine house) 81 84 85 87; and Fumé Blanc (ripe, rich with the melony flavors of Sauvignon) 84 85 86.
→*Pinot Noir (pale, understated); Cabernet Sauvignon (typical ripe, fleshy Alexander Valley Cabernet); Blanc de Pinot Noir (dry, made only in cool years).
NYR: Brut Rosé (deep pink, dry, packed with flavor in its first release).

JADE MOUNTAIN WINERY Sonoma   T $7–$12
The winery of Dr. Douglass Cartwright has undergone a long gestation. He bonded a cellar on his 34-acre vineyard in the Alexander Valley in the late 1960s, but did not produce a bottling for sale until a set of 84s. In 1988 he altered the course of vineyard and winery alike to focus more on Rhôneish varieties because the climate at Cloverdale seems to call for them. Current production is 5,000 cases a year.
NYR: Cabernet Sauvignon, Mourvedre, Sauvignon Blanc.

JAEGER WINERY, THOMAS San Diego   T $7–$9
The same William Jaeger who is otherwise involved in Freemark Abbey, Jaeger-Inglewood, and Rutherford Hill is one of the partners in this cellar, located in what began life as San Pasqual Vineyard. The goal is to make wine only from San Diego County grapes, including a vineyard at the winery, and sell it only in the home county. Production in 1988 was 4,500 cases; the plan is to double that in 1989.
NYR: Chardonnay, Chenin Blanc, Muscat Canelli, and White Zinfandel.

JAEGER–INGLEWOOD VINEYARD Napa   T
$15.50   One of the principals of Freemark Abbey and Rutherford Hill, William Jaeger, sort of moonlights in an estate-bottled Merlot at a 4,000-case cellar on the vineyard near St. Helena that yields the grapes.
NYR: Merlot (dark, round, distinctly varietal in flavor).

JEFFERSON CELLARS
Occasional second label for MONTICELLO.

JEKEL VINEYARD Monterey   T $6.75–$17.95
Bill Jekel has been a passionate spokesman for Monterey, especially the Arroyo Seco AVA, since he and his twin, August, planted the first blocks of a 140-acre vineyard and built a 20,000-case winery near Greenfield in 1978. Simultaneous with the addition of 210 acres on the w. side of the Salinas River and a jump in production to 60,000 acres, the focus has sharpened to Chardonnay, Cabernet Sauvignon, and Riesling as of 1988. Pinot Noir, Pinot Blanc, and other early trials have gone by the way.
*** Johannisberg Riesling (fat, succulent, ripe to taste, and well off-dry at about 2% r.s.; this is the familiar style); Johannisberg Riesling–Late Harvest (concentrated by *Botrytis* into a nectar).

** Chardonnay (well-wooded, often slightly harsh in texture, even with age); Cabernet Sauvignon–Estate, Cabernet Sauvignon–Estate Reserve (both polished and deftly balanced, but strong with regional vegetative flavors redoubled by those from American oak); Muscat Canelli (spot-on varietal only at the winery).
NYR: Dry Johannisberg Riesling (begun with a light, rather crisp, altogether understated 87), and Sweet-Styled Johannisberg Riesling (at +4% r.s., pneumatically soft in its 87 debut outing, but still understated in fruit flavors).

JEPSON VINEYARDS Mendocino T,S
$7.50–$16 In 1985, Chicago businessman Robert S. Jepson, Jr., bought a well-established 108-acre vineyard alongside the Russian River n. of Hopland, and the beginnings of a winery building. The cellar is now complete and scaled to do 30,000 cases a year of estate white and sparkling wine.
NYR: Chardonnay and Chardonnay Reserve (attractive fruit flavors, full-bodied); Sauvignon Blanc (pale, lean); Brut (some of the hearty fruit flavors of pre-French California).

JFJ WINERY Stanislaus T,S $2–$4.50
A 2-million case winery e. of Modesto has kept to the course it charted for itself when it opened in 1973: good-value generic wines from San Joaquin Valley grapes, mostly packaged in liter and larger bottles, and more recently, in bag-in-a-box formats. The winery is owned by the brothers Joseph, Fred, and John Franzia, hence the initials. The wines are sold under two labels, JFJ and CC.
* Chablis, Rhine, Blush Chablis, Rosé, and Burgundy, plus Brut and Extra Dry Charmat Champagnes.

JOHANNISBERG RIESLING
The best-known but not most accurate of three synonyms for a white grape and its varietal wine. *See* WHITE RIESLING.

JOHNSON-TURNBULL VINEYARDS Napa T
$14.50 The owning partners, a lawyer and an architect, started with an 81 Cabernet Sauvignon from their 20-acre vineyard at the Oakville winery, limited themselves to one wine until they added an 86 Chardonnay from Turnbull's 18-acre property in Knights Valley, and divided the Cabernet into two lots based on the age of the vines used to make them.
*** Cabernet Sauvignon (old school, minty-ripe, fleshy, 100% varietal; to be known as VS 67—after the year of planting—from 86 onward) 81 83 84.
NYR: Chardonnay; Cabernet Sauvignon (from younger vines than VS 67, much less minty in its debut vintage, 86).

JOHNSON'S OF ALEXANDER VALLEY Sonoma T
$4–$12.50 Three brothers started in 1975 to develop the rustic winery that takes the crop from a 40-acre, valley-floor vineyard. Now the cellar is entirely in the hands of one of them, Tom, and his wife, Gail. Their daughter makes the wine in a manner as straightforward and unassuming as the barn-cum-winery in which she works. Most of the annual 5,000 cases are sold at the cellar door.
** Chardonnay, Pinot Noir, Cabernet Sauvignon, Zinfan-

del, and a bit of Johannisberg Riesling. White Zinfandel is a sometimes entrant.

JORDAN VINEYARD AND WINERY Sonoma T
$17.50–$19 Petroleum geologist Tom Jordan and family built a stunning châteaulike, 75,000-case estate winery on a hilltop in the Alexander Valley in 1976. The plan was to make memorable but immediately accessible Cabernet Sauvignon. Their success is well documented. Chardonnay joined the roster in 1981. Both are estate-bottled wines from the Jordan's 276 acres on the valley floor below the winery.
*** Cabernet Sauvignon (early tendency to strong herbaceous flavors has moderated with maturity in the vineyard; wines always beautifully balanced, polished) 81 84 85; Chardonnay (ultratoasty initial style has moderated to show off more fruit) 85 86.

JORY WINERY Santa Clara T,S $16.50–$20
Dan Lewis is the coproprietor with his son-in-law of a 1,500-case winery that focuses on two Chardonnays from Santa Clara County, but also produces a sparkling wine, plus a Pinot Noir from Oregon grapes. The winemaking goes on in leased space. The first vintage: 86.
NYR: Chardonnay–San Ysidro Vineyard, Chardonnay–San Ysidro Vineyard Reserve (both big, ripe, noticeably marked by wood in their first outings); Brut nonvintage (curiously perfumey and sweet in the first try).

JUG WINES
Wines packaged in large bottles for sale at modest to outright cheap prices; often miscalled bulk wines.

KALIN CELLARS Marin T $10–$22
Full-time microbiologist, part-time winemaker Terry Leighton started as a ceaseless experimenter with 76s, but has begun to settle into a style in recent vintages. He produces 6,000 cases a year in a Novato warehouse, all from bought grapes.
** Chardonnays (five a year from Dry Creek Valley, Livermore Valley, Potter Valley, Russian River Valley, each designated by cuvée letters keyed to source vineyards, all definitely toasty); Alexander Valley Pinot Noir (uncommonly husky, good ager); Dry Creek Valley Cabernet Sauvignon; Potter Valley Sauvignon Blanc; Livermore Valley Semillon (well-wooded).
NYR: Brut Rosé (80% Pinot Noir, 20% Chardonnay).

KARLY WINES Amador T $5.75–$12.50
Buck Cobb turned away from defense engineering to Sierra-foothills Zinfandel in 1980. His 20-acre vineyard in the Shenandoah Valley contributes an enlivening dollop of Petite Sirah to old-vines Zinfandel bought from three, sometimes four nearby vineyards, and is also a substantial source of Sauvignon Blanc. Total annual production is slightly more than 11,000 cases. The winery is named after Karly Cobb, Buck's wife.
→*Zinfandel (splendid fruit subtly touched by oak; plenty big but has polished textures) 83 84 86; Petite Sirah (sold only at winery, same style as Zinfandel) 86.

** Sauvignon Blanc (sturdy, well-wooded); White Zinfandel.
NYR: Zinfandel-Reserve (added with 86, from Sadie Upton vineyard); Chardonnay (heavy, quick-aging thus far).

KEENAN WINERY, ROBERT Napa T $12–$18
Wines from Robert Keenan's cellar and vineyard on Spring Mountain were woody and overweight to outright thuddy from the 77s through 81s; more recent vintages have trimmed down. The 46-acre estate plantings of Chardonnay, Cabernet Sauvignon, and Merlot are supplemented by bought-in Napa Chardonnay to bring production to 12,000 cases. Keenan plans to top out at no more than 20,000.
→*Cabernet Sauvignon (recently supple, distinctively varietal) 82 84 85; Merlot (echoes the Cabernet Sauvignon).
** Napa Valley Chardonnay (ripe, rich, well-wooded), Estate Chardonnay–Ann's Vineyard (paler, clearer fruit flavors).

KENDALL-JACKSON VINEYARD Lake, Mendocino T $8–$20 One of the startling growth stories of recent years began as a modest local winery near Clear Lake in 1981, and grew to a 400,000-case enterprise by 1988. Half of the production is barrel-fermented Chardonnays. Proprietor Jess Jackson owns 85 acres of vines at his winery in the Clear Lake AVA. He has interests in another 32 in Mendocino's Anderson Valley AVA (originally the Edmeades vineyard, acquired in 1988), and 710 acres of what was planted as Tepusquet in the Santa Maria AVA of Santa Barbara County (also bought in 1988, *see* CAMBRIA VINEYARDS). Both of these parcels have separate wineries on them. In 1989 he acquired another winery and 100 acres (originally Stephen Zellerbach) in Sonoma County. With all that, Jackson and winemaker Jed Steele still buy grapes.
*** Mendocino Zinfandel (at times overrun by new oak perfumes, more often splendidly varietal and perfectly balanced, at peak in individual-vineyard bottlings labeled Zeni, DePatie-DuPratt, Ciapusci, Pacini, and Mariah) 84 85 86; Clear Lake Sauvignon Blanc, Jackson Vineyard (lovely melony flavors in youth) 85 86 87 88.
** Chardonnay–Proprietor Reserve, Chardonnay–Vintner Reserve (ripe, fat with a touch of r.s., toasty, noticeable notes from new wood); Lake County Cabernet Sauvignon, Cabernet Sauvignon–Proprietor Reserve, Cabernet Sauvignon–Vintner Reserve, Cabernet Sauvignon–Cardinale (clear, straightforward varietal flavors); California Sauvignon Blanc (clear Sauvignon flavors, sometimes a touch of spritz); Muscat Canelli; Santa Barbara Johannisberg Riesling (well off-dry).
NYR: Sonoma Valley Chardonnay–Durrell Vineyard; Syrah; Merlot.

KENNEDY WINERY, KATHRYN Santa Clara T $25 A tiny specialist in estate Cabernet Sauvignon has an 800-case winery and 5-acre vineyard a few blocks from the heart of Saratoga, just at the edge of the Santa Cruz Mountains AVA. The first vintage was 79. Kathryn's son, Martin Mathis, makes the wine.

** Cabernet Sauvignon (consistently dark, pungently herbaceous).

KENWOOD WINERY Sonoma T $4.50–$30

The Martin Lee family bought the old Pagani country jug winery at Kenwood, in the upper Sonoma Valley, in 1970 and transformed it into a modern cellar by 1975. From that time on, they have simultaneously expanded the capacity and refined production to include a number of vineyard-designated wines. Production has grown to 150,000 cases, all from Sonoma County vineyards save for Clarksburg AVA grapes in the Chenin Blanc. Most of the fruit is bought-in; the Lees own 135 acres at the winery and are partners in the 100-acre Yulupa Vineyard. Sauvignon Blanc is far and away the specialty of the house.

[***] Sonoma Sauvignon Blanc (polished, understated, ultrareliable) 85 86 87 88; Sonoma Valley Zinfandel (splendid smack of berries mates with firm, lively textures) 82 83 84 85 86 87.

[**] Chenin Blanc (from Clarksburg and Sonoma grapes; always off-dry, fresh, and appealing); Chardonnay (direct varietal aromas, always well-balanced in both regular Sonoma Valley and individual-vineyard Beltane Ranch and Yulupa Vineyard bottlings); Cabernet Sauvignon–Sonoma Valley (neatly balanced and well-flavored of Cabernet), and Sonoma Valley Pinot Noir.

** Cabernet Sauvignon–Jack London Vineyard and Cabernet Sauvignon–Artist Series (both always dark, tannic, and heady); Pinot Noir–Jack London Vineyard (echoes vineyard-designated Cabernet Sauvignon from same source).

KENWORTHY VINEYARDS Amador T

$5.50–$7.70 Burly John Kenworthy makes wines pretty much in his own image at a 1,000-case-a-year cellar in the Shenandoah Valley. Most of the grapes are bought-in within the home county, but some come from neighboring El Dorado. The label dates from 1979.

** Zinfandel-Amador (hearty, heady in the local tradition); Cabernet Sauvignon–El Dorado (echoes the Zinfandel). Also: Semillon–El Dorado, Chardonnay–El Dorado, white table wine, and red table wine.

KERR WINES, JOHN

A winemaker's label. Proprietor John Kerr is employed as winemaker and assistant winemaker at two Santa Barbara cellars when he is not moonlighting in leased space. His first vintage was 86; current production is about 500 cases of $13.50–$15 wines, mostly from Santa Maria Valley grapes. NYR: Chardonnay (barrel-fermented, malolactic, long in oak); Syrah (bold style again).

KIRIGIN CELLARS Santa Clara T $5–$7.50

Nikola Kirigin Chargin trained in his native Yugoslavia and has somehow kept his original sense of style though many transplantings. He has now settled into a 45-acre vineyard and 3,000-case "retirement" winery in Hecker Pass by way

of a production job at a large winery in the San Joaquin. All of the wines are estate.
** Opol Rosé, Burgundy, Pinot Noir, Zinfandel (all bone-dry, subdued in fruit, and reflective of long aging in well-seasoned wood).

KISTLER VINEYARDS   Sonoma   T $15–$20
Ambitious young partners set out in 1979 to make grand style Chardonnay in their mountaintop winery at the head end of the Sonoma Valley; they have since added Cabernet Sauvignon and Pinot Noir, but Chardonnay remains much the dominant wine in an annual production edging toward 9,000 cases. Most of the wines are vineyard-designated from Sonoma County properties, one from their own 30 acres at the winery. Kistler also has 20 acres in the Russian River Valley, newly planted to Chardonnay in 1988.
** Chardonnay (separate bottlings from Kistler Estate, Dutton Ranch, and Durrell Vineyard in the Sonoma Valley AVA, and McCrea Vineyard in the Sonoma Mountain AVA; all are barrel-fermented, malolactic, toasty heavyweights).
NYR: Cabernet Sauvignon–Estate, Pinot Noir–Dutton Ranch, and Pinot Noir–McCrea Vineyard.

KLEINBERGER
An offbeat white grape variety possibly related to Riesling. GUNDLACH-BUNDSCHU's planting in the Sonoma Valley is the only one in California from which a varietal wine is made.

KNIGHTS VALLEY AVA
Small, upland Sonoma AVA snuggled between Napa Valley's n. end and Alexander Valley's s. tip. Beringer has dominated there since the early seventies (and done very well with Cabernet Sauvignon and Late Harvest Johannisberg Riesling); others have begun to explore it. Total acreage is about 1,000, mostly in Cabernet Sauvignon, but with appreciable amounts of Riesling and Sauvignon Blanc.

KONOCTI CELLARS   Lake   T $5–$8
A co-op of 26 local vineyardists and John Parducci (of PARDUCCI WINE CELLARS in Mendocino) are the operating partners in a 40,000-case winery that draws only on the owner/growers' vineyards in the Clear Lake AVA. The label dates from 1979, Parducci's participation from 1983. Since the early years, Konocti's fame has rested with its Sauvignon Blanc. In 1988 the winery began pushing harder in that direction and also placing new emphasis on Cabernet Sauvignon.
[**] Sauvignon Blanc (light, hovers between grassy and melony flavors); Cabernet Sauvignon (pleasing flavors, balance).
• Merlot, White Riesling, Chardonnay, and White Cabernet.

KORBEL & BROS., F.   Sonoma   S $10–$12.50
Three Korbel brothers founded the winery as a sparkling wine house in 1882; three Heck brothers bought the Russian River Valley property in 1954. The family of one of the Hecks still holds the reins at what is now (by a considerable margin) California's largest champagne-method sparkling

wine producer with 1.2 million cases, nearly all of it from bought grapes.

[**]Brut, Blanc de Blancs (100% Chardonnay), Blanc de Noirs (100% Pinot Noir), Natural (no sweetening dosage), Sec (a sweet rarity among champagne-method sparklers in California these days), Extra Dry (very similar to the Sec), and Rosé. All cling vigorously to a long-standing style that emphasizes ripe grape flavors and textures.

KORNELL CHAMPAGNE CELLARS, HANNS Napa S $8.99–$15 Hanns Kornell emigrated from Germany in 1939 with the equivalent of lunch money. He worked for others, started small in Sonoma in 1952, and moved to the Napa Valley in 1961. Since then, he and his family have built an 85,000-case sparkling wine house near Calistoga more out of grit than gravy. All of the cuvée wines are bought, originally with Hanns's Germanic sense of style, lately with broader ideas in mind.

*** Sehr Trocken (an original; very dry, and distinctly flavored by the tastes of well-aged Riesling).

** Brut (all Pinot Noir in recent seasons but still hints at the same tastes that developed Sehr Trocken), and Rouge (as good as red sparklers get, only at the winery).

NYR: Blanc de Blancs (all Chardonnay, new with an 80, still settling into its style), and Blanc de Noirs (all Pinot Noir, also finding its niche).

KRUG WINERY, CHARLES Napa T,D $5.75–$18 One of Napa's great pre-Prohibition names has belonged since the 1930s to the family of Cesare Mondavi. From the mid-1960s it has been directed by Cesare's youngest son, Peter, and Peter's family. Properties include the historic 1861 winery at St. Helena, and a bit more than 1,200 acres of vineyards in 10 parcels that dot the length of the valley from the winery at St. Helena s. into Carneros. Production is at 200,000 cases.

[**] Cabernet Sauvignon (consistently varietal, well-balanced).

** Cabernet Sauvignon–Vintage Selection (back on track in vintages since 80, richer, firmer than regular); Chardonnay (pleasantly fruity young, quick to age in recent times); Sauvignon Blanc (recently renamed from Fumé Blanc and restyled with all the emphasis on varietal fruit, no oak aging). Also: Chenin Blanc (well off-dry), Johannisberg Riesling (also off-dry), Pinot Noir–Carneros.

NYR: Carneros Chardonnay–Brown Ranch, and Carneros Chardonnay–Cabral Ranch (introduced with 86s).

A $4–$7 second label, CK-Mondavi, covers *→** varietals and * jug generics, the latter mostly from San Joaquin grapes. Included in the roster: Chardonnay, Chenin Blanc, Sauvignon Blanc, White Zinfandel, Cabernet Sauvignon, Zinfandel, Burgundy, Chablis, Rhine, Bravissimo, Vin Rosé, Barberone, and Fortissimo.

KRUSE WINERY, THOMAS Santa Clara T,S $4.50–$12 A onetime academic in Chicago transplanted himself to the Hecker Pass district in 1971 to make wines a shade finer than the country jugs for which the region had been known. Now old guard, Tom Kruse produces close to 4,000 cases a year from bought Gilroy and Morgan Hill district grapes.

*→** Chardonnay, Blanc de Noir (a blended blush), Gilroy White, Gilroy Red, Cabernet Sauvignon, Zinfandel (honest country wines every one), and Blanc de Blanc (a rustic champagne-method sparkler from Chardonnay).

LA BELLE
Second label for fine-value $4.50–$5.75 California Chardonnay, Sauvignon Blanc, and Cabernet Sauvignon from RAYMOND VINEYARDS.

LA CASCADA San Luis Obispo T $4.50–$12
A new name for a Paso Robles winery that has been operating as El Paso de Robles signals the new ownership in 1988 of Jeff Strickland. The winery has been making 5,000 cases. His plan is to build quickly to 10,000, more slowly to 15,000, all with Paso Robles grapes. He owns 11 acres of Zinfandel and buys the rest.
NYR: Cabernet Sauvignon, Merlot, Late Harvest Zinfandel, and White Zinfandel.

LA CIENEGA AVA
AVA in San Benito County developed by Almaden, which soon after sold off as much of its 330 acres as it could and abandoned the rest. At least two wineries still draw on small vineyards within its boundaries.

LA CREMA Sonoma T $4.95–$18
The winery has changed owners and winemakers and dropped "Vinera" from its name since it was founded in 1979, but remains committed to the most practical of the original programs. New Yorker Jason Korman, the owner since 1985, has done away with vineyard-designated wines in favor of regular and reserve bottlings, but stuck with barrel fermentation and other Burgundian techniques of his predecessors; grapes continue to come from Mendocino and Monterey as well as Sonoma. Korman is moving the winery from Petaluma to Graton during 1989, and planting the first of a 70-acre vineyard near Forestville in the Russian River AVA. Production has climbed to an annual 80,000 cases.
NYR: Chardonnay (impressive first outing), Chardonnay Reserve, Pinot Noir, Pinot Noir Reserve, and Select White Table Wine (remarkably fine barrel-fermented blend of Chardonnay, Semillon, and Chenin Blanc).

LA JOTA VINEYARD CO. Napa T $10–$18
William and Joan Smith set out with the vintage of 82 to produce grand Cabernet Sauvignon at their 1,800-case winery and 30-acre vineyard in the Howell Mountain AVA. Cabernet remains the mainstay, but their first grand success is a mere 85 cases of 86 Viognier, one of California's first two.
NYR: Cabernet Sauvignon (thus far dark, tannic, and marked by overtones of the farmyard); Zinfandel (follows Cabernet's lead); and Viognier (enticing floral perfumes from the grapes, neatly balanced).

LA REINA Monterey T $13.50
The only wine is a Chardonnay, part of it from the once-

affiliated, now-separately-owned vineyard of the same name, all of it from Arroyo Seco AVA grapes. The first vintage was 84; production approaches 8,000 cases a year.
NYR: Chardonnay (plenty of fruit, plenty of the toasty notes of barrel fermentation in its first three vintages).

LA VIEILLE MONTAGNE   Napa   T $7–$12
The label began with an 81 Cabernet from bought-in Sonoma grapes, but Shawn and John Guilliams launched their estate winery toward the top of Spring Mountain with 84s. Planned annual production from 7 acres is 1,000 cases.
NYR: Cabernet Sauvignon (blended with Cabernet Franc and Merlot), and White Riesling.

LAKE SONOMA WINERY   Sonoma   T $4.50–$12
Vineyardist Robert Polson's winery in Dry Creek Valley AVA uses grapes from his own 20 acres plus other Sonoma County ranches he farms under contract. The label dates from 1985; the business is an outgrowth of Diablo Vista Winery (still used as a second label), for which Polson was a major grower from 1978 until he bought the assets in 1985.
NYR: Chardonnay, White Table Wine, Cabernet Sauvignon, and Zinfandel.

LAKESPRING WINERY   Napa   T $8–$12
An 18,000-case winery at Yountville is producing a steadily more illustrious list of wines. Winemaker Randall Mason uses all bought-in Napa grapes, except for 8 acres of Chardonnay belonging to the owners, three brothers Battat. The label began with 80s.
[***]Merlot (enticing varietal flavors neatly complicated by wood, firmly structured, well-balanced for aging) 83 84 85.
[**] Cabernet Sauvignon (same graceful style as Merlot, as or more likely to age well); Sauvignon Blanc (emphasizes grassy side of the variety); and Chardonnay (often agreeably varietal but can be a bit woody and heady).

LAMBERT BRIDGE   Sonoma   T $10–$12
Gerard Lambert's 119 acres of vineyard, in three separate blocks in the Dry Creek Valley AVA, have yielded distinctively flavored wines across the board through several changes of winemakers since the beginning in 1975. Production is at 25,000 cases.
[**→***] Chardonnay (faint, almost Sauvignon-like hints of fresh asparagus among the fruit flavors are one hallmark, balance the other).
** Cabernet Sauvignon (delicately structured, distinctively herbaceous), and Merlot (echoes the Cabernet Sauvignon). There is an occasional Late Harvest Johannisberg Riesling when *Botrytis* develops in a low-lying block near the creek.

LAMBORN FAMILY VINEYARD   Napa   T $8
Bill Lamborn started out as a pure grower, developed a grower label for his 82, and finally bonded his own winery in time for the 84. His 9 acres are the highest up in the lofty Howell Mountain AVA, on a property that made Zinfandel of enough substance to win a medal in the Paris exposition of 1890. Annual production is edging past 1,500 cases.
NYR: Zinfandel (shaky 84, hearty, likable 85 and 86).

LANDMARK VINEYARDS   Sonoma   T $10
Part-owner/winemaker Bill Mabry started narrowing his
focus soon after his debut vintage, 74; by 1984, the list was
down from five wines to just one, Chardonnay. Most of
Landmark's annual 15,000 cases comes from his family's 77
acres of vineyards in the Russian River, Alexander Valley,
and Sonoma Valley AVAs. In 1989 the winery began moving to Kenwood, in the Sonoma Valley, driven out of its
original location in the burgeoning residential town of
Windsor.
[**] Chardonnay (a bit erratic, but splendidly varietal in the
finest vintages).
Cypress Lane is Landmark's 15,000-case second label.
[*→**] $5–$6 Chardonnay, Sauvignon Blanc, and White
Zinfandel are all designed to be immediately drinkable.

LAS MONTANAS   Sonoma   T $9–$13
Aleta Apgar uses no additives in producing an annual 1,000
cases of red wine at her cellars on the Sonoma side of Mt.
Veeder. Her first vintage as Las Montanas was 81; she began making wine with 79s. A Sonoma Valley Pinot Noir is
to join the other two reds on her short list.
** Sonoma Valley Zinfandel (big, dark) and Cabernet Sauvignon (from Mt. Veeder, also big and dark).

LAS VINAS WINERY   San Joaquin   T $4–$11
Grower/winemaker John Cotta and two vineyardist broth-
ers made their first wines in 86, all from their own Lodi
AVA grapes. First-year production was 12,000 cases.
NYR: Chardonnay (barrel-fermented); Symphony (very at-
tractive in first outing); Amorosa (a blush blended from
Chenin Blanc, Symphony, and Zinfandel); Cabernet Sauvi-
gnon; and Zinfandel.

LATE-HARVEST
A label term with no precise definition or legal standing. On
whites (Johannisberg Riesling, Gewürztraminer, Semillon,
Sauvignon Blanc) it usually signifies a sweet, *Botrytis*-
affected wine, but may only signify sweetness. On reds (especially Zinfandel) it sometimes suggests sweetness, but
more surely denotes alcohols in excess of 14%.

LAUREL GLEN   Sonoma   T $20
Violist-turned-winegrower Patrick Campbell devotes nearly
all of his winery and 40-acre vineyard high up on Sonoma
Mountain to Cabernet Sauvignon, though he has saved a
few rows for Cabernet Franc, Merlot, and Tempranillo to
see if they will improve the breed. (Only Cabernet Franc
goes into the finished wine so far.) The label began with an
81; the vines reached bearing age in 1974. Production stands
at 5,000 cases. Counterpoint is a second label for Cabernets
deemed by Campbell not to be worthy of the Laurel Glen
name.
*** Cabernet Sauvignon (richly varietal, silky smooth, accessible early but rewards a wait) 81 83 84 85.

LAVA CAP   El Dorado   T $5.50–$10
David Jones and family opened a 4,000-case winery to take
grapes from their 26-acre vineyard high up on Apple Hill,

n.e. of Placerville. David's University of California–Davis–trained son, Tom, is the winemaker. First vintage: 86.
NYR: Chardonnay, Sauvignon Blanc, White Zinfandel, White Cabernet, Cabernet Sauvignon, and Lava Cap Red (Zinfandel-Cabernet blend). Also: a nonestate Johannisberg Riesling.

LAZY CREEK VINEYARDS   Mendocino   T
$6.50–$9.50 Longtime San Francisco waiter Hans Kobler launched his 15-acre Anderson Valley vineyard and 1,500-case winery as a retirement hobby in 1979. As of 1989 he is up to 20 acres and 2,000 cases and building new structures.
[***] Gewürztraminer (superior varietal flavors, dry, flawless balance for keeping 4 years, maybe more) 85 86 87.
[**] Pinot Noir (sometimes a bit rough-hewn, but full of agreeable flavors from the grapes); Chardonnay.

LE DOMAINE
The longtime second-label sparkler of Almaden has been revived as of 1988 by Heublein as a stand-alone brand for Charmat-method Brut and Extra Dry.

LE VIN CELLARS
A merchant label belonging to a San Francisco family named Le Vin covers $6.25–$10.50 NYR Sonoma Chardonnay, Sauvignon Blanc, Cabernet Sauvignon, and Blushing Zinfandel made in leased space in Sonoma County. The first vintage was 84. Production is about 1,500 cases a year, and gaining.

LEEWARD WINERY   Ventura   T $5.75–$15
Partners Chuck Brigham and Chuck Gardner chose to put their winery in Ventura in 1979 not because it was so far from the nearest vineyard but because the climate was exactly what they wanted for barrel-fermenting their Chardonnays. They have added and dropped other wines, but most of the annual 18,000 cases is of the wine that put them where they are.
–→* Chardonnay–Edna Valley, Chardonnay–Central Coast (distinct fruit plus toasty notes).
** Blanc de Pinot Noir (from the Santa Maria AVA), Cabernet Sauvignon–Alexander Valley (softened with a bit of Merlot).

LEFRANC, CHARLES
The prestige label for Almaden from the midseventies until the company's sale to Heublein in 1987 is now used by the latter for a separate line of $3.99–$4.99 California-appellation wines made with Almaden and Inglenook Navalle at Madera. The first releases in 1988 were Sauvignon Blanc, White Cabernet, White Zinfandel, and Cabernet Sauvignon.

LIBERTY SCHOOL
Second-label for CAYMUS VINEYARDS was expanded in 1988 to cover imports from Chile as California sources fell short of the needs. The California entries are good-value $5.50–$7.50 Chardonnay, Sauvignon Blanc, and Cabernet Sauvi-

gnon from variable sources. Annual volume is about 80,000 cases.

LIME KILN VALLEY AVA

Tiny, one-winery sub-AVA at the s. tip of La Cienega AVA in San Benito County. ENZ VINEYARDS developed it.

LIVE OAKS WINERY Santa Clara T $5–$7

One of the oldest family jug wineries in the Hecker Pass district now has a second owner, Richard Blocher, who bought it from Peter Scagliotti in 1986. Blocher has spruced up the buildings, but kept longtime winemaker Mitsuo Takamoto and the whole roster of wines. He has expanded grape sources beyond Gilroy to Monterey, Paso Robles, Santa Barbara, and Amador counties. Annual production is around 3,500 cases.

*→** Chenin Blanc Extra Dry, Medium Dry, and Dolce; Grenache Rosé Extra Dry and Medium Dry; Sweet Grenache; Burgundy; Sauterne; Haut Sauterne; Muscat; Chardonnay; Gewürztraminer; Johannisberg Riesling; White Zinfandel; Zinfandel.

LIVERMORE VALLEY AVA

One of coastal California's oldest commercial wine districts is anchored on the Alameda County town of Livermore, in hills e. of San Francisco Bay. Nearly all of 1,800 acres of vineyard there are planted in a 600-foot-deep dry wash full of stones ranging from pebbles up to boulders the size of melons. The valley has been most famous for whites, particularly Sauvignon Blanc and Semillon, since the 1880s, but does have modest plantings of Cabernet Sauvignon, Petite Sirah, and other reds. The wineries that have sustained it through a long period of suburban growth are the historic ones, Concannon Vineyards and Wente Bros. Another six smaller cellars also call it home.

LIVERMORE VALLEY CELLARS Alameda T $5.95–$12

As a retirement venture Chris Lagiss makes 2,000 to 3,000 cases of estate wine a year from his 30 acres of dry-farmed old vines s.e. of Livermore town. Every drop is white. His first vintage was 78.

*→** Chardonnay, Grey Riesling, French Colombard, Fumé Blanc, Blanc de Blanc, Golden Seco (generic), Servant Blanc (which Lagiss believes to be the only planting in the U.S. of a Mediterranean grape widely cultivated for table use in Europe). Generics: Blanc de Blanc and Golden Seco (fuller).

LIVINGSTON Napa T $24

John Livingston makes only Cabernet Sauvignon from his own 8 acres, called Moffitt Vineyard, s. of St. Helena. The first vintage was 84; winemaking is still in leased space, but the rehabilitation of pre-Prohibition H. W. Helms cellars is the proprietor's current project.

NYR: Cabernet Sauvignon–Moffitt Vineyard (bit heavy in debut).

LLORDS & ELWOOD

An old label mainly known for creditable flor sherry-types

while it was family-owned and operated out of Weibel Vineyards in Alameda County, but also a source of varietal table wines. It was bought in 1986 by MONTICELLO CELLARS, which has revamped the table wines (now good-value $5–$8 Napa Chardonnay, Sauvignon Blanc, and Cabernet Sauvignon and California White Zinfandel) and continued with the excellent-value $5–$5.75 dessert types (Dry Wit Sherry, Judge's Secret Cream Sherry, and Ancient Proverb Port).

LODI AVA
One of the San Joaquin Valley's durable growing regions pivots on the town of Lodi, at the junction of the Mokelumne and San Joaquin Rivers. The dominant grape variety on Lodi's flat to gently rolling terrain is Zinfandel. Chardonnay, Sauvignon Blanc, and Cabernet Sauvignon are rapidly supplanting Tokay, once a favorite for brandies and sherry types.

LOHR, J.   Santa Clara   T $5–$14.50
The winery started in 1975 as Turgeon and Lohr, with all of the wines coming from a proprietor-owned vineyard at Greenfield, in what is now Monterey's Arroyo Seco AVA. Jerry Lohr bought out his partner in 1984. Both vineyard holdings and wine production have been growing ever since. The Monterey property (335 acres called Cypress Vineyard) has as company 225 acres in the Clarksburg AVA, 280 (plus a new fermenting winery) in the Paso Robles AVA, and 34 in the Napa Valley AVA at St. Helena. When all plantings are complete total acreage will be more than 1,000. The winery buys grapes in the same regions to round out 200,000 cases of production a year.
** Monterey Chardonnay, Chardonnay-Reserve, Chardonnay–Cypress Vineyard; Monterey Johannisberg Riesling; Monterey Gamay (luscious fruit, almost viscously rich in texture); California Cabernet Sauvignon, and Napa Valley Cabernet Sauvignon Reserve–Carol's Vineyard.

LOLONIS WINERY   Mendocino   T $7.50–$11
Three brothers—Nicolas, Petros, and Ulysses—and their families grow 300 acres of vines in the Redwood Valley; their father planted the first 4 in 1920. They select from that to make 8,000 cases of wine a year using their own equipment and cooperage but in leased space in another Mendocino winery. Their first vintage, 82, was all white. Zinfandel and Cabernet Sauvignon joined the roster in 88.
• Chardonnay; Fumé Blanc; Late Harvest Sauvignon Blanc.

LONE OAK VINEYARDS
A new-in-1988 second label for SMITH & HOOK covers a $5 Monterey Chardonnay from a vineyard called Lone Oak, and a $6 Monterey Cabernet Sauvignon from the Smith & Hook vineyard. Both are made at Smith & Hook; annual production is 15,000 cases.

LONG VINEYARDS   Napa   T $9–$36
This 3,000-case winery on the same hill e. of St. Helena as Chappellet belongs to Bob Long and Zelma Long. It started with only Chardonnay and Johannisberg Riesling from the Long family's 17-acre vineyard, but soon branched out to

make other wines with grapes bought elsewhere. First vintage: 77.
*** Chardonnay (thoroughly toasty) and Johannisberg Riesling (richly varietal, well off-dry); Late Harvest Johannisberg (as the seasons permit, splendid when it comes).
NYR: Sauvignon Blanc–Chalk Hill (introduced with an 83), and Cabernet Sauvignon (from the University of California vineyard at Oakville, begun with a 79).

LONGORIA WINES, RICHARD
The winemaker label of Richard Longoria (The Gainey Vineyard) started with 82 Chardonnay and Pinot Noir made while he was at J. Carey, and resumed with a $14 Santa Barbara Pinot Noir 85. A Chardonnay is in the works. Lots will remain in the 250-case-per-wine realm at least through the 89s.

LOS HERMANOS
Jug-wine label of BERINGER VINEYARD.

LOST HILLS WINERY San Joaquin T,D
$2.49–$4.99 Lost Hills made a new start in 1988 when Jason Korman—the New Yorker who also owns LA CREMA—assembled a group that bought it with the plan of turning it into a half-million-case producer of bargain-priced varietals from coastal grapes within two years. The label goes back through several owners before Korman and company to a large grower in the San Joaquin. The winery, in the village of Acampo n. of Lodi, goes back another owner still, Dino Barengo having started it in 1944 under his own name. First-year volume under the new regime was about 100,000 cases, from coastal and San Joaquin Valley grapes.
NYR: Nonvintage Chardonnay, Fumé Blanc, Johannisberg Riesling, White Zinfandel, Cabernet Sauvignon, and red, white, and blush. Barengo still exists as a label, in current use for Estate Ruby Cabernet and dessert wines sold only at the winery.

LOWER LAKE WINERY
The original name of the winery now operating as STUERMER.

LUCAS WINERY, THE San Joaquin T $6.50
Dave and Tamara Lucas grow 30 acres of Zinfandel on Lodi's w. side. They sell some of the grapes, but hang on to enough to make an annual 1,200 cases, almost all sold direct. Their first vintage was 78.
** Zinfandel (pleasantly polished, Lodi's typical hint of weight augmented by new French-wood flavors).

LYETH VINEYARD & WINERY Sonoma T
$12–$22 New-in-1987 owners of an ambitious vineyard and winery project in the upper Alexander Valley near Cloverdale began shifting the style of their wines but not the basic course. The 30,000-case winery was started by the late Munro (Chip) Lyeth with the idea of making a Cabernet Sauvignon–based red and Sauvignon Blanc–based white from his adjoining 115-acre vineyard, but not as varietal types. The vineyard is now separately owned, but remains the source of Lyeth wines. The first vintage: 81.

→* Lyeth Red (original ultrawoody style is giving way to one concentrated more on the flavors of a Cabernet Sauvignon–Merlot–Malbec blend, and toward more refined balances) 84 85; Lyeth White (Sauvignon Blanc–Semillon–Muscadelle blend also now less woody in flavors, more delicate in texture) 85 86.

LYTTON SPRINGS WINERY Sonoma T $10
This Alexander Valley specialist in hearty, heady, old-vines Zinfandels dates from 1976 and has not bent to any change in the winds from its powerhouse first vintage onward. The base vineyard is proprietor Richard Sherwin's own patch called Valley Vista. Production runs about 15,000 cases a year, including small lots of other wines sold only at the winery.
→* Zinfandel (intense flavors, heavy-duty tannins, and throat-warming alcohols appeal to linebacker types) 85 86. Also: Chardonnay, Sauvignon Blanc, White Zinfandel, and Late Harvest Zinfandel (just off-dry, and 16.7% alcohol).

MACROSTIE
The winemaker label of Steve MacRostie (longtime Hacienda Wine Cellars, since 1986 a consulting enologist) goes on only one wine, a $14.50 Carneros Chardonnay (seamless marriage of fruit and wood and polished texture in debut 87). Annual volume will grow slowly from startup 1,300 cases until he moves from leased space to his own cellar.

MADEIRA
A seldom-used name for a generic dessert wine made, in California, in much the same way as the drier sherry-types.

MADERA AVA
In the San Joaquin Valley is a sprawling AVA that encompasses much of Madera County and the northern edge of Fresno County. The great acreages in Madera County are 17,680 of French Colombard, 6,060 of Chenin Blanc, 4,155 of Grenache, and 2,780 of Barbera. However, some of the most impressive wines from the region have been port types from tiny plantings of traditional Portuguese varieties, and sherry types from 405 acres of Palomino.

MADRONA VINEYARDS El Dorado T $5–$10
Richard Bush's 35 acres e. of Placerville are, at 3,000 feet elevation, the loftiest and thus coolest in the Sierra foothills, and the sole source of grapes for his 10,000-case winery on the property. The vines date from 1973, the cellars from 1980.
→* Chardonnay (fine fruit aromas, well-balanced) 86.
** Johannisberg Riesling, Gewürztraminer (only at the winery); Cabernet Sauvignon; Cabernet Franc; Merlot; Zinfandel, and season permitting, Select Late Harvest Johannisberg Riesling.

MAGNOLIA RIDGE
A new-in-1987 second label of CHARLES F. SHAW for $3.99–$7.99 Napa Valley Chardonnay, Sauvignon Blanc, and Gamay.

MAISON DEUTZ San Luis Obispo S $15
When Deutz & Geldermann established its California arm, André Lallier brought along the most traditional equipment and traditional champagne-method techniques to make sure the wines had the qualities of traditional Champagnes if not the exact characters. The first few wines (reserve lots go back to 83) have come from Santa Maria AVA grapes while his own 300 acres of vines mature at Arroyo Grande in southernmost San Luis Obispo County. The first cuvée, released in 1986, was 1,900 cases; the plan was to go quickly to 25,000.
NYR: Brut (Pinot Blanc, Pinot Noir, and Chardonnay form a cuvée that was attractive in its first two outings).

MALBEC
A black grape variety, and rarely, its varietal wine. A distinctly secondary variety in Bordeaux but the primary one of Cahors. In its brief post-Prohibition career in California it has yielded dark, tannic wines used mostly in Cabernet Sauvignon–based blends. Its performance has been uneven enough for several growers to write off experimental plots while others clamor for more. Acreage is a scant 68, of which 27 are in the North Coast counties, the other 41 in Stanislaus County in the San Joaquin Valley.

MALOLACTIC FERMENTATION (m-l)
A bacterial fermentation that can be spontaneous or induced, simultaneous with the primary alcoholic fermentation or later. It converts comparatively tart malic acid to the less brisk lactic acid. The twin effects are to soften wine and add immediate complexity to its flavors. Some say it does not add flavors, but tempers dominant ones so as to allow more subtleties to shine through. Malolactic, m-l for short, is much used in California reds and Chardonnays.

MALVASIA BIANCA
The Muscat-related white grape variety and its varietal wine. Malvasias usually are made as off-dry to dessert-sweet table wines, but some wineries add brandy to make dessert wines by the legal definition. Of 2,240 acres planted to Malvasia, more than 1,700 are in the San Joaquin Valley; among coastal counties only Monterey has substantial acreage, 430.

MANZANITA
A cross between a winemaker and a merchant label belongs to winery designer Steve Koster and winery CPA Bob Holder, who make 2,300 cases a year of $15 Napa Chardonnay and Cabernet Sauvignon in leased space in Napa. First vintage: 80.

MARIETTA CELLARS Sonoma T $4.99–$10
Chris Bilbro established his label and cellars w. of Healdsburg in 1978, has moved them once since, and is now planning their permanent home on a 40-acre Geyserville vineyard he bought in 1987. Annual production: 15,000 cases.
[**→***] Zinfandel (estimably rich in the berryish flavors of Zinfandel, hearty in texture, and well-balanced) 78 79 82

84 85; Cabernet Sauvignon (echoes the style but leans to the herbaceous side of Cabernet).
• Old Vines Red (a field blend) and White Zinfandel.

MARILYN MERLOT
A merchant-label $13 Merlot made by a partnership in Napa, with a different picture of Marilyn for each vintage.

M. MARION   Sonoma   T $5.99–$6.99
Dennis Marion started out in 1978 with a pure merchant label using mostly Central Coast grapes. Now he makes wine in leased space in Geyserville, primarily from Sonoma grapes. (There was a short interlude in the old cellars of the onetime Jesuit Novitiate at Los Gatos.) Production approaches 75,000 cases.
[*→→*] M. Marion Artist Series Chardonnay, Fumé Blanc, Johannisberg Riesling, White Zinfandel, and Cabernet Sauvignon and Pinot Noir.

MARK WEST VINEYARDS   Sonoma   T,S
$5.95–$18   Bob and Joan Ellis were among the pioneer growers and winemakers when the western edge of the Russian River Valley started to be a seriously regarded region for Burgundian and Germanic grape varieties. Their first vintage was 76. Current production is about 22,000 cases a year, much of the Chardonnay, Pinot Noir, and Gewürztraminer from their own 62 acres n. of Forestville.
*** Gewürztraminer (pungent with varietal perfumes, nearly dry, always willing to age 3 to 5 years) 85 86.
** Sonoma County Chardonnay, Estate Chardonnay, Estate Chardonnay–Reserve, Estate Chardonnay–Artist Series; Johannisberg Riesling; Pinot Noir Blanc; Sonoma County Pinot Noir, Estate Pinot Noir (both dark, firm to slightly rough-textured, often a bit earthy); Zinfandel–Sonoma County (middle-of-the-road); Pinot Noir Blanc; and as the seasons allow, Late Harvest Gewürztraminer. There is an occasional champagne-method Blanc de Noir.

MARKHAM WINERY   Napa   T $7–$12
H. Bruce Markham assembled three vineyard properties totalling 250 acres (two at Yountville, one at Calistoga) in the early 1970s, bought an old winery in 1977, refurbished it, then sold the lot to Sanraku of Tokyo in 1988. The new owners have kept all intact, including the house style. Annual production is 20,000 cases.
** Chardonnay (steady, deftly tinted by wood); Sauvignon Blanc; Muscat Blanc; Cabernet Sauvignon (estate-grown in the Yountville vineyard, ripe, definite notes from wood, held 4 to 5 years before release); and Merlot.
Vinmark is a Markham second label for episodic lots of wines not quite up to the house standard.

MARSALA
An increasingly rare label designation for an ultrasweet rather raisiny-tasting dessert wine patterned after a Spanish original.

MARTIN BROTHERS   San Luis Obispo   T
$5.50–$12   The winemaking brother, Domenic, is one of several who itches to make California Nebbiolo into a wine

to be reckoned with. While the rest of the world waits to take notice, Martin also makes more familiar varietal types. Production stands at 9,000 cases, all from Paso Robles AVA grapes, a fair proportion from 68 acres of owned vineyards at the winery e. of Paso Robles town. The first vintage was 81. ** Chardonnay (ripe, noticeably touched by new oak); Chenin Blanc (well off-dry, pleasingly fruity); Mozart (Sauvignon Blanc–based proprietary); Zinfandel (pale, lean, tart); Nebbiolo (well marked by new wood) and Estate Nebbiolo (packed with flavors of fresh berries).

MARTINI, LOUIS M. Napa T,D $5.85–$18
One of the Napa Valley's great keepers of the flame since 1933, especially in reds. The careers of Louis M., his son Louis P., and grandson, Michael, have a constant thread: their wines have often been dismissed early as too light, then treasured for the next two or three (or four) decades as demonstrations that distinctive character is not synonymous with raw power. The 235,000-case winery draws heavily on family vineyards—Las Amigas and La Loma in Napa Carneros, Monte Rosso on a Sonoma Valley mountaintop, Los Vinedos del Rio in the Russian River Valley, and Glen Oak in Napa's Chiles Valley. In sum, their acreage is 800. A Lake County ranch is under development. The winery is a notable source of older vintages.
[***] Cabernet Sauvignon–Monte Rosso (true Cabernet nose, ripe, almost luscious in texture, long-lived) 78 80 81 82; Merlot, Merlot–Vinedos del Rio (from cool Russian River Valley vines; both are lean, tart, packed with flavor) 82 84 85; Zinfandel (spot-on Zinfandel polished smooth) 78 79 80 82 84 86; Barbera (Italianate red suffused with grace notes from old wood, warm sun, and long age) 76 78 81 83; Cream Sherry (old, old stocks give it wonderful depth, warmth); and Moscato Amabile (honeysuckle nectar from Muscat).
[**→***] Cabernet Sauvignon–North Coast (the regular bottling, always balanced, polished, and ready to age in bottle longer than bigger wines) 74 76 78 79 82 83 84 85; Pinot Noir (spotty in the seventies but regaining form, especially in individual-vineyard bottlings from Las Amigas Vineyard).
[**] Chardonnay (from Russian River and Carneros grapes, much improved in the last few vintages) 86 87; Gewürztraminer (old standby with impeccable varietal character in favorable years) 86; Folle Blanche (California's nearest answer to a well-made Soave); Johannisberg Riesling. Also: Chenin Blanc, Merlot Blanc, White Zinfandel (clean, affable sippers, all). GLEN OAKS is a Martini second label for $3.50 generics.

MARTINI & PRATI Sonoma T,D $2–$5
This longtime bulk producer in the Russian River Valley w. of Santa Rosa produces small lots under its own name, primarily for local sale. The proprietors bottle what they need from lots made principally from Sonoma but also Lake, Mendocino, and Napa County grapes. Most of it goes under the Martini & Prati label, but some Cabernet Sauvignon

appears under the famous pre-Prohibition name of Fountaingrove, now theirs.

*→→** Cabernet Sauvignon, Pinot Noir, Zinfandel, Burgundy, Chardonnay, Johannisberg Riesling, Chablis, Port, Sherry, Muscat.

MASSON VINEYARD   Monterey   T,S,D
$4.50–$8.50   Before and just following Prohibition, Paul Masson was a famous man, and his winery in what is now the Santa Cruz Mountains AVA was just as well-known. The label faltered in recent years until it became known for jugs more than for fine wine. Now, under the ownership of Vintners International, it is being pushed back toward loftier ranks. The Masson Vineyards label goes only on Monterey varietal wines, most of them from 4,000 affiliated acres. The Paul Masson label goes on generics meant to be phased slowly over to the sister TAYLOR CALIFORNIA CELLARS label. Current Masson production at a winery at Gonzales, in the Salinas Valley, is 6 million cases and planned to grow smaller as it becomes more select.
NYR: Masson Vineyards Chardonnay (pleasantly straightforward), Sauvignon Blanc, Cabernet Blanc, Cabernet Sauvignon (appealing, straightforward Cabernet flavors from vineyards in warm, southern Monterey County).
[**] Paul Masson Rare Cream Sherry and Rare Souzao Port.
*→→** Paul Masson Chenin Blanc, French Colombard, Chablis, Emerald Dry, Rhine Castle, Rosé, White Zinfandel, Zinfandel, Burgundy, Champagne-Brut, Champagne–Centennial Cuvée, Madeira, and others.

MASTANTUONO   San Luis Obispo   T $5.50–$20
Pasquale Mastan moved to Paso Robles from Chicago to make Zinfandel. He has branched out a bit since 1977, but when he is inspired to do something particular he keeps returning to the variety that brought him w. Production is about 15,000 cases a year, all from Paso Robles AVA grapes.
→→* Zinfandel nonvintage, Zinfandel-Templeton, and Estate Zinfandel (the wines start rich and dark and keep getting more so as the sources become more specific).
• Fumé Blanc, White Zinfandel, Muscat Canelli.
NYR: Cabernet Sauvignon.

MATANZAS CREEK WINERY   Sonoma   T
$11.50–$18   The considerable fame of Sandra and William MacIver's winery rests most especially on its Chardonnays, but critics have had trouble finding any weak spots in their roster, especially in the vintages since 84. Production has climbed swiftly from 6,000 to 27,000 cases a year since the winery was founded in 1978; the plan is to stay close to the latter level for some time. A 46-acre estate vineyard s. of Santa Rosa is supplemented by grapes bought from the Russian River Valley, Sonoma Valley, Carneros, and Sonoma Mountain AVAs.
→→** Chardonnay (restrained, complex, balanced) 85 86 87.

*** Merlot (dark, full of flavor, tannic among its kind) 85.
→* Sauvignon Blanc (rich with the melony side of Sauvignon, and crisply textured; peaks young) 85 86 87.

MATROSE
The winemaker label of Jamie Meves (Pat Paulsen, Château de Baun) will go inactive when the last of his admirable 85 Alexander Valley Gewürztraminer sells out.

MAYACAMAS Napa T $10–$20
At a virtual aerie high in the Mayacamas Mountains, Bob and Nonie Travers grow 48 acres of Chardonnay and Cabernet Sauvignon, and he makes 5,000 cases of those and two, sometimes three other wines, all of uncommonly individual character. The buildings predate Prohibition; the label started in 1948; the Travers have owned Mayacamas since 1968.
*** Chardonnay (for years woodily weighty, more recently livelier and more aromatic of its grapes) 85; Cabernet Sauvignon (for years fiercely tannic, with 85 supple but still full of flavor). Also: Sauvignon Blanc, Pinot Noir, sometimes Zinfandel.

MAZZOCCO VINEYARDS Sonoma T
$10–$16.50   Mazzocco got off to an impressive start with a pair of 85 Chardonnays—one estate and one not—and has kept the pace since. Owner Tom Mazzocco has 45 acres of vineyard in three patches, two in Dry Creek Valley, one in Alexander Valley. The privately owned 20,000-case winery began making Zinfandel and Cabernet Sauvignon with the vintage of 86.
NYR: Chardonnay–Sonoma County; Chardonnay–River Lane Vineyard.

MCDOWELL VALLEY AVA
This one-winery AVA cupped in hills above the main Russian River Valley floor e. of Hopland in Mendocino County has just less than 1,000 acres planted to a broad spectrum of grape varieties. Its short, warm growing season is versatile but appears to favor Syrah and Zinfandel.

MCDOWELL VALLEY VINEYARDS Mendocino T
$5.25–$10.85   Since 1978 Karen and Richard Keehn and their brood of children have done much of the work in building their solar-powered, 100,000-case cellar in the small pocket valley for which the winery is named. In spite of their 600 acres of vineyard, the Keehns buy some Chardonnay and Sauvignon Blanc.
** Syrah (deep, dark, the best red for aging); Zinfandel (sturdy, sun-kissed); Cabernet Sauvignon (most attractive when youthful flavors and baby fat make it a mouth-filler). Also: Fumé Blanc, Estate Chardonnay (a bit weighty and quick to mature), Zinfandel Blanc, and Grenache Rosé.
NYR: A proprietary blend of Syrah and Grenache called Le Tresor, and California Chardonnay.

MCHENRY VINEYARD Santa Cruz Mountains T
$14   At their weekend winery two generations of McHenrys make as much as they can coax out of 4 shy-bearing

acres near Felton, the maximum having been 400 cases to date.

NYR: Pinot Noir, Chardonnay.

MCLESTER WINERY Los Angeles T $3.50–$15
Another of the indomitable trio at the end of LAX's runway 25R (the other two are DONATONI WINERY and PALOS VERDES WINERY) produces 3,000 cases a year 300 feet under the bellies of departing jetliners. The McLesters have been at it since 1980. The wines come principally from San Luis Obispo grapes. Nearly all are sold close to home.
• Fumé Blanc, Merlot, Cabernet Sauvignon, Zinfandel, Sweet 13, Runway White, Runway Red.

MEADOW GLEN WINERY
This joint venture of Eric Russell (RABBIT RIDGE) and his marketing company is producing 5,000 cases a year of $4.75–$8 Chardonnay, Sauvignon Blanc, White Zinfandel, Cabernet Sauvignon, and Zinfandel, all from Napa and Sonoma grapes. The first red was 85, the first white 86.

MEEKER VINEYARD Sonoma T $9–$18
The name is the owning family's, not a characterization of the wines from a steep 215-acre property in Dry Creek Valley. The winery began with 83s. Annual production is 4,000 cases.

NYR: Zinfandel (a bit erratic in early vintages); Chardonnay (conventional, a bit rustic); Cabernet Sauvignon (up and down in early outings).

MELIM Sonoma T $6–$10
A family-owned vineyard and estate winery in the Chalk Hill AVA near its boundary with Alexander Valley, Melim began producing with 87s. Debut volume was 1,400 cases; the potential approaches 10,000 from 60 acres.

NYR: Chardonnay (first one strongly perfumed by new wood); Fumé Blanc, and Cabernet Sauvignon.

Maacama Creek is a second label for Cabernets deemed not up to the standard of the main label.

MENDOCINO AVA
A blanket AVA encompasses all of Mendocino's particular AVAs—ANDERSON VALLEY, COLE RANCH, MCDOWELL VALLEY, and POTTER VALLEY—as well as plantings in Mendocino County's share of the Russian River drainage from Redwood Valley s. to Sonoma.

MENDOCINO VINEYARDS Mendocino T
$3.99–$6.99 Once a second label, it is now the principal one at GUILD WINERIES' Mendocino cellars in Ukiah (until recently known as Cresta Blanca). The same growers and the same winemaking team appear to be keeping the same styles that have prevailed to date. Annual production is 45,000 cases.
** Chardonnay, Fumé Blanc, White Zinfandel, and Cabernet Sauvignon (all Mendocino appellations).
[*→**] Timber Ridge Red, Salmon Point Blush, Eagle Creek White.

MENGHINI WINERY San Diego T $5–$10

Mike Menghini opened his winery in 1982 after working as a winemaker in Temecula. Annual production is 1,500 cases from Temecula and local grapes, all of it sold locally.
• White Riesling; Sauvignon Blanc; Julian Mist (a blush from Gamay Beaujolais); Julian Blossom (a blush from Napa Gamay); Cabernet Sauvignon.

MERCED AVA
A large AVA at the San Joaquin Valley's midsection. Thus far, seldom a source of identified wine.

MERIDIAN VINEYARDS   San Luis Obispo   T
$10–$12   Charles Ortman, a longtime consulting enologist, sold his Meridian label to Wine World, Inc. (also Beringer Vineyards and Château Souverain), then signed on to direct a new version of Meridian housed in the former Estrella River winery e. of Paso Robles. Ortman is drawing on more than 700 acres of vineyard at the winery plus other Central Coast properties to produce some 30,000 cases of Chardonnay plus smaller lots of Cabernet Sauvignon and Syrah. The first vintage under the new arrangement was 88.

MERITAGE
A trademarked name for blended white and red wines using only the principal Bordelais grape varieties. Its use is open to any who accept certain restrictions imposed by the trademark owners.

MERLION   Napa   T $9–$13.50
Proprietor George Vierra and winemaker John McKay are a veteran team in the Napa Valley, having been together at Charles Krug and then Vichon before they launched the Merlion label with a set of 85s. They have fermented their wine in leased space all along and aged it in their own cellars s. of Napa city since 1988. The plan is to unify the proceedings for 1989, or 1990 at the latest. Annual production is at 16,000 cases.
NYR: Chardonnay (stylish to date); Sauvrier (a refined but rich 50/50 blend of Semillon and Sauvignon Blanc, tops in 86); Chevrier (pure Semillon by its other name, splendid 85); Coeur de Melon (affably fruity example of Melon de Bourgogne, or Pinot Blanc); Blanc Doux; Cabernet Sauvignon; and Pinot Noir (introduced with an 86 released in 1989).
Piccolo is a second label for $7–$7.50 Chardonnay and Sauvignon Blanc–Semillon.

MERLOT
The black grape variety, and increasingly, its varietal wine. Long the principal variety of St. Emilions and Pomerols in France, plantings of it in California increased from fewer than 100 acres in 1970 to more than 2,880 in 1987. Napa has much the largest plantings at 1,145 acres. Sonoma has 750 acres; Monterey trails with 260. The grapes have proven difficult to grow in almost every region, the wines difficult to make distinctive. The variety was planted to soften Cabernet Sauvignon, thus the first varietals were made as fat, soft reds. More tannic wines came later. The more complicated the ideas about style have become, the

harder it is to generalize about what Merlot is, or ought to be in California.

MERRY VINTNERS, THE Sonoma T
$9.75–$14.75 After tours of duty at Mount Eden Vineyards and Matanzas Creek, Merry Edwards launched her own label with 84s at a 7,000-case cellar in the Russian River Valley w. of Santa Rosa. The bold to gigantic style she demonstrated earlier has been and continues to be tempered.
→* Sonoma County Chardonnay (replaces the Vintage Preview label ... comparatively light, straightforwardly varietal); Chardonnay-Reserve (bold, more markedly flavored by barrel fermentation, lees contact, and other winemaking routines than by grapes, will be relabeled Merry Edwards Reserve commencing with 87).
NYR: Chardonnay–Sylvan Hills Vineyard (first vineyard-designated bottling from 87); Pinot Noir (introduced with 86 Oregon-California blend carrying an American appellation); and Late Harvest Sauvignon Blanc (in 86 and the next time there is a textbook *Botrytis* infection).

MERRYVALE VINEYARDS Napa T $21–$25
A partnership produces only Cabernet Sauvignon–based red table wine and Chardonnay, using grapes bought from several vineyards and leased cellar space. The first vintage was 83. Production is 2,500 cases a year of each.
NYR: Red Table Wine (Cabernet Sauvignon–Cabernet Franc–Merlot blend); Chardonnay.

MÉTHODE CHAMPENOISE
This traditional method of producing sparkling wine requires that the wine undergo its secondary fermentation in a bottle, then be kept in that same bottle through the subsequent steps of aging, riddling (clarifying), disgorging (removal of spent fermentation yeasts), and dosage (adjustment of final sweetness by addition of a liqueur). California wines so produced are identified on their labels by the words "*méthode champenoise*" or "fermented in this bottle."

MEV
A second label of MT. EDEN VINEYARDS going out of use in 1989.

MIHALY WINERY, LOUIS
Recent name of a Napa winery now called SILVERADO HILL.

MILANO WINERY Mendocino T $12.50–$18
Owner Jim Milone started in 1977 largely as a red wine house and since has gravitated primarily to Chardonnay. Production is 10,000 cases a year, in a onetime hop kiln just s. of the town of Hopland.
→* California Chardonnay, Sonoma County Chardonnay–Vine Hill Ranch, Mendocino Chardonnay–Hopland Cuvée (all sometimes a bit big and slightly rough, but always pleasingly full of Chardonnay flavors) 84 85 86.
NYR: Mendocino Cabernet Sauvignon–Sanel Valley Vineyards. Milone makes *Botrytis*-affected Riesling and Chardonnay in favorable years; in 85 he achieved an Ice

Wine from Anderson Valley Chardonnay (still available at $60 per half-bottle).

MILAT VINEYARDS   Napa   T $5.25–$9.50
Two brothers whose family is among Napa's veteran growers built a 2,500-case estate winery in 1986 to take the grapes from their 22 acres at St. Helena's s. side.
NYR: Chardonnay (debut 88 is not estate but 89 will be as vines bear); Chenin Blanc; White Zinfandel (cleanly made, well off-dry, richly fruity 87); Cabernet Sauvignon (well-balanced, straightforward 86).

MILL CREEK VINEYARDS   Sonoma   T
$5.50–$11   Charles Kreck and family own 65 acres of vines just w. of Healdsburg, on the boundary between the Russian River Valley and Dry Creek AVAs, and make 15,000 cases of estate wine a year at a cellar just uphill from their vineyard. They started with 77s. The plan is to grow just a bit more.
[**] Cabernet Sauvignon (herbaceous, approachable early) 82 84; and Merlot (same style as Cabernet).
** Chardonnay, Sauvignon Blanc, Gewürztraminer (lightly spicy, off-dry), Cabernet Blush.

MIRASSOU VINEYARDS   Santa Clara   T,S
$3.50–$15   One of California's oldest winemaking families is now in its fifth generation, but only the great-great-grandchildren of Pierre Pellier and great-grandchildren of Pierre Mirassou have concentrated their efforts on building the family label. The winery has always been in or near the city of San Jose; the vineyards once were, but the Mirassou's have had 1,100 acres of vineyard at Soledad in the Arroyo Seco AVA since the early 1970s. To fill out 350,000 cases of a full-range of varietal table wines and champagne-method sparklers, the family buys, especially red grapes, from widely scattered sources in both the Central and North coasts.
[**] Family Selection Chardonnay (straightforwardly fruity, approachable), Harvest Reserve Chardonnay (firmer touch of wood); Harvest Reserve Cabernet Sauvignon (84 and 85 from Napa well made, distinctly varietal).
** Au Naturel (dry, no-dosage Champagne), Blanc de Noirs, Brut, and Brut Reserve (2 years longer on yeast than Brut); Harvest Reserve Pinot Noir and Zinfandel; Family Selection Fumé Blanc, White Burgundy (all Pinot Blanc), Gewürztraminer, Johannisberg Riesling, Chenin Blanc, Monterey Riesling, White Zinfandel, Pastel (low-alcohol proprietary blush), Cabernet Sauvignon, Gamay Beaujolais, Petite Sirah, Pinot Noir, Dry White, Dry Red, and Petite Rosé.

MISSION
California's first wine grape—brought from South America by Franciscan missionaries, hence the name—and rarely, its varietal wine. Current acreage is 1,880 and fading. Of that, San Bernardino County (the Cucamonga district) has 570, San Joaquin County 495, and Fresno and Stanislaus about 215 apiece. The only intriguing wines of recent years have come, however, from Amador County's 34 acres. *See* HARBOR WINERY.

MISSION VIEW WINERY San Luis Obispo T $7–$12 The name goes back a few years, but a private corporation of locals elected to start all over when they bought the property in 1988. They made 9,000 cases of 88 from 40 acres of vines at the winery in San Miguel, in the Paso Robles AVA.
NYR: Chardonnay, Sauvignon Blanc, Muscat Canelli, Cabernet Sauvignon, and Zinfandel.

MONDAVI WINERY, ROBERT Napa/San Joaquin T $4.25–$33 Robert Mondavi is still, after all these years, a tireless experimenter, and better, a brilliant innovator. His ultramodern winery n. of Oakville is dedicated to turning out wines on a large scale, but with as much or more distinction than counterparts from tiny cellars. Strikingly frequent success comes from diligent attention to everything—Teflon edges on crusher paddles, fermentation temperature curves, the techniques of coopers—everything. A long third of the fruit for an estimated 500,000 cases of Napa Valley varietals comes from 1,050 acres of family-owned grapes around the winery and in a separate block s.e. of Yountville; the rest is bought from local growers. In 1988, the Mondavis bought 450 acres of Carneros land soon to be planted. California appellation wines recently relabeled Robert Mondavi–Woodbridge are produced separately at a winery in the Lodi AVA; industry observers put the volume of those at 1.5 million cases.
→* Cabernet Sauvignon (delicate yet firm textures, fine Cabernet flavors subtly wooded) 73 74 75 78 80 83 85. Cabernet Sauvignon Reserve (plush textures, well marked by new oak) 73 74 75 80 83 85.
*** Pinot Noir Reserve (years of trials began paying off with fine 84, 85); Chardonnay (supple, polished, at peak early) 81 83 85; Chardonnay Reserve (bigger, oakier than regular); Fumé Blanc (the grassy side of the variety for flavors, honed perfectly smooth) 85 86 87.
→* Fumé Blanc Reserve (big, sometimes a bit heady, but always intriguingly rich with fruit, oak flavors).
** Chenin Blanc, Johannisberg Riesling (sipping sweet), Moscato d'Oro (fine light Muscat).
[*] Red (well-balanced, full of Cabernet flavors); White (well made, faint Sauvignon character); Rosé (off-dry, from Gamay); and White Zinfandel.

MONDEUSE
A black grape variety, also known as Refosco, blended almost entirely into generic reds. Once fairly widely planted, it now occupies fewer than 100 acres, too little to earn it a citation in grape acreage surveys.

MONT ST. JOHN CELLARS Napa T $6.50–$15 The cellar in Carneros dates from 1979, but Lino Bartolucci and family have been growers and winemakers in Napa since 1922, using the Mont St. John label as early as 1934. The current winery, directed by Lino's son, Andrea (Bucky) Bartolucci, dates from 1978 and makes about 20,000 cases of wine a year. Six of nine wines are estate grown in the family's 160-acre Madonna Vineyard, also in Carneros; the

other three are from bought grapes of varieties not planted in Madonna.
** Estate Chardonnay, Sauvignon Blanc, Gewürztraminer, Johannisberg Riesling, Muscat Canelli, Pinot Noir. Non-estate Cabernet Sauvignon, Petite Sirah, and Zinfandel. All sound, with emphasis on grape flavors. DOMAINE FELIPE is a second label for Mont St. John.

MONTE VERDE
A second label for Arciero covers $5.85–$6.50 Chardonnay, Chenin Blanc, Fumé Blanc, White Zinfandel, and Cabernet Sauvignon, all from San Luis Obispo County grapes.

MONTEREY AVA
A blanket AVA for all of Monterey County's grape-growing regions, including the Arroyo Seco, Carmel Valley, Chalone, and San Lucas AVAs.

MONTEREY PENINSULA WINERY   Monterey   T
$5–$14   A pair of local dentists named Deryck Nuckton and Roy Thomas have delighted in producing big to gigantic wines, mostly from Monterey grapes, since 1974. Current production is 12,000 cases a year.
** Chardonnay, Pinot Blanc, White Burgundy, Cabernet Sauvignon, Merlot, Zinfandel, Barbera, Black Burgundy.

MONTEREY VINEYARD, THE   Monterey   T,S
$3.99–$10   The label and winery have had something of a wayward history since 1974. Both started out as showcases for partner-growers of almost 10,000 acres of vineyard in the Salinas Valley, then went to new owners with less voluminous plans shortly thereafter. Finally in 1983, they were bought by Seagrams to become a prestigious name in the entire Central Coast, not just Monterey. In 1988, the company bought the 1,100-acre Paris Valley Ranch in southern Monterey County as the primary source of grapes. It will provide 40% of 500,000 to 550,000 cases a year. In 1988, the roster was divided into the generally distributed Classic line and a small-lot program called Limited Release.
** Classic Chardonnay (ripe, full-bodied, deftly touched by wood in 86); Sauvignon Blanc (ultragrassy flavors typical of the region); and Cabernet Sauvignon (straightforward, pleasant). Chenin Blanc, Johannisberg Riesling, and Pinot Blanc are available at the winery.
[*] Vintage Classic White, Vintage Classic Red, Vintage Classic White Zinfandel.
NYR: Limited Release Chardonnay and Cabernet Sauvignon, and Petite Fumé (a Sauvignon-based proprietary). Pinot Noir is coming (88 debut).

MONTEVIÑA   Amador   T $4.50–$9
Here is a wheel come full circle. Bob Trinchero, of Napa's Sutter Home, resurrected Amador Zinfandel in 1974, and Monteviña was the first new winery built there to take advantage of that boom. In 1988, Sutter Home bought Monteviña and its 250 acres of mature vineyard in the Shenandoah Valley AVA. Reds are all Amador, whites not. The Trincheros intend to keep the 50,000-case winery on its existing course.

** Zinfandel (the relative lightweight, but still sturdy); Reserve Zinfandel (some polish, fair balance as a heady wine); Barbera (hearty enough); Reserve Barbera (big but some polish); White Zinfandel; California Chardonnay, California Sauvignon Blanc (perfumey-ripe, slightly heavy).

MONTICELLO CELLARS Napa T $7.50–$20
Jay Corley admires President Thomas Jefferson for many reasons. His winery, no surprise, pays particular homage to Jefferson the architect and the wine connoisseur. The label began with 81s made in the shell of a building under construction, from vines planted 9 years earlier. Annual production is 25,000 cases, all but the Cabernet from 225 acres around the winery in the Big Ranch Road district n. of Napa city.
*** Sauvignon Blanc (splendid in grassy style in 81 and no letdown since) 81 82 83 85 87; Chevrier (Semillon under its alternate name, and curiously leaner and tarter than Sauvignon at the coolest edge of its range); Gewürztraminer (powerful varietal aromas in the cool vintages) 83 85.
→** Cabernet Sauvignon–Jefferson (polished, deftly balanced, marked by a seamless marriage of fruit and wood) 81 84 85; Cabernet Sauvignon–Corley Reserve (austerely firm, woody, slow to evolve).
** Chardonnay-Jefferson (pleasant fruit, well marked by wood), and Chardonnay–Corley Reserve (bigger, harder, marked even more by aromas of wood and notes from barrel fermentation).
NYR: Pinot Noir (promisingly rich 85).
See also LLORDS & ELWOOD, DOMAINE MONTREAUX.

MORGAN WINERY Monterey T $8.50–$16
Dan Lee started Morgan as a moonlighting job in 1982 while he was the winemaker at Jekel, but swiftly turned it into his full-time occupation. He buys all of the grapes for an annual 20,000 cases, most of them in Monterey but some in Sonoma's Alexander Valley and some in Carneros.
→** Chardonnay (well marked by wood, lean, sometimes even austere); and Sauvignon Blanc (originally labeled St. Vrain but now Morgan, neatly balanced, classic Sonoma grassy flavors).
NYR: Pinot Noir (blend of Monterey, Carneros grapes begins with 87) and Cabernet Sauvignon (from Carmel Valley, debut vintage is 86).

MORRIS WINERY, J. W.
The second label and company name of a Sonoma winery that prefers to be known as BLACK MOUNTAIN VINEYARD, the name that goes on owner Ken Toth's premium wines and his vineyard. The J. W. Morris label covers $3.50–$8 everyday Chardonnay, Sauvignon Blanc, Cabernet Sauvignon, red and white—and carefully crafted $12 Vintage Port and $22 Late Bottled Vintage Port, both from the owner's vineyard.

MOSCATO AMABILE
Label name for a dessert-sweet, low-alcohol, sometimes slightly fizzy wine made from members of the Muscat family of grapes.

MOSCATO D'ORO
Label name for dessert-sweet, low-alcohol table wine made from Muscat grapes.

MOUNT EDEN VINEYARDS   Santa Cruz Mountains
T $14–$25   The winery and 22 acres of vines in steep hills of the Santa Cruz Mountains originally belonged to Martin Ray but became a separate property in the mid-1970s. The style has always been for tiny lots of big-bodied, intensely flavored estate wines. As the former MEV label becomes part of Mt. Eden, annual production goes to about 4,000 cases.
*** Chardonnay-Estate (huge, buttery, toasty); Chardonnay–Edna Valley (the former MEV is not quite the scale of its running mate, but close); Pinot Noir–Estate (intensely flavored by the variety, always big, sometimes heady); Cabernet Sauvignon.

MOUNT PALOMAR WINERY   Temecula   T,D
$4.50–$9   The winery has come from rustic early efforts—it dates from 1975—to a place very near the forefront in the region as of 1988. The 15,000-case cellar draws on owner John Poole's adjoining 100-acre vineyard for most of its grapes, but the owners buy Cabernet Sauvignon in other districts.
[**] Chardonnay, Sauvignon Blanc (both well made, varietal). Also: Johannisberg Riesling, Chenin Blanc, White Cabernet, and Nouveau Gamay Beaujolais.
NYR: Semillon (87 an excellent first try); Cabernet Sauvignon (85 from Napa, 86 from Dry Creek Valley AVA).

MT. VEEDER VINEYARD   Napa   T $14
Henry and Lisille Matheson bought Mt. Veeder from Michael and Arlene Bernstein in 1982, and kept the wines on the track the founders started to lay down beginning with the 73s—to the point of hanging on to the original winemaker. FRANCISCAN VINEYARDS acquired the property in 1989 and plans few or no changes. The Cabernet (and the other Bordelais grapes blended into it) grows in the winery's own 26 acres; the Chardonnay comes half from the estate, half from the neighbor next door.
→* Cabernet Sauvignon (recently supple, polished, rich in Cabernet flavors) 81 82 84.
** Chardonnay (pungently woody and toasty).

MOUNTAIN VIEW VINTNERS
A San Francisco–based merchant label is doing 150,000 cases a year of $5–$9.99 Monterey Chardonnay, Mendocino Sauvignon Blanc, Mendocino Cabernet Sauvignon, Carneros Pinot Noir, Amador Zinfandel, and California White Zinfandel, plus Mendocino Red and Monterey White. All of it is custom-crushed in the regions of origin. The label dates from 1978; the current volume is a recent development.

MOURVEDRE   (also: Mataro)
A black grape and its varietal wine. Mostly known as Mataro in California, the grape has origins in the Rhône and has just begun to be a varietal as Mourvedre as a boom in

Rhône types begins to gather force in the late 1980s. Total acreage is 456; Contra Costa County's 178 acres lead the way.

MURPHY-GOODE Sonoma T $7.50–$16
Seasoned Alexander Valley growers Tim Murphy and Dale Goode joined forces on a winery in time to make an 85 Fumé Blanc. The current production of 25,000 cases does not strain 350 acres of vines owned by the two partners. NYR: Fumé Blanc (ripe Sauvignon flavors, well marked by wood, full-bodied); Chardonnay (same style as Fumé); Merlot; and Cabernet Sauvignon. A Reserve Fumé Blanc 87 sold only at the winery; a larger supply of 88 will go to general markets.

MUSCAT BLANC, MUSCAT CANELLI, MUSCAT DE FRONTIGNAN
The grape variety is Muscat Blanc; Canelli and Frontignan have been alternative names for the varietal wine. The federal government is ruling out all but Muscat Blanc for future wines, though proprietary coinages such as Moscato Amabile, Moscato d'Oro, etc., remain legal. California acreage of Muscat Blanc is 1,531; the variety has performed particularly well in San Luis Obispo (171 acres), Napa (109), and Sonoma (82). Other major plantings are in Fresno (208), Madera (210), and Tulare (355).

MUSCATEL
A semivarietal name, as it were, for brandy-fortified dessert wines made from one or more members of the extended family of Muscats. Usually used on cheap, quickly made wines, the name has appeared from time to time on well-crafted, long-aged bottlings of considerable quality. In fact, California's closest counterparts to the great Rutherglen Liqueur Muscats of Australia have appeared under this rather than more specific varietal names.

NALLE Sonoma T $9.50
Doug Nalle has shown a master's touch with Zinfandel since his first try, an 82 for Balverne. It is the only wine under his label. The first vintage was 84. Annual production is 2,000 cases, all from Dry Creek Valley grapes.
*** Zinfandel (rich, complex fruit flavors, fine balance, good young, better with time in bottle) 84 85 86 87.

NAPA CELLARS
The original name of a winery now called DEMOOR, and now its second label.

NAPA CREEK WINERY Napa T $7–$12.50
After a long career as a wine salesman, Jack Schulze decided in 1980 to get over to the production side. His cellar on the Silverado Trail e. of St. Helena turns out an annual 12,000 cases, all from bought Napa Valley grapes.
** Chardonnay, Johannisberg Riesling, Gewürztraminer, Cabernet Sauvignon, and Merlot.

NAPA GAMAY
Alternative name for the black grape sooner known as GAMAY.

NAPA RIDGE
The commercial brand of Wine World, Inc. (also Beringer Vineyards, Château Souverain, Meridian Vineyards). Goes on 2 million cases of $3–$7 Cabernet Sauvignon, Merlot, Chardonnay, Sauvignon Blanc, White Zinfandel, and red and white table wine. The reds have been more distinctive.

NAPA VALLEY AVA
California's first and still premier AVA lies directly n. across the bay from San Francisco. The cooler southern end overlaps the CARNEROS AVA and is increasingly devoted to Chardonnay and Pinot Noir; the warmer northern end, around Calistoga, is better suited to Cabernet Sauvignon and Sauvignon Blanc, perhaps best suited to Zinfandel and Chenin Blanc; the center from Napa to St. Helena is a versatile climatic middle ground, but especially suited to Cabernet Sauvignon. Chiles and Pope Valleys, upland areas to the e. of the main valley, also fall within the AVA boundaries. By plantings, prime varieties within the AVA's 30,000 acres are Chardonnay (7,715 acres) and Cabernet Sauvignon (7,435). Others of importance are Sauvignon Blanc (3,640), Pinot Noir (2,470), Chenin Blanc (2,216), Merlot (1,150), and Zinfandel (2,060). Gaining: Semillon (267), Cabernet Franc (416).

NAPA VALLEY PORT CELLARS   Napa   D $15
Merchant turned producer Sean Denkler launched his label with an 84 Port aged in wood two years in the way of the Portuguese, but using Napa Cabernet Sauvignon, Petite Sirah, and Zinfandel as his grapes, and French oak for his wood. Volume is 500 cases a year, ready to go to 1,000. NYR: Vintage Port.

NAPA VINTNERS   Napa   T $5–$12
Don Charles Ross began making wine in a rented warehouse in Napa city in 1978 and is still there, but looking for higher ground after recent winter floods. His annual production is 6,000 cases, all from bought-in Napa Valley grapes.
• Chardonnay, Sauvignon Blanc, Cabernet Sauvignon, and Zinfandel.

NAPOLI CELLARS   Sonoma   T $8–$12
A small grower in the Sonoma Valley, Napoli Lehnert, and his family make about 2,000 cases a year, nearly all of it sold in their roadside fruit and fruit-products stands near Sonoma town. The first vintage was 75.
• Chardonnay, Cabernet Sauvignon, Zinfandel.

NATURAL   (or Naturel)
See CHAMPAGNE.

NAVARRO VINEYARDS   Mendocino   T,S
$4.50–$15   Ted Bennett and Deborah Cahn picked their spot in the Anderson Valley because they thought it would be perfect for Gewürztraminer, which it is, but they have made their fame with Chardonnay anyway. They make most of Navarro's 12,000 cases from their 30 rolling acres w. of Philo, but buy bits and pieces from other growers, especially for Cabernet Sauvignon. The first wines were 75s.

*** Chardonnay (regular and reserve both beautifully scented by Chardonnay, lightly touched by oak, tart, and firm enough to last) 84 85 86 87; Gewürztraminer (barely off-dry, perfumed with the licheelike aromas of the grape, able to age to its profit) 82 83 85 86 87; Johannisberg Riesling (lean, firm textures and rich varietal flavors) 85 86 87. Late-harvest Gewürztraminer and Riesling worth special hunt when made.

[**] Edelzwicker (fine value, aromatic blend of Riesling, Gewürztraminer).
** Pinot Noir (begins to have Pinot's aromas, still a bit rough, especially when young); Cabernet Sauvignon (steady).

NEBBIOLO
A black grape and its varietal wine. The great variety of Italy's Piedmont is beginning to be explored in California—again, earlier tries in the 1880s and 1940s having ended in disappointment. MARTIN BROTHERS in the Paso Robles AVA grows 8 acres and buys more to make the only steadily available bottlings as of late 1989. State acreage is less than 100.

NERVO WINERY
An old Alexander Valley winery now operated as a second label by GEYSER PEAK, with sales only at the tasting room.

NEVADA CITY WINERY   Placer   T,S
$4.95–$13.50   A partnership-turned-corporation bought the winery from its founder in 1986, when it was six years old. Several of the owners are growers; they supplement their own grapes with bought-in fruit, most of it from the home county in the Sierra foothills, but some from as far away as Sonoma. Current production is 8,000 cases a year; the new owners plan to grow to 14,000 cases.
NYR: Chardonnay (separate Napa and Nevada County bottlings), Fumé Blanc, Gewürztraminer (mostly Sonoma grapes), Cabernet Sauvignon, Pinot Noir, Douce Noir (a proprietary name for a Charbono), Zinfandel (impressive 86), and Rough and Ready Red. There is a tiny bit of a champagne-method Brut.

NEWLAN VINEYARDS AND WINERY   Napa   T
$11–$19   A former engineer and home winemaker turned 30 acres of vineyards near Napa city and a 5,000-case winery into a second career beginning in 1977. He and partners started earlier under another label.
** Pinot Noir (increasingly stylish); Cabernet Sauvignon (well-balanced, gentle); and Chardonnay. Late Harvest Johannisberg Riesling is an episodic specialty.
NYR: Pinot Noir–Vieilles Vignes (tiny lots); Red Table Wine–Century Selection (proprietary red from graybeard vineyards).

NEWTON VINEYARDS   Napa   T $14.65–$16.65
A stunning and stunningly ambitious 62-acre vineyard on some of the steepest slopes of Spring Mountain yields most of the grapes for the annual 15,000 cases from this winery dug deep into the same hill. Owner Peter Newton was a

founding partner of STERLING VINEYARDS before launching out on his own. The first wines were 78s.

→* Cabernet Sauvignon (ripe, fleshy, noticeably tinged by new French oak) 84 85; Merlot (same style but softer).

** Chardonnay (scaled large, forcefully wooded, has aged rather quickly in some vintages). Sauvignon Blanc drops from the list after the 87 is gone (ripe and markedly woody).

NEYERS WINERY Napa T $14
Bruce Neyers makes 7,000 cases of wine a year for his own account as a sideline to his main job as a marketing and sales executive at Joseph Phelps Vineyards. His cellar is just e. of his executive desk. The first vintage: 80.
NYR: Cabernet Sauvignon (supple, polished) 84 85; Chardonnay (enticing fruit, well-balanced) 84 85 86.

NICHELINI VINEYARDS Napa T $3–$12
The last of the old-time, drop-in, country jug wineries in Napa now belongs to Jo-Ann Nichelini Meyer, great-granddaughter of the founder. She makes a bit more than 4,000 cases a year of the wines her father taught her, nearly all from family vineyards in Chiles Valley. She began at her father's side in 1979 and took over the whole job after his death in 1985.
*→*** Chenin Blanc, Sauvignon Vert, Cabernet Sauvignon, Napa Gamay, Petite Sirah, and Zinfandel.

NIEBAUM COLLECTION, GUSTAVE
In 1989, in tribute to the founder of Inglenook Vineyards, Heublein, Inc. established this label to show off its finest Napa Valley properties. An impressive collection of 87 whites and 85 reds introduced Chardonnay–Laird Vineyards, Chardonnay Reserve–Bayview Vineyard, Chevrier–Herrick Vineyard, Cabernet Sauvignon–Reference (all Rutherford), Cabernet Sauvignon–Mast Vineyard, and Cabernet Sauvignon–Tench Vineyard. Production is about 20,000 cases; prices range from $11.50 to $18.

NIEBAUM-COPPOLA ESTATES Napa T $35
Famed movie producer Francis Ford Coppola bought one of the three traditional vineyards of Inglenook in 1976 and developed an estate-grown, Cabernet Sauvignon–based proprietary red called Rubicon beginning with 79. Coppola has been keeping a low profile with the wine ever since, though annual production has grown from less than 1,000 to 5,000 cases.
NYR: Rubicon (only 79 and 81 released to date).

NOBLE MOLD
Common name for BOTRYTIS CINEREA.

NOBLE HILL VINEYARDS Santa Cruz Mountains
T $8–$15 One of several weekend wineries in the Santa Cruz Mountains belongs to electronics execs Russ and Barbara Schildt. They make 5,000 cases a year, part from their own 5 acres, most from Napa and Sonoma grapes. The first vintage: 86.
NYR: Chardonnay (separate Estate, Sonoma County, and

Russian River Valley–Dutton Ranch bottlings); Sauvignon Blanc (Sonoma); Cabernet Sauvignon (Napa); and Pinot Noir (estate). First whites impressive.

NONINI WINERY, A.   Fresno   T $2.76–$3.15
A family winery built in the 1930s has slaked the thirsts of local folk and passing Basque shepherds since then with old-fashioned, unchanging, straightforward Big Valley reds that lend themselves to drinking from tumblers or botas. Annual production, now in the hands of the third generation, is 30,000 cases. All of it comes from the Nonini family's 200-acre vineyard w. of Fresno.
* Chablis Blanc, Golden Chasselas, White Zinfandel, Barbera, Grenache, Zinfandel, and others.

NORTH COAST AVA
A blanket AVA encompassing all of the vineyards in Mendocino, Lake, Sonoma, Napa, Solano, and Marin counties.

NORTH YUBA AVA
A one-winery AVA in Sierra foothills e. of Marysville.

OAK RIDGE WINERY   San Joaquin   T $4–$8
The label is relatively new, but belongs to East-Side Winery, a 50-plus-year-old incorporated grower co-op. All of the members have their vineyards within the Lodi AVA. In an earlier era, it turned out worthy dry reds and admirable, sometimes splendid dessert wines under the name of Royal Host—still in use for generics. (The dessert wines now go by the name of HANDEL & METTLER.) Current production under the Oak Ridge label is about 175,000 cases.
** Chardonnay, Dry Chenin Blanc, Sauvignon Blanc, White Zinfandel, Cabernet Sauvignon, and Gran Sirah (100% Duriff).

OBESTER WINERY   San Mateo   T $7–$12
From 1977 until 1989, Paul and Sandy Obester trucked most of their grapes from Mendocino County to their cellar in the fishing village of Half Moon Bay to make 8,000 cases of wine a year. In the latter year they bought a vineyard and winery in Mendocino's Anderson Valley, though they will keep the original winery in operation to make wines from Central Coast grapes. The Obesters also own GEMELLO, for red wines.
→** Sauvignon Blanc (delicately grassy, light, crisp).
• Chardonnay (impressive 87), Gewürztraminer, Johannisberg Riesling (from Monterey, off-dry and all fruit to taste).

OFF-DRY
Sometimes seen on labels to indicate wines of 0.5 to 1.5% r.s.

OJAI WINERY   Ventura   T $10–$13
Adam Tolmach, a partner in Au Bon Climat, developed the 1,500-case Ojai label to satisfy his interest in wines from grapes with origins in the Rhône. Tolmach has planted his vineyard to Marsanne, Viognier, Mourvedre, and Syrah. Only Syrah appears in his first vintage, 83.
NYR: Sauvignon Blanc (has the regional, cooked-asparagus aromas) and Syrah (dark, fat, plummy).

OLD CREEK RANCH WINERY   Ventura   T
$5.50–$10   A small winery with mostly local sales grows
Chenin Blanc and Sauvignon Blanc on its own 10 acres,
buying in the Santa Maria AVA to round out its 1,800-
to-2,000-case annual production. The first vintage was 81.
• Chardonnay, Chenin Blanc, Johannisberg Riesling, Sauvignon Blanc, Cabernet Sauvignon, and Merlot.

OLIVE HILL WINERY
A grower label based in 45 acres at Fallbrook, San Diego
County, began with 83s. It is being held at 2,000 cases per
year pending a decision to build a winery or back away.
$3.75–$7.50 Chardonnay, Johannisberg Riesling, Sauvignon Blanc, Cabernet Blanc, and Cabernet Sauvignon are
the list.

OLSON VINEYARDS   Mendocino   T $5–$10
This Redwood Valley winery started out trying to be as
Norwegian as possible. But founder Don Olson and his
winemaker, both Norse, changed Viking Zinfandel to just
Zinfandel to placate Italian restaurateurs who liked the wine
even before the Olsons sold to new, non-Norwegian owners
in 1989. Most of the grapes come from the 34-acre estate;
bought grapes will remain all Redwood Valley as the winery
grows from 7,000 to a planned 14,000 cases. The first vintage: 82.
** Chardonnay, Fumé Blanc, Glacier (proprietary blended
white), Northern Lights (blush from Napa Gamay), Cabernet Sauvignon, Petite Sirah, and Zinfandel.

OPICI WINERY
A Cucamonga merchant label has a long list of conventional
$2.55–$9.95 table wines made to its style at several wineries; sales are mostly along the Atlantic seaboard.

OPUS ONE   Napa   T $50
The joint venture of Napa's Robert Mondavi and Bordeaux's Philippine de Rothschild produces 10,000 cases of a
Cabernet Sauvignon–based proprietary red designed to be
neither typical Napa nor typical Medoc, but a synthesis of
the two. A separate cellar is under construction; meanwhile
the wine is made at Mondavi. An eventual estate vineyard
has joined a select block of Mondavi vines at Oakville in
recent vintages. Opus One debuted with 79.
**** Opus One (soft, lush textures lean it toward Napa;
so, increasingly, do ripe varietal flavors noticeably tinged by
new French oak) 81 83 85.

ORLEANS HILL WINERY   Yolo   T $4.50–$8
The legal name of James Lapsley's winery is Orleans Hill
Vinicultural Association, which brings back to life a modestly famous pre-Prohibition name. The name was reborn
with an 80 Amador Zinfandel; the winery got going in time
for the 82s. From that time, all of the grapes have come
from the affiliated Rieff Vineyard in the home county. Current production is 22,000 cases a year. A certain lightheart-
edness governs the names of the wines.
• Sunday Chardonnay, Dry Colombard (Bunny Blanc at
Easter), Sauvignon Blanc (Grape Pumpkin at Hallowe'en),

White Zinfandel (Noel Blanc at Christmas), Saturday Cabernet Sauvignon, Cajun White, and Cajun Red (the latter two designed to ward off spicy heat).

PACHECO RANCH WINERY Marin T $9.50
Marin's only estate winery takes grapes from 15 acres to make 1,000 cases a year of Cabernet Sauvignon. Jamie Meves (Pat Paulsen, Château de Baun) has made the wine from 79 on.
• Cabernet Sauvignon.

PAGE MILL WINERY Santa Clara T $9–$14
Dick Stark buys some Chardonnay close to home, but reaches as far n. from Los Altos Hills as the Napa Valley and as far s. as the Santa Maria Valley for grapes to make 2,500 cases of wine a year. The first crush was 76.
• Napa Cabernet Sauvignon, Napa Zinfandel, Napa Chardonnay, Santa Cruz Mountains Chardonnay, and San Luis Obispo Sauvignon Blanc. Santa Barbara Pinot Noir may join the list.

PALOS VERDES WINERY Los Angeles T
$6.95–$9.95 Herbert Harris's 2,000-case winery is one of three in a row in a warehouse at the end of LAX's runway 25R. Like his neighbors, Harris gets most of his grapes from the Central Coast, but also buys in Sonoma. He bonded his winery in 1982 after 20 years of home winemaking.
NYR: Chardonnay (one from MacGregor Vineyard in Edna Valley, another from Bien Nacido in Santa Maria Valley); San Luis Obispo Sauvignon Blanc, and Sonoma Cabernet Sauvignon.

PAPAGNI VINEYARDS Madera T,S,D $4.50–$8
Angelo Papagni launched his noble effort to bring truly dry table winemaking to the San Joaquin Valley in 1975, but has kept his hand in the sweet game as well. All of his wines come from vineyards he and his family developed in southern Madera and northern Fresno counties. Papagni does not disclose production figures.
[**] Alicante Bouschet (transcends its variety); Moscato d'Angelo (lively sparkler in the vein of Asti Spumantes); Dry Sherry (intriguing smack of new oak), and Cream Sherry.
*→** Chardonnay (a bit heavy); Sauvignon Blanc (also a bit weighty but true to Sauvignon); Zinfandel; and Brut and Extra Dry Champagne.
[*] Burgundy, Chablis, Rosé (only in 1.5-liter bottles).
NYR: Fiamma (10-year-old fortified Muscat made once to date).

PARADISE VINTNERS Butte T $5–$12
Owner Wilson Bruce does not make much of any one wine at his new-in-1986 cellar in the town of Paradise, but his list runs to 40 items. All sales are local, most at the winery.
NYR: Aleatico, Cabernet Sauvignon, Chardonnay, Dago Red, Palomino, Sauvignon Vert, Tokay, and many more.

PARDUCCI WINE CELLARS Mendocino T
$4–$9.50 The keeper of the flame for Mendocino County from the end of Prohibition until the early 1970s has plenty

of company now, but still concentrates as always on providing good value. Though John Parducci and family no longer own the firm outright—a teacher's retirement fund bought in as partners in 1973—the Parduccis still make the wine as if the place were theirs. Most of the grapes for an annual production of 350,000 cases come from 400 winery-owned acres at the winery near Ukiah, at Talmage, and near Hopland. The Cellarmaster label designates small special lots.

[**→***] Sauvignon Blanc (fine Sauvignon flavors, just enough off-dry to feel rich, not enough to taste sweet) 86. [**] Cellarmaster Cabernet-Merlot, Cellarmaster Petite Sirah, Chardonnay, French Colombard, Petite Sirah, Zinfandel, Barbera, Charbono (all sound, straightforward, balanced).

** Gamay Beaujolais, Cabernet Sauvignon, Merlot, Muscat Canelli, Chenin Blanc, Gewürztraminer, Vintage Red, Vintage White, White Zinfandel. Also: Pinot Noir, Champagne.

PARSONS CREEK WINERY   Mendocino/Sonoma
T,S $10–$13   Founding partner Jesse Tidwell—still the winemaker—gets some of the credit—or blame, depending on point of view—for making a critical success of off-dry Chardonnay (0.5 to 0.8% r.s.) with his 80. In 1988 a Canadian group bought the Ukiah winery and started planning a move to Sonoma County. They are already developing a 150-acre vineyard in Alexander Valley and scouting for another. The winery will follow. Meanwhile, most of the grapes are bought-in. Annual production is at 25,000 cases and planned to grow.

** Chardonnay (marked by wood but strong on fruit and perceptibly off-dry), and Brut (distinct fruit flavors in the old California Champagne style).

NYR: Cabernet Sauvignon (85 the debut vintage).

PARTRIDGE EYE
A color-descriptive term for BLUSH sometimes used on labels in English or in the original French (*oeil de perdrix*).

PASO ROBLES AVA
A sprawling AVA anchored on the San Luis Obispo County town of Paso Robles, but ranging mostly eastward from it toward the boundary with Kern County. Most of the terrain is rolling grassland; a western fringe is wooded coastal hill country that shelters the region from sea air, producing one of coastal California's warmest summer climates. Not surprisingly, the AVA has been at its peak with Cabernet Sauvignon, Sauvignon Blanc, Muscat Blanc (recent introductions since 1970), and Zinfandel (with a history dating back to the 1850s). Also planted are Chardonnay, Chenin Blanc, Barbera, Syrah, and a promising patch of Nebbiolo. Plantings approach 6,000 acres; more than 20 wineries are here.

PASTORI   Sonoma   T $2.50–$6
A longtime winemaker for Nervo Winery when it was family-owned, Frank Pastori took some of the red wines he made there to launch his own label in 1974. He makes small

lots of old-style wine each year at his winery n. of Geyserville in the Alexander Valley, and he still has a few bottles of some of his old-timers to sell for comparison.
• Cabernet Sauvignon, Burgundy, Zinfandel, White Zinfandel, Johannisberg Riesling, and Sherry.

PAULSEN VINEYARDS, PAT Sonoma   T
$5.50–$12   The only candidate in the United States who finds humor in running for the presidency is indeed the founder of the Alexander Valley winery bearing his name. A little less than half of the grapes for an annual 21,000 cases come from a winery-owned vineyard s. of Cloverdale; the rest are bought in Sonoma County, primarily in Alexander Valley.
[**] Muscat Canelli (subtle, off-dry); Refrigerator White (cleanly made, pleasantly fruity generic).
** Chardonnay (well-wooded); Sauvignon Blanc (distinct flavors of both grapes and oak barrels); and Cabernet Sauvignon (strong charred taste from oak barrels outweighs Cabernet flavors).

PECOTA WINERY, ROBERT Napa   T
$5.75–$16   Pecota grows all of his Cabernet Sauvignon and much of his Sauvignon Blanc on 40 acres at his 18,000-case winery just n. of Calistoga. He buys the rest of his grapes, all or nearly all in the Napa Valley. The first vintage was 78.
** Estate Cabernet Sauvignon–Kara's Vineyard (fleshy, ripe); Sauvignon Blanc (round to soft, melony); Muscato di Andrea; Chardonnay–Canepa Vineyard (well-wooded small-lot specialty); and Nouveau Beaujolais (small lot of carbonic maceration wine made each year to mark the harvest).

PEDRIZZETTI WINERY Santa Clara   T
$3.59–$8.75   This old-line family firm in the Santa Clara Valley at Morgan Hill was primarily in the bulk business for many years, but turned to bottled varietals early in the 1970s. Since then it has developed most of its market in Canada. The Pedrizzettis buy grapes in San Luis Obispo, Monterey, Napa, and the Clarksburg AVA for an annual 100,000 cases.
*→** Chardonnay, Chenin Blanc, Gewürztraminer, Johannisberg Riesling, White Zinfandel, Barbera, Cabernet Sauvignon, Petite Sirah, and Zinfandel (all sound, a bit rustic).

PEDRONCELLI WINERY, J. Sonoma   T
$2.99–$12   A family-owned winery on the ridge separating Dry Creek Valley from Alexander Valley has turned increasingly in the 1980s to its own 135 acres of vines in the Dry Creek Valley AVA for its varietal wines—and to independent growers there for what it does not grow itself (excepting Alexander Valley Chenin Blanc). Annual production is 125,000 cases. Like many of the other Sonoma wineries with origins in the late 1920s or early 1930s, Pedroncelli began bottling under its own name only after a long career in the bulk trade.

[**→***] Zinfandel (firm, sound, true to the variety in regular bottlings; similar but bigger in the Reserves). Fumé Blanc (ripe, fresh melony) 86 87 88.

[**] Cabernet Sauvignon (both regular and Reserve are firmly structured, subtly flavored, able to go 20 years in more vintages than not) 78 79 84 85; Pinot Noir (un-Burgundian firmness of texture, ripe flavors); Gewürztraminer (gentle flavors, well off-dry); White Riesling (same vein as Gewürz); Zinfandel Rosé (drier than most, ringingly true to berryish flavors of Zinfandel); White Zinfandel (sweeter than the Rosé, just as aromatic); and Chardonnay (distinctly oaky but well-balanced).

[*] Sonoma Red, White, Blush (solid everyday performers). NYR: Brut Rosé (first-ever champagne-method sparkler released in 1989 is 100% from Pinot Noir).

PEJU PROVINCE Napa T $7.50–$18

A family-owned winery began with an 82 Cabernet Sauvignon. After a couple of hiccups in succeeding years, Tony Peju got his annual production leveled out at 3,000 cases, nearly all from his 30-acre vineyard at Rutherford.

NYR: Cabernet Sauvignon, Cabernet Sauvignon–Special Selection (both estate grown); Sauvignon Blanc (pale, delicate, purely varietal); Chardonnay; and Carnival (proprietary French Colombard). Also: White Cabernet only at the winery.

PEPI WINERY, ROBERT Napa T $8–$16

The owning Pepi family originally intended to specialize in Sauvignon Blanc and Semillon from their 70 acres between Yountville and Oakville. They have done well with those two varieties since the debut 81s, but have enjoyed as much if not more praise for Chardonnay and Cabernet Sauvignon added later.

→* Sauvignon Blanc (definite cool-Napa, sweet-grassy aromas and flavors in a lean, firm wine); and Semillon (less lush than most in both flavors and textures, and so perhaps more versatile).

NYR: Chardonnay (subtle fruit and wood flavors marry neatly, well-balanced) 85 87; Cabernet Sauvignon–Vine Hill Ranch (classical Napa Cabernet flavors, supple textures) 84.

PESENTI WINERY San Luis Obispo T,D

$4.98–$12.98 The family-owned winery's traditional role since the thirties was to supply rustic Zinfandel and generics to a local market in and around Paso Robles. In recent years it has broadened its line to include a number of varietals and has upped the prices, but without changing the style or basic audience. Most of the grapes come from the family's 65 acres at Templeton, but some come from the Santa Maria Valley AVA.

* Gray Riesling, Johannisberg Riesling, Gewürztraminer, Zinfandel Rosé, Cabernet Sauvignon Rosé, White Zinfandel, Cabernet Blanc, Muscat Canelli, Cabernet Sauvignon, Zinfandel, generics.

PETITE SIRAH

The black grape variety and its varietal wine. The variety has recently been reidentified as Duriff (and sometimes goes by that name now), but is and always will be Pets or Petty Sarah to veteran growers and winemakers. For most of the years since prohibition, much more of its annual tonnage has gone into generic blends than varietal wines because the firm acidity and stout tannins are accompanied by a relatively low flavor profile. However, varietals have been steadily available since the mid-1970s, and the recent blossoming of interest in Rhône types is giving it yet another life. Statewide plantings are 5,000; major acreages by county are San Joaquin (1 170), Monterey (790), Napa (675), Sonoma (480), and Mendocino (360).

PHELPS VINEYARDS, JOSEPH　Napa　T　$8–$35
Joseph Phelps, the man, got into the wine business because he saw the charms of it while his Colorado-based construction company was building a winery in the Napa Valley for somebody else. The first wines out were 73s, and a lofty reputation came quickly on the broad deck of a *Botrytis*-affected Johannisberg Riesling from that great vintage. His winery has since found other ways to make a mark, but none better. Production, currently at 60,000 cases, comes largely from winery-owned vineyards. The largest surrounds the winery e. of St. Helena; four others are divided equally between the w. and e. benchlands from Rutherford s. to Stag's Leap.
***　Late Harvest Johannisberg Riesling (rich), and Special Select Late Harvest Johannisberg Riesling (honey-rich).
→*　Early Harvest Johannisberg Riesling and Johannisberg Riesling (both gentle, off-dry); Gewürztraminer (lean, underplayed); Zinfandel (splendid fruit, bottled young) 84 85 86; Chardonnay and Sonoma Chardonnay–Sangiacomo Vineyard.
**　Cabernet Sauvignon (recently supple, full of Cabernet flavors); Cabernet Sauvignon–Eisele Vineyard (the ultratannic model for people who wish to wait); Insignia (a proprietary usually based in Cabernet but not limited to it, and habitually very ripe and quite woody); and Syrah.

PHILLIPS FARMS　San Joaquin　T　$2.99–$8.50
W. of Lodi town, the winery is small at 2,600 cases a year, but the owning family has 130 acres of Lodi AVA vineyard to draw on, and another 40 coming. The first vintage was 84.
NYR: Chardonnay, French Colombard, Symphony, Cabernet Sauvignon, Carignane, and Syrah, plus tiny lots of Pinot Noir, Merlot, and Semiree Blanc (Semillon-Sauvignon).

PHILLIPS VINEYARDS, R. H.　Yolo　T
$2.99–$10　A go-ahead vineyard and winery in the Dunnigan Hills some 35 miles w. of Sacramento, at the foot of hills separating the Sacramento River Valley from Clear Lake in Lake County. The goal—achieved steadily in a no-frills cellar in a region of low land cost—is value for money. From the start-up 83s at least through the 89s, the owning Giguiere family's 250 acres are the backbone—but not the whole supply—of grapes for 175,000·cases per year. The intent, as the vineyards double in size early in the 1990s, is to become an estate winery.

→* Reserve Semillon (understated but complex, firm).
[**] Night Harvest Sauvignon Blanc (cleanly made, distinctly Sauvignon); Dry Chenin Blanc (understatement is its particular charm); Chardonnay (subtle barrel-fermented notes, bolder fruit flavors); Vin Blanc; and Vin Rouge.
NYR: Reserve Syrah; Night Harvest Cuvée (red based in Syrah); Cabernet Sauvignon; and Night Harvest Blush.

PICONI WINERY, LTD. Temecula T $6–$10
John Piconi is one of Temecula's pioneer growers, with plantings going back to 1968, but he launched his label with an 80 Petite Sirah and built his 8,000-case winery just in time to crush the 81s. The grapes come from Temecula and Santa Barbara.
• Chardonnay, Chenin Blanc, Fumé Blanc, Rosé of Cabernet Sauvignon, and Petite Sirah from Temecula; Johannisberg Riesling and Merlot from Santa Maria Valley AVA.

PIÑA CELLARS Napa T $9
The four brothers Piña pick and choose small lots of grapes from the Napa vineyards they manage for their own winery. Thus far they produce about 1,200 cases a year of Chardonnay; beginning with 88 Cabernet Sauvignon joins the list. The first vintage, in leased space, was 79; their cellar e. of Oakville was ready for the 83.
** Chardonnay (big, woody).

PINE RIDGE Napa T $6.75–$40
Since the beginning 81s, proprietor/winemaker Gary Andrus has kept a certain focus on Cabernet and Merlot at his winery in the Stag's Leap district, but found time to do well by Chardonnay, indicated by the fact that two of his six ranches grow that variety. Aggregate winery-owned acreage is 125. Production has climbed to 50,000 cases.
*** Cabernet Sauvignon–Rutherford, Cabernet Sauvignon–Stag's Leap (Rutherford slightly the firmer of two handsomely matched running mates, but both supple, polished, layered with flavors) 81 83 84 85; and Merlot (softer, but similar).
→* Chardonnay–Stag's Leap Cuvée; Chardonnay–Knollside Cuvée (balanced, slightly toasty).
*→** Chenin Blanc (off-dry, texture, flavor a bit heavy).
NYR: Cabernet Sauvignon–Andrus Reserve (only when Andrus finds a special lot, inaugural 85 splendid); and Cabernet Sauvignon–Diamond Mountain (in selected years).

PINK CHABLIS
An alternative to the dreaded name "rosé," once important, now much outstripped by White Zinfandel and its kin.

PINK CHAMPAGNE
Almost invariably sweet, cheap, Charmat sparkling wine. *See also* CHAMPAGNE.

PINOT BLANC
The white grape and its varietal wine. Diligent scholarship now suggests that some, even much, of what has been known as Pinot Blanc might in fact be Melon. Whether the vineyards grow one variety or two, the varietal wine is a leaner, tarter, more subtly flavored cousin of Chardonnay.

Yet those who think California Chardonnays are too full of themselves have ignored this perfect recourse. Only a handful of producers make it, most of them fitfully, grumblingly, or both. Statewide acreage is 2,030, of which 1,040 is in Monterey County. Other counties where its wine has shown real turns of speed are Mendocino (43 acres), Napa (235), and Sonoma (210); examples from all three counties have aged well. Much of the crop goes into sparkling wines.

PINOT CHARDONNAY

The universal name for CHARDONNAY until genetic research separated it from the family of Pinots in the 1970s.

PINOT NOIR

The great black grape of Burgundy shows all manner of faces in California: sometimes deplorable, sometimes outstanding, but mostly a tease. The finest wines from it show a minty overtone of flavor against a meaty texture; a faintly raisiny note further marks many of the most fetching examples of these. Of 7,670 acres in the state, more than 80% are in just three counties: Sonoma (2,700), Napa (2,330), and Monterey (1,165). The cooler parts of these three counties, Santa Barbara (630 acres), and Mendocino (440) are where most of the hope has rested and still rests. At Pinot Noir's best it has yielded extraordinary red wines capable of aging 15 years, but its frequent shortcomings as a red have led to most of the annual crop's being used in champagne-method sparkling wines, blushes, and rosés.

PINOT NOIR BLANC

A varietal BLUSH or BLANC DE NOIRS from Pinot Noir grapes.

PINOT ST. GEORGE   (also Red Pinot)

A black grape and its varietal red wine. The variety appears to have origins in Burgundy. The finest of its 130 acres are in the Russian River Valley, Carneros, and the Mayacamas Mountains in Napa. Alone, it makes an agreeable, sometimes surprisingly durable red. It has also produced admirable results blended in small proportions into Pinot Noir.

PIPER-SONOMA   Sonoma S $13.99–$29

A champagne-method producer founded in 1980 as a joint venture of Sonoma Vineyards and Piper Heidsieck became a wholly owned subsidiary of Piper Heidsieck in autumn, 1988, without changing the roster of wines, vineyard sources (mostly Russian River Valley but other parts of Sonoma as well), production volume (125,000 cases), winemakers (Chris Markell with counsel from Michel Lacroix), or prices. The cellars are at Windsor.

→** Brut (subtle but persistent flavors, light on the tongue); Blanc de Noirs (slightly richer in flavor and texture than the Brut for the presence of a larger proportion of Pinot Noir), and Tête de Cuvée (superior lots from Brut). In years of no Tête de Cuvée, there may be a Brut Reserve.

PLAM VINEYARDS   Napa   T $8–$24

One of the veritable horde of family-owned Napa Valley wineries started in recent years owns six acres of Chardonnay at Yountville and buys the rest of its grapes locally to produce an annual 10,000 cases. The first vintage was 84.

NYR: Chardonnay, Sauvignon Blanc–Sacrashe Vineyard, and Cabernet Sauvignon.

POMMERAIE VINEYARDS   Sonoma   T
$4.50–$6.75   A family-owned, 2,000-case winery w. of Sebastopol in the Russian River Valley that has since 1979 carved out a fair reputation for both of its wines. Owner/winemaker Ken Dalton buys all of his grapes, most from the Alexander Valley.
[**] Cabernet Sauvignon (dark, intensely varietal) 81 83 84; and Chardonnay.

PORT
Usually a generic wine type patterned after the Oportos of Portugal, but sometimes made as a varietal port-type. These and other dessert wines are enjoying a resurgence in the upscale market. Among those priced to reflect craftsmanship, the generics are labeled Ruby (from red grapes, usually bottled fairly young, but with a proportion of older stocks blended in); Tawny (often with a proportion of white grapes, bottled after some aging and blending with older stocks); and Vintage (some bottled after two years in the Portuguese tradition, some late-bottled). The varietal port-types include Tinta and Tinta Madeira (using traditional Portuguese varieties); Zinfandel (fairly common); and Cabernet Sauvignon (comparatively rare). Inexpensive and cheap port-types also go by the names Ruby, Tawny, and White Port (usually Muscatty).

PORTER CREEK   Sonoma   T $6–$12.50
George Davis's family-owned, 2,000-case winery and 20-acre vineyard in the Russian River Valley started with 82s. The plan is to go to 8,000 cases.
NYR: Chardonnay, Pinot Noir Blanc, Pinot Noir.

POTTER VALLEY AVA
A small upland valley n.e. of Ukiah in Mendocino County that has fewer than 1,000 acres of vineyard, all or virtually all of them planted since 1970. At present all of the crop is made into wine outside its boundaries. In its short history it has won its greatest fame for Sauvignon Blanc.

PRADEL CELLARS, BERNARD   Napa   T
$11–$15   Burgundy-born Bernard Pradel settled in the Napa Valley in time to make—when in Rome—an 84 Cabernet Sauvignon. He added Chardonnay the following year. Pradel grows half his own Cabernet, buys the rest in Rutherford, and buys all of his Chardonnay grapes. Production is 3,000 cases.
NYR: Cabernet Sauvignon and Chardonnay.

PRAGER WINERY   Napa   T,D $12.50–$30
A small producer at St. Helena specializes in varietal port-types from bought local grapes and also makes table wines. Production is about 3,400 cases. The first vintage was 80.
NYR: Noble Companion (from Cabernet Sauvignon), Royal Escort (from Petite Sirah), and Summer Port (from Pinot Noir)—the style in all three cases relatively dry and high in tannin. Chardonnay, Gewürztraminer (dry, added in 87), and Cabernet Sauvignon are the table wines.

PRESTON VINEYARD & WINERY Sonoma T
$6–$12   Lou Preston started as a grower in the Dry Creek
Valley in 1973. Between 1975 and 1985 the winery grew
from 2,500 to 25,000 cases a year, always with estate
grapes. The family vineyard is 125 acres on the valley floor
not far downstream from Warm Springs Dam.
*** Sauvignon Blanc (husky in the beginning, lately subtler
in flavor and polished smooth) 85 86 87 88.
[**] Cuvée de Fumée (appealingly fruity, off-dry
Sauvignon–Chenin Blanc blend); Cabernet Sauvignon; Zin-
fandel (steady, a bit underplayed for fruit); Sirah-Syrah
(blends Petite Sirah and Syrah to pleasing effect); Muscat
Canelli (sweet sipper).
** Dry Chenin Blanc, Gamay Beaujolais.
NYR: Barbera (debut 83 to be followed by 85); Muscat
Brûlé (a late-harvest wine).

QUADY WINERY Madera D $9–$18
One of a handful that has acted on the belief that California
can make outstanding dessert wines started out with port
types in mind in 1975 and quickly branched out into the
fertile field of Muscats. Andrew Quady's 15,000-case winery is at Madera; all of the grapes are bought from the San
Joaquin Valley and Sierra foothills.
→* Vintage Port–Frank's Vineyard (from Tinta Cao
and Tinta Amarela grown in Amador County); Vintage Port
(mostly from Zinfandel but the composition can vary); Port
of the Vintage (wines that come up one shade lighter than
Quady wants for his Vintage series); Port (nonvintage, lightest of the port types); Essensia (a pale, young wine from
Orange Muscat rich with the flavors of that grape); Elysium
(a dark-red counterpart to Essensia, from Muscat Hamburg).

QUAIL RIDGE Napa T $14–$15
The winery was launched as a family-owned Chardonnay
specialist with a 78. It later became a partnership of founder
Elaine Wellesley and Leon Santoro, then, in 1988, was
bought by The Christian Brothers. Heublein, Inc. acquired
it in 1989 as part of its purchase of The Christian Brothers.
Chardonnay has been joined by other wines at each step.
Wellesley remains at the controls. Production is about
15,000 cases and growing slowly; all of the grapes are
bought-in from Napa growers.
** Chardonnay (ripe, toasty-woody school); Cabernet Sauvignon (fat to slightly weighty, perfumed by new wood).
NYR: Sauvignon Blanc (firm, fine Sauvignon flavors subtly
complicated by oak in debut 87); and Merlot (new with 85).

QUIVIRA Sonoma T $8.50–$9.75
Henry and Holly Wendt launched their Dry Creek Valley
winery with a pair of 83s, one red, one white. Most of the
grapes come from their own 90 acres, but they have bought
some local Grenache and Syrah as part of the early explo-
rations for a Rhône-inspired proprietary to be called
Regñum. Production is at 12,000 cases on the way to a
planned peak of 26,000.

NYR: Sauvignon Blanc (balanced, polished) 86 87 88; and Zinfandel (excellent varietal flavors, built to last) 85 86 87. Cabernet Sauvignon joins the list with 87.

QUPÉ   Santa Barbara   T $12–$20
Owner/winemaker Bob Lindquist started with Chardonnay, but leans mostly toward grapes with origins in the Rhône at his 4,500-case cellar. Lindquist founded Qupé in a temporary location in 1982; it stayed transient until 1989, when it settled into permanent quarters on Bien Nacido vineyard, its principal grape source, in the Santa Maria Valley.
• Chardonnay and Chardonnay Reserve.
NYR: Paso Robles Syrah, Santa Ynez Valley Syrah–Los Olivos Vineyard, Santa Maria Valley Syrah–Bien Nacido Vineyard, and Santa Ynez Valley Marsanne–Los Olivos Vineyard.

RABBIT RIDGE   Sonoma   T $7.50–$16
All of Rabbit Ridge's grapes come from owner Eric Russell's 45-acre vineyard in the Russian River Valley w. of Healdsburg. A 10-year veteran winemaker before he started his own label (while still an assistant winemaker elsewhere), Russell produces 4,000 cases a year. The first vintage: 81.
NYR: Chardonnay, Cabernet Sauvignon, Cabernet Franc, and Zinfandel.

RADANOVICH WINERY   Mariposa   T $?
George Radanovich established his as the first winery in Mariposa in 1986. He makes 1,200 cases a year, partly from his own grapes, partly from bought-in Mariposa grapes.
NYR: Sauvignon Blanc, White Zinfandel, and Zinfandel. A Chardonnay and a proprietary based in Cabernet are to come.

RAFANELLI WINERY, A.   Sonoma   T $7–$8
Dave Rafanelli has taken up where his late father Americo left off, producing reds from 60 acres of family vines in the Dry Creek Valley AVA. The label began with Zinfandel and Gamay in 79; the new generation has added Cabernet Sauvignon and dropped Gamay. Production is 6,000 cases.
→* Zinfandel (hearty, straightforward, soul-warming red for winter nights) 82 85.
** Cabernet Sauvignon (much the same vein as the Zinfandel).

RANCHO DE PHILO
Label for sweet sherries produced by onetime Brookside owner Philo Biane from Cucamonga-area grapes.

RANCHO SISQUOC WINERY   Santa Barbara   T
$6.50–$10   Rancher James Flood started a small winery in 1978, mainly to show off the quality of grapes from his 200-acre vineyard at the eastern boundary of the Santa Maria Valley AVA. Public response has production up to 4,000 cases a year, nearly all of it sold to a mailing list.
** Chardonnay, Sauvignon Blanc, Johannisberg Riesling, Franken Riesling, Merlot, and Cabernet Sauvignon. Special Late Harvest Johannisberg Riesling ($18 per half-bottle)

joins the roster in years favorable to *Botrytis* (all steady, all able to show a turn of speed).

RAPAZZINI WINERY Santa Clara T $5.50–$25
Jon Rapazzini's wines have been a fixture in Gilroy under various names since 1962. The family name went on the label in 1982, two years after a fire destroyed the original winery and all the wine in it. Production is 6,500 cases, all sold locally. The grapes come from growers in the Central Coast, mainly Monterey.
*→** Chardonnay, Sauvignon Blanc, Johannisberg Riesling, Gewürztraminer, Muscat Canelli, White Zinfandel, Gewürztraminer Rosé, Merlot, Cabernet Sauvignon, Mellow Burgundy, May Wine, Apribella, Crème Marsala, Cream Sherry, and Château de Garlic (unmistakably what it says it will be, garlic-flavored wine).

RASMUSSEN WINERY, KENT Napa T $11–$18
The owner/winemaker worked in Australian, South African, and other Napa wineries before he put his name on a Carneros winery he built in time to make a quartet of 86s. All of the grapes are bought, the Burgundian varieties from Carneros, the Bordeaux varieties from farther up the Napa Valley. Production is 3,000 cases.
NYR: Chardonnay, Pinot Noir, and Sauvignon Blanc. Cabernet Sauvignon is a temporary member of the list through 89.

RAVENSWOOD Sonoma T $4.99–$26
The mainstay of a 15,000-case winery in Sonoma town is Zinfandel in varying heavyweight styles. Owner/winemaker Joel Peterson started with a 76. He buys all of his grapes, mostly from the Dry Creek Valley, but also Sonoma Valley and Napa Valley.
** Sonoma County Zinfandel, Napa Valley Zinfandel–Dickerson Vineyard, Sonoma Valley Zinfandel–Old Hill Ranch (all big, tough, old-vines reds), and Vintners Blend Zinfandel (the gentlest member of the Zinfandel tribe).
NYR: Sonoma Cabernet Sauvignon; Sonoma Mountain Cabernet Sauvignon; Pickberry (a Cabernet-based proprietary from Sonoma Mountain and Knights Valley grapes); and Sonoma Valley Chardonnay-Sangiacomo (the big, toasty school).

RAY VINEYARDS, MARTIN
A legendary name when the late Martin himself ran the aerielike vineyard and winery in the Santa Cruz Mountains above Saratoga. The current owners are selling old inventory (mostly Cabernet Sauvignon and Merlot); no wine has been made since the 83s.

RAYMOND VINEYARD & CELLAR Napa T
$4.50–$18   The winery seemed to burst on the scene with a fine set of wines from the dramatic vintage of 74, but the proprietors were a long way from novices. Roy Raymond, Sr., had been with Beringer Vineyards from 1933 until 1970, and his sons, winemaker Walter and vineyardist Roy, Jr., had grown up in the business. Two reserve wines are estate grown on their 90 acres just s. of St. Helena. The Raymonds

buy Napa grapes for their primary varietals, and elsewhere for generics and a third Chardonnay. Production
is 110,000 cases including wines sold under a second label,
LA BELLE.
→* Cabernet Sauvignon, Cabernet Sauvignon–
Reserve (rich varietal flavors deftly complicated by wood,
excellent balance for aging; Reserve firmer, slower to evolve,
but not by much) 75 78 79 81 84 85.
*** Chardonnay, Chardonnay-Reserve (rich Chardonnay
with almost a sweetening note from toasty wood) 81 82 84
85 87; Sauvignon Blanc (all on the melony side of Sauvignon).
[**] California Chardonnay (same style as Napa bottlings),
Vintage Select White, Vintage Select Red.

REDWOOD VALLEY
Though not an AVA, Redwood Valley is a well-defined district directly n. of the town of Ukiah, in Mendocino County's portion of the Russian River drainage. Much of the
terrain is steep slopes; none is dead flat. Cabernet Sauvignon
and Zinfandel have been the most-praised wines from here.
Pinot Blanc could rank high if the type were more popular.

RENAISSANCE VINEYARD AND WINERY   Yuba
T $7–$9.50   Vineyard and winery are owned by a com-
munal society dedicated to collecting and creating fine
works of art. Planting of the 365-acre vineyard in foothill
country n.e. of Marysville began in 1975; the first wines
were 82s. Production exceeds 5,000 cases; the planned peak
is 30,000.
NYR: Sauvignon Blanc (ripe, weighty, well-oaked 85) and
White Riesling (dry). Late-harvest White Riesling and Sauvignon Blanc are in half-bottles at $25 per. Cabernet Sau-
vignon will be the primary wine starting with an 82 due out
in 1989.

RESIDUAL SUGAR OR REDUCING SUGAR   (r.s.)
Grape sugar remaining in an incompletely fermented wine,
or other sugar added as part of the dosage of sparkling
wines. Dry wines may have 0.1 to 0.2% r.s. in the form of
unfermentable sugar. Typical levels in off-dry wines
(Gewürztraminers, Chenin Blancs, etc.) are 0.4 to 1.5%; in
overtly sweet wines (most White Zinfandels, Muscat Canel-
lis, port types, sherry types) 2.0 to 8.0%. In late-harvest
specialties (Rieslings, Sauvignon Blanc–Semillon blends),
r.s. can range all the way to 30%. *See also* CHAMPAGNE.

RETZLAFF VINEYARDS   Alameda   T
$5.95–$9.95   The Livermore Valley's newest and smallest
winery is a moonlighting venture for research chemist Robert Taylor and his wife Gloria (née Retzlaff). Their first
vintage was 85; all of the wines are estate from the family's
10 acres; production is 3,000 cases.
NYR: Gray Riesling, Chardonnay (added in 86), and Cabernet Sauvignon (first made in 88).

REVERE VINEYARD   Napa   T $22
John Kirlin makes Chardonnay and nothing but, all from

his own small vineyard e. of the city of Napa. A tiny lot of 84 launched the label, the outgrowth of 10 years of successful home winemaking. Winemaking still is a relaxation from his regular career as a university professor.
NYR: Chardonnay (big, toasty, woody through 86).

RHINE
Fading generic name for off-dry to sweet blended whites.

RICHARDS WINERY, L. W. El Dorado T,S
$5–$9 Production at a small, weekend winery e. of the village of Somerset is 1,200 cases; the first vintage was 85. All of the grapes are locally bought.
NYR: Chenin Blanc, White Zinfandel, Cabernet Sauvignon, and sparkling White Zinfandel. Chardonnay debuts with an 88.

RICHARDSON VINEYARDS Sonoma T $9–$14
Dennis Richardson started on the sales side of wine and swapped for production because that was where the fun was. He makes 1,500 to 2,000 cases a year, all red wine since Chardonnay and Sauvignon Blanc fell out of the lists. Pinot Noir from Carneros is the focus; all of the grapes come from there or the adjacent Sonoma Valley. All are bought-in.
** Pinot Noir, Merlot, and Zinfandel (all big, heady). The last Cabernet Sauvignon for a time at least was the 86.

RIDGE VINEYARDS Santa Cruz Mountains T
$12–$40 From a ridge-top site in the Santa Cruz Mountains high above the town of Cupertino, Ridge reaches far and wide for grapes to make area- and vineyard-designated red wines. Small lots of white come from much closer to home. The winery was founded by a partnership in the 1960s; it was bought in 1987 by a Japanese firm, Otsuka Pharmaceutical, which has kept longtime winemaker Paul Draper in charge of the cellars. Ridge makes about 40,000 cases of wine a year.
→→ Santa Cruz Mountains Cabernet Sauvignon–Montebello, Santa Cruz Mountains Cabernet Sauvignon–Jimsomare, Napa Valley Cabernet Sauvignon–York Creek, Santa Cruz Mountains Cabernet Sauvignon (regional characteristics modify the flavors, but the style every time is for dark, tannically hard wines meant to age for years in bottle); Alexander Valley Zinfandel–Geyserville, Alexander Valley Zinfandel–Lytton Springs, Howell Mountain Zinfandel, Paso Robles Zinfandel, and Napa Valley Zinfandel–York Creek (somewhat more quickly approachable than the Cabernets, but still big, firm to hard wines built to last); and Napa Valley Petite Sirah–York Creek (same style). Sold only at the winery are two Chardonnays (Howell Mountain and Santa Cruz Mountains) and a Barbera.

RIESLING
Once only a label designation for wines blended from all varieties with Riesling in their name, it is now used increasingly on varietal wines from WHITE RIESLING.

RITCHIE CREEK Napa T $11–$15
Richard Minor makes only estate wines from 10 steep-to-

plummeting acres high on Spring Mountain. He has been at it since 74, when the only wine was a Cabernet. Production is 1,000 cases.

** Cabernet Sauvignon (always dark and firm in the way of hillside Cabernets from Napa).

NYR: Chardonnay (joined the roster in 83) and Viognier (the first tiny lot came from 86).

RIVER OAKS VINEYARDS

A recently discontinued second label for CLOS DU BOIS.

RIVER ROAD VINEYARDS   Sonoma   T $4.50–$6

Gary Mills makes 10,000 cases of wine a year under both the River Road and Sandy Creek Labels. The main label started with a 77. All of the grapes are bought.

• Sonoma Chardonnay, Sonoma Sauvignon Blanc, California White Zinfandel, and Monterey Cabernet Sauvignon.

RIVER RUN VINTNERS   Santa Cruz   T $6–$10

Christine Arneson's 2,500-case winery is but a hop from Santa Clara, a skip from San Benito, and a jump from Monterey. The annual 2,500 cases come from grapes bought in these counties and Mendocino. The winery dates from 1978, Arneson's ownership from 1982.

• Chardonnay, White Riesling, Cabernet Sauvignon, Zinfandel, and Late Harvest Zinfandel.

RIVERSIDE FARM

A second label of LOUIS J. FOPPIANO for $3.50–$4.50 varietals and generics of variable quality. The star of the show is a sound, solid Zinfandel, and a Sauvignon Blanc is reliable. Also: Chenin Blanc, White Zinfandel, and Cabernet Sauvignon.

ROCHIOLI VINEYARDS   Sonoma   T $7–$16

The Rochioli family has been growing grapes on their 130 acres in the Russian River Valley since 1936, but made their first commercial wine only in 1985, when Tom, the grandson of the vineyard's founder, launched the family label. Production is 4,500 cases, virtually all from Rochioli vines.

NYR: Chardonnay, Sauvignon Blanc, and Pinot Noir. Small lots of Gewürztraminer (from the only bought-in grapes) and Zinfandel sell only at the winery.

ROEDERER ESTATE   Mendocino   S $16

An ambitious new sparkling wine house in the Anderson Valley belongs to the famous French firm Champagne Louis Roederer. It released its first Brut in autumn 1988 after six years of trials; the oldest lots in it are from 85. Roederer's California arm has planted 380 of an eventual 450 acres of vineyards in four parcels and has built a winery planned to yield 90,000 cases per year.

NYR: Brut nonvintage.

ROLLING HILLS VINEYARDS   Ventura   T
$5.99–$11

Owner/winemaker Edward Pagor, Jr., makes 1,500 cases a year from bought-in grapes, most of them from Paso Robles and Santa Barbara County. The first vintage was 81.

NYR: Chardonnay, Cabernet Sauvignon, Merlot, Petite Sirah, and Pinot Noir.

ROMBAUER VINEYARDS Napa T $12.50–$35
Proprietor Koerner Rombauer is one of an ever-growing
roster of former commercial pilots who have found second
careers in wineries. His first vintage was 82, when the winery made 3,000 cases from bought-in grapes. With the
88s, production was 15,000 cases a year, half of that from
four winery-owned vineyards ranging from Calistoga to
Yountville.
** Chardonnay, Chardonnay-Reserve (Reserve replaces
French Vineyard bottlings; both regular and reserve have
been of the ultratoasty school), Cabernet Sauvignon (dark,
firmly tannic but well polished and so approachable).
NYR: Merlot (enters lists with an 86), and Meilleur du Chai
(a Cabernet-based proprietary similar in style to the varietal).

ROSÉ (Vin Rosé)
A generic table-wine type traditionally colored by crushing
red grapes and allowing the skins to macerate in the juice
for a period of several hours before commencing a fermentation and aging program in the style of white wine.

ROSE FAMILY VINEYARD Sonoma T $5–$12
Bill Rose buys grapes only from vineyards he can see from
a cellar located on one of those properties between Healdsburg and Windsor in the Russian River Valley. His first
vintage was 81; annual production is 1,500 cases.
** Chardonnay–Cameron Vineyards, Gewürztraminer,
Sauvignon Blanc, and Pinot Noir Blanc. Pinot Noir is a
dropout.

ROSENBLUM CELLARS Alameda T,S $5–$15
The less-than-10,000-case avocational winery of an
Alameda veterinarian and his family dates from 1978. The
grapes—all bought—are trucked from Sonoma, Napa, Contra Costa, Monterey, and Amador to a downtown Alameda
warehouse-turned-winery. Most of the wines are vineyard
designated; in most vintages there are two or more bottlings
of Zinfandel; the exact roster varies year to year.
• Johannisberg Riesling, White Zinfandel, Zinfandel Nouveau, Zinfandel (big, heady, woody), Cabernet Sauvignon,
and sparkling Gewürztraminer.

ROSSI, CARLO
A second label for E. & J. GALLO for its least-expensive generic
table wines.

ROUDON-SMITH VINEYARDS Santa Cruz Mountains T $4.50–$15 The winery began as a hobby for
a two-family partnership in 1972 and blossomed in fairly
short order into a source of consistently individual wines.
Current production is 10,000 cases a year, all from grapes
bought in from as far n. as Mendocino and as far s. as San
Luis Obispo. The early habit of designating each lot by
vineyard has yielded to more general appellations.
** Chardonnay (in three bottlings . . . California, Mendocino, and Estate); Johannisberg Riesling (a wavering member of the roster, mostly from Monterey); Cabernet
Sauvignon (usually separate California and Santa Cruz

Mountain lots); Pinot Noir (Santa Cruz Mountains); Petite Sirah (San Luis Obispo); Zinfandel (Sonoma, in small lots only); and Claret.

ROUND HILL Napa T $3.50–$11.75
Good value appears to be Goal #1 for a winery that began mostly as a bulk buyer in 1977, but capped a steady progression toward producing most of its own wine by building a substantial new cellar e. of Rutherford in 1987. The annual 300,000 cases come in three distinctly separate lines, the top two all Napa grapes including those from 150 acres belonging to partners and stockholders. The third line (House) is assembled from several regions under a California appellation.
** Rutherford Ranch: Chardonnay, Sauvignon Blanc, Cabernet Sauvignon, Merlot, and Zinfandel.
[**] Round Hill Napa Select: Chardonnay, Gewürztraminer, Cabernet Sauvignon, and Zinfandel.
[*→**] Round Hill–House: Chardonnay, Fumé Blanc, Cabernet Sauvignon, White, Red, and Blush.

RUBY CABERNET
A black grape variety developed for warm regions at U.C.–Davis by Dr. H. P. Olmo, and its varietal wine. Though the wines from warm-climate vineyards age well and taste distinctly—perhaps too much—of the Cabernet family, they failed to catch on during the 1970s and are only occasionally seen now. Total acreage is 9,320, the largest plantings in Fresno (2,460 acres), Kern (2,115), Merced (1,310), and Stanislaus (1,745) counties.

RUBY PORT
A generic Red dessert wine. *See* PORT.

RUDD CELLARS, CHANNING Lake T $12–$16
A commercial artist, Rudd is trying to work things around to full-time winemaking at the same time he is pioneering a vineyard district high on the flanks of the mountains looking down onto Clear Lake from the s.w. He made fewer than 1,000 cases from 10 acres of young vines in 88.
NYR: Chardonnay, Cabernet Sauvignon. An as-yet-unnamed Cabernet-based blend is in the works.

RUSSIAN RIVER VALLEY AVA
One of several AVAs through which the Russian River flows, this AVA is well w. in Sonoma County, most of it gently rolling, all of it in cool, often foggy climate regimes. Planted acreage approached 8,400 acres in 1988; Chardonnay and Pinot Noir for both still and sparkling wines are the most praised as well as the most planted varieties throughout the AVA. Gewürztraminer has also done uncommonly well as a dry white, and White Riesling has been special as a late-harvest type. The eastern boundary offers warmer, more versatile growing conditions than the chilly western edge.

RUSTRIDGE Napa T $5.99–$12.99
In the late 1970s the owners planted 54 acres of their much larger horse ranch in the Chiles Valley to vineyard. The first

wines were 84s made in leased space; the winery went up in 1985. Production is 1,500 cases a year, nearly all from family vines. Proprietor Stan Myer is his own winemaker.

NYR: Chardonnay, Sauvignon Blanc, Cabernet Sauvignon, and Zinfandel. Johannisberg Riesling is sporadic, sometimes as a late harvest, sometimes just as an off-dry.

RUTHERFORD ESTATE

A second label for INGLENOOK–NAPA VALLEY. In essence it covers what used to be the least expensive tier of Inglenook's Napa wines (subtitled Cabinet while they were under the primary label). The good-value $4–$6.25 roster includes red, white, Chardonnay, Sauvignon Blanc, Cabernet Sauvignon, all with Napa Valley appellations.

RUTHERFORD HILL WINERY Napa T

$7.25–$25 Winemaker Jerry Luper, like his predecessors, has some 800 acres of vineyards belonging to the winery's owning partners from which to select grapes. Annual production is 100,000 cases. Rutherford Hill, which substantially overlaps ownership with Freemark Abbey, has managed to carve out a separate niche from its sister cellar since it was bought in 1976. Previous owners operated it as Souverain Cellars. The first Rutherford Hill wines were 74s.

*** Cabernet Sauvignon (dark, firm, flavorful) 81 83 84 85; Merlot (dark, a bit firmer than most); Chardonnay, Chardonnay–Jaeger Vineyard, Chardonnay-Reserve (always sound, recently subtle and stylish with deft touches of new wood) 85 87; and Gewürztraminer (barely off-dry, splendid lichee flavors from vineyards near Napa) 84 85 86.

** Sauvignon Blanc (lean, firm, perceptibly marked by new wood, able to age).

NYR: Cabernet Sauvignon–XVS (the new kid in the block begins with an 85 released in 1989).

RUTHERFORD RANCH

The premium brand of ROUND HILL.

RUTHERFORD VINTNERS Napa T

$7.75–$13.50 Bernard Skoda had a long tenure as an executive at Louis M. Martini before he opened his own winery in 1977 with wines going back to 74. Either he shared the Martini preference for understated balance going in, or he learned it there. His 12,000-case winery s. of St. Helena draws on his own 31 acres of vines (in two parcels, both at Rutherford) plus Napa grapes bought from close-by close friends.

→** Cabernet Sauvignon, Cabernet Sauvignon–Château Rutherford (supple, balanced, noticeably marked by oak but dominated by Cabernet) 74 77 78 79 81.

** Chardonnay, Johannisberg Riesling, Sauvignon Blanc. Muscat of Alexandria (delicate, sweet) sells only at the winery.

SADDLEBACK CELLARS Napa T $7.75–$11

Winemaker Nils Venge (Groth Vineyards) moonlights in his own cellar, using only grapes from his 17 acres e. of Oakville to make 1,800 cases of wine a year. He started with 82s.

NYR: Chardonnay, Pinot Blanc, and Cabernet Sauvignon.

SAGE CANYON WINERY Napa T $8
Gordon Millar abandoned his original two wines—White Zinfandel and dry Chenin Blanc—in favor of an annual 500 cases of Carneros Chardonnay. His first wines were 81s; he shifted to Chardonnay with 85. The grapes are bought-in. NYR: Chardonnay.

ST. ANDREWS WINERY Napa T $9–$14
Estate-grown Chardonnays are the main event at St. Andrews, but the winery makes Sauvignon Blanc and Cabernet Sauvignon from bought-in Napa grapes. The estate vineyard is 63 acres on the Silverado Trail just n. of Napa city. Imre Vizkelety founded St. Andrews in 1980 and sold it to the owners of Clos du Val in 1988. Production is 15,000 cases a year and meant to hold at that level.
*** Chardonnay–Estate Bottled (subtle fruit, fine grace notes from the winemaking, balanced to age) 83 84 85 86.
[**] Napa Valley Chardonnay (from the home vineyard, emphasizes fresh flavors from the grapes); Sauvignon Blanc; Cabernet Sauvignon.

ST. CARL
A second label of BRANDER VINEYARD, mostly for blush types.

ST. CLEMENT VINEYARD Napa T $9.50–$16
Founded by Dr. William Casey in 1975 and sold to Sapporo USA in 1987, St. Clement has bought grapes from throughout the Napa Valley for all its annual 10,000 cases since the founding. However, the new owners bought a 20-acre Carneros vineyard of Chardonnay and Merlot in time for St. Clement's longtime winemaker Dennis Johns to include that fruit in his 88s. Production is planned to increase to 15,000 cases over the next several years.
*** Sauvignon Blanc (full-bodied, full-flavored, readily able to age) 84 85 87.
** Chardonnay (always plays noticeable wood against the fruit); Cabernet Sauvignon (leans to the dark, tannic side). NYR: Merlot.

ST. FRANCIS Sonoma T,S $7.50–$16
Most of the wines come from proprietor Joe Martin's 100-acre vineyard flanking the cellars in the town of Kenwood, but a portion comes from grapes bought elsewhere in the Sonoma Valley, and—beginning with 88—a tiny bit comes from Monterey. Production is at 34,000 cases, with a long-term goal to peak at 55,000.
** Estate Merlot, Estate Merlot–Reserve; California Chardonnay, Barrel Select Chardonnay; Johannisberg Riesling; Gewürztraminer; Muscat Canelli; Cabernet Sauvignon.

ST. SUPERY VINEYARDS & WINERY Napa T $7.50–$12 A high-powered French business family named Skalli has developed 300 acres of vineyard in Pope Valley and built a 200,000-case winery at Rutherford. The first wines—88 Chardonnay and Sauvignon Blanc—appeared during 1989; an 87 Cabernet Sauvignon is due out in 1990. Initial volume is to be around 20,000 cases a year, growing as the vineyard expands to its full 500 acres. The name comes from the 1880s owner who first planted the winery property to vineyard.

NYR: Chardonnay, Sauvignon Blanc (attractive in debut vintage).

SAINTSBURY Napa T $9–$14
The old professor would not be likely to complain about Richard Ward and David Graves borrowing his name for their Carneros-district winery, which, forgetting an annual two barrels of marc, produces only Chardonnay and Pinot Noir, all from Carneros grapes. Since the first vintage, 81, production has climbed to within 3,000 cases of the planned maximum 35,000.

*** Chardonnay (distinctly toasty but counterbalanced by intriguing flavors from the grapes and ever well-balanced) 84 85 86 87; Pinot Noir (after an uncertain beginning, neatly married flavors of fruit and oak, big and tannic enough to demand some bottle age) 85 87; Pinot Noir–Garnet (a lighter, fresher, fruitier Pinot meant for earlier drinking but sometimes the longer ager anyhow) 83 84 85 86 87.

SAN ANTONIO Los Angeles T,S,D $3–$11
For many years a source of everyday, buy-em-at-the-door wines in downtown Los Angeles. It turned up the volume in the late 1970s with a roster of consistently agreeable varietal wines labeled Maddalena, then moved into broader distribution. The owning Riboli family now sells 400,000 cases a year of a list with 91 wines on it.

[**] Maddalena Chardonnay (Napa and Central Coast bottlings); Cabernet Sauvignon (Sonoma County and Sonoma County–Reserve bottlings); Chenin Blanc, Johannisberg Riesling, White Zinfandel (all Central Coast, all well off-dry).

* San Antonio Chablis, Rosé, Burgundy, Sherry, Madeira, Marsala, Port, Angelica, and many others.

SAN JOAQUIN VALLEY
The great interior valley of California extends from San Joaquin County on the n. to Kern County on the s. Its reliably dry climate—warm in the north, hot in the south—and rich soils have made it the source for much of the state's everyday table wine and nearly all of its port and sherry types. San Joaquin County contains the LODI AVA, Merced County the MERCED AVA, and Madera County plus a slice of Fresno County the MADERA AVA.

SAN LUCAS AVA
One of several AVAs launched by Almaden Vineyards before the winery changed hands and departed the Central Coast. The name seldom appears on labels, but covers major vineyards totaling more than 15,000 acres in southern Monterey County not far n. of the Paso Robles AVA, and similar in climate.

SAN MARTIN WINERY Santa Clara T,D $3–$9
One of the old-line producers in the Central Coast has kept doing pretty much the same thing under a succession of owners during the past 10 years, offering good-value table

wines from its sizable cellars in southern Santa Clara County. New World Wines, the current owner, buys grapes in Monterey, San Luis Obispo, Santa Barbara, and Mendocino for an annual production of 240,000 cases.

[**] Chardonnay, Sauvignon Blanc, Johannisberg Riesling, White Zinfandel, Cabernet Sauvignon, Zinfandel, and Late Harvest Johannisberg Riesling (all vintage-dated, all reliably well made).

NYR: Chardonnay, Johannisberg Riesling, Sauvignon Blanc, White Zinfandel, Cabernet Sauvignon, Zinfandel, Blanc, Claret, and Blush (all newly added nonvintage bottlings).

SAN PASQUAL VALLEY AVA

A tiny district at the s.e. corner of Escondido, in San Diego County, was developed by a now-disappeared winery of the same name. It contains about 100 acres of vineyards.

SAN SABA

The grower label of a Texan with 70 acres of Cabernet Sauvignon on the w. benchlands of the Salinas Valley. He has his $18 wines made by next-door neighbor Smith & Hook in the same smooth-textured, forcefully regional style as their own. Annual production is 5,000 cases; the first vintage was 81.

SANFORD WINES   Santa Barbara   T $7.50–$15

The winery appeared to burst from the blocks with excellent 81s, but in fact proprietor Richard Sanford has been making wine in Santa Barbara County since 1977 and knew what he was about. All of the grapes have been bought from growers in the Santa Maria Valley AVA, but Sanford's first 10 acres at the winery, in the lower Santa Ynez Valley w. of Buellton, bore their first crop in 89. Production is virtually at the planned limit of 30,000 cases a year.

*** Pinot Noir (layered with Pinot and regional flavors deftly harmonized by new wood, bears but does not demand bottle age) 81 84 85.

→* Chardonnay (big, bold); Sauvignon Blanc (regional asparaguslike flavors plus notes from wood); Vin Gris of Pinot Noir (dry, oak-aged). Merlot bows out with a final 85.

SANTA BARBARA WINERY   Santa Barbara   T

$6–$13.50   What began in 1962 as a source of local jug wines for the townsfolk of Santa Barbara has evolved into a producer of 28,000 cases a year of reliably attractive varietal wines sold all over the country. The plan is to expand only to 35,000 cases, much of that from owner Pierre Lafond's own 75 acres in the lower Santa Ynez Valley, most of the rest from a nearby vineyard his firm manages.

[**] Chardonnay (pleasing fruit flavors) and Sauvignon Blanc.

** Chardonnay-Reserve (toastier than the regular); Sauvignon Blanc–Reserve; Pinot Noir–Reserve; Beaujour (a carbonic maceration Zinfandel); Dry Chenin Blanc (barrel-fermented, wood aged); Johannisberg Riesling (off-dry, pleasingly floral); Paradis (a dry Riesling); Zinfandel.

SANTA CRUZ MOUNTAIN VINEYARD Santa Cruz Mountains T $9.75–$15 One of a considerable (and still growing) number of seekers of the perfect Pinot Noir grows all of the grapes for that variety in 12 acres high in the Santa Cruz Mountains, and buys grapes from Santa Cruz Mountain neighbors for Cabernet Sauvignon and Chardonnay. Annual production at Ken Burnap's winery is about 2,500 cases a year, pretty much what it has been since the start-up 75s.
→* Pinot Noir (dark, huge, heady, heavily tannic . . . the sort of reds they used to make in Burgundy according to legend).
** Chardonnay (the big, toasty school); and Cabernet Sauvignon (not quite as huge as the Pinot Noirs, but up there).

SANTA CRUZ MOUNTAINS AVA
The long n.-s. ridge that protects first San Francisco Bay then the Santa Clara Valley from sea air has been home to famous vineyards since pre-Prohibition times, but never many of them. That remains the case, with little more than 100 acres scattered among miles of alternating meadows and woodlands. The AVA spans three counties, San Mateo, Santa Clara, and Santa Cruz, and stays uphill from the towns along San Francisco Bay and beyond. Cabernet Sauvignon, Pinot Noir, and Chardonnay claim the most attention.

SANTA MARIA VALLEY AVA
California's only pure e.-w. river valley parallels Santa Barbara County's boundary with San Luis Obispo, just far n. enough for the eternal sea fogs of the latitude to sweep its full length day after summer day. Thus, in spite of its southerly location, it is one of the coolest and cloudiest of all the coastal wine valleys in the state, and one of the most hospitable growing regions for Chardonnay, Pinot Noir, and—especially where *Botrytis* is wanted—Johannisberg Riesling. Current acreage is about 7,500. No more than six wineries are located in it, a majority of them founded after 1984.

SANTA YNEZ VALLEY AVA
Santa Barbara's second, more southerly AVA forms a long dogleg that touches the Santa Maria Valley at its inland end but is separated from its neighbor by more than 20 miles at its seaward limit. Increasing elevation and a sharp curve divide it into two distinct climate zones. The foggy lower end, running close to e.-w., does well with Chardonnay and Pinot Noir. The sunny upper end, running closer to n.-s., has performed notably well with Sauvignon Blanc and shows promise with Merlot and Cabernet Franc. Though much larger in area than the Santa Maria Valley, the Santa Ynez's plantings are just short of 2,000 acres. Contrarily, the winery population of 14 more than doubles that of the Santa Maria Valley.

SANTA YNEZ VALLEY WINERY Santa Barbara T $6–$14 The winery earned instant fame with a debut 77 Sauvignon Blanc of arrestingly intense flavor. Since then it has settled down to producing an annual 20,000 cases of appealing but less dramatic wines. From the 80 vintage onward, all of the grapes have come from 100 acres surrounding the winery. Those vines still belong to the original owners of the cellars, who, in 1987, sold the winery to Doug Scott, already the proprietor of Santa Barbara–based merchant labels called Stearns Wharf Vintners, Vikings Four, and Warner West.

** Chardonnay, Gewürztraminer, Johannisberg Riesling, Sauvignon Blanc, Semillon, Blanc de Cabernet Sauvignon, Cabernet-Merlot, and Zinfandel Nouveau. Also: small amounts of champagne-method sparkling wine, Cabernet Sauvignon Port, and episodic Late Harvest Johannisberg Rieslings.

SANTINO WINERY Amador T $9–$12

In the long run Nancy Santino intends to have a red Zinfandel winery devoted to wines from nearby vineyards in the Shenandoah Valley and Fiddletown AVAs. In the short run it has grown to a 30,000-case-a-year cellar by anticipating then riding the fad for White Zinfandel. German-trained winemaker Scott Harvey also keeps Late Harvest Riesling in the list.

*** White Harvest (white Zinfandel; can't be done better as a fresh, drink-it-now, off-dry wine that captures all the enticing berrylike flavors of the grape) most recent.

** Zinfandel-Fiddletown, Zinfandel–Shenandoah Valley, Zinfandel–Grand-père (all dark, ripe, a bit heady in the Amador tradition, the last-named from the winemaker's own century-old vineyard next door to the winery); Barbera; and Muscat Canelli.

Also: Late Harvest Riesling (at equivalent sugars to German Trockenbeerenauslesen, from wherever Harvey can find grapes he likes, mature as soon as it is released, current edition priced at $18 per half-bottle); and Lisa Marie (a sweet, brandy-fortified Zinfandel with not quite enough alcohol to qualify as a port).

SARAH'S VINEYARD Santa Clara T $22–$45

Marilyn Otteman approaches each vintage hunting for small lots of grapes that somehow intrigue her. The objective results are an ever-shifting roster, and an annual volume of about 2,000 cases at prices Gilroyans are not used to seeing on wines from the Hecker Pass district, where countrified generic jugs long have ruled. Otteman started Sarah's Vineyard with 78s, but has balked categorization of style or anything else ever since.

• Estate Chardonnay (the fixture, from 7 acres at the winery); Merlot (from a vineyard at Templeton in the Paso Robles AVA); Cadenza (Hecker Pass grapes blended to make a wine in the Rhône style).

SATIETY Yolo T $5.25–$9.50

Probably the only 15,000-case winery begun as a prelude to a restaurant. Owner Sterling Chaykin started with 83s and still looks, long term, to opening a fine restaurant at the winery w. of Davis, but meanwhile is a winemaker. The grapes come from his own 29 acres plus another 21 he leases.

NYR: White Table Wine (bone-dry blend of Colombard,

Chenin Blanc, Orange Muscat); Blush (also dry); and Cabernet Sauvignon (in various styles from, as Chaykin says, "Beaujolais to Burgundy").

SATTUI WINERY, V. Napa T,D $7.75–$15.75
Daryl Sattui built his winery at St. Helena in 1975 because he wanted to get back into the business his grandfather Vittorio had enjoyed. He decided to combine it with a picnic ground and deli because that was a niche nobody else had filled. His current production is 27,000 cases, part of it from 34 acres of vines he owns near the winery, the rest from bought-in Napa grapes. All sales are direct.
[**→***] Dry Johannisberg Riesling (reliable, rich in varietal flavors) and Johannisberg Riesling (off-dry, just as rich); and Napa Valley Cabernet Sauvignon, Napa Valley Cabernet Sauvignon–Preston Vineyard (husky, full of Cabernet, complicated by notes from wood) 78 79 81 83 84 85.
** Chardonnay, Sauvignon Blanc, Gamay Rouge (a blush in spite of the name), White Zinfandel, Howell Mountain Zinfandel.

SAUCELITO CANYON VINEYARD San Luis Obispo
T $8.25–$9.50 In 1982, after 10 years as a grower, Bill Greenough built a 1,000-case winery on his ranch e. of Edna Valley. He makes only estate wines from 25 acres of vines.
• Cabernet Sauvignon and Zinfandel (the latter the more expensive one).

SAUSAL WINERY Sonoma T $3–$12
After a long, honorable career in the bulk trade, the owning Demostene family began making wine for its own label with a fine Zinfandel 74. Dave, the winemaking brother in the family, has followed his original success with a long string of others. The cellars sit spang in the middle of 75 acres of Alexander Valley vineyard that—with another 50 family-owned acres nearby—supply it with grapes. Current production is 14,000 cases, on the way to a planned maximum of 20,000.
[**] Zinfandel (big, fleshy, rich with ripe fruit aromas); White Zinfandel (fresh berry flavors, off-dry).
** Chardonnay; Sausal Blanc; Cabernet Sauvignon.
NYR: Reserve Zinfandel.

SAUTERNE
Longtime term for generic wines, mostly in jugs. Dry Sauterne is more or less that; Haut Sauterne promises and delivers more than 2% r.s. The term is not much in use except at the lowest end of the price scale.

SAUVIGNON BLANC (also Fumé Blanc)
The white grape and its varietal wine. The varietal flavors are distinctive to the point of being unmistakable, yet subject to marked regional variations. The overall flavor association is herbaceous, or grassy, yet wines from Sauvignon can evoke distinct memories of some of the muskier melons and at times even approach floral aromas. At the other end of the pole they transcend the merely herbaceous to become asparaguslike. Even within districts the differences can be

marked: witness the grassy Sauvignons of cooler southern Napa versus the melony ones from the warmer northern end of the valley. In one of these guises or another, the variety is widely adapted to the coastal counties and performs creditably in the Sierra foothills and much of the San Joaquin Valley. Statewide acreage is 15,190. Major plantings by county include: Napa (3,750 acres), Sonoma (2,025), Monterey (1,595), San Joaquin (1,210), and Mendocino (800). Other counties in which the grape fares particularly well are Alameda (235 acres) and Lake (605 acres).

SAUVIGNON VERT
Some students regard Sauvignon Vert as Golden Chasselas in disguise. However, the white grape variety is counted separately in grape acreage reports, and the name is used on varietal table wines by a handful of producers. Statewide plantings are 210 acres, of which 110 are in Sonoma and another 60 in Napa County.

SCHARFFENBERGER CELLARS   Mendocino   S
$14–$18   From the inaugural 81s onward, John Scharffenberger has cast a bio-geographer's eye across the whole of Mendocino County in search of the ideal mix of climates and soils to produce complex wines. The search keeps leaning more and more to the Anderson Valley, but the wines continue to include grapes from more easterly quarters, especially Potter Valley. Volume is up to 25,000 cases and meant to grow a bit more after a period of digesting the recent growth that got him where he is. The winery was bought in 1989 by the French champagne house of Pommery.
→**   Brut (robust flavors, textures), Blanc de Blancs (ditto).
NYR: Brut Rosé and Cremant (softly bubbly, and sweet).

SCHRAMSBERG   Napa   S $17.85–$27.95
As a name, Schramsberg goes back to the 1880s, when Robert Louis Stevenson was one of the first systematic winery tourists in the Napa Valley. It even had a short run as a sparkling-wine cellar before Jack and Jamie Davies bought it in 1965 and set about the earnest work of turning it into a premier name for California Champagne. They started at well less than 10,000 cases and now are at 50,000. Some of the grapes for their four Brut styles come from their own 40 acres at the winery, in hills w. of Calistoga, but these are outweighed by grapes bought from growers in the southern third of the Napa Valley. All of the wines are vintage dated, something of a rarity among California sparkling wines of any stripe.
→**   Reserve (subtle flavors, richly textured from Pinot Noir) 80 82 84 85; Blanc de Blancs (firm, bold) 81 82 84; Blanc de Noirs (slightly less intense echo of the Reserve) 80 82 84; Cuvée de Pinot (dry, in the traditional rosé style of France).
→**   Cremant (Flora-based, sweet, gently bubbly).
NYR: an as-yet-unnamed prestige cuvée releasing in 1990.

SCHUG CELLARS   Napa   T $13–$14
Walter Schug has led a charge of German-born, German-

trained winemakers toward making California wines from grapes of Burgundian origin. He started his label with 81s, abandoning Johannisberg Riesling even though that variety had made his fame during his years at Joseph Phelps Vineyards. The 8,000-case cellar was to move from Yountville to Carneros in 1989 or 1990, to a vineyard Schug bought there. He had been buying all of his grapes.

** Chardonnay-Beckstoffer (from a Carneros ranch, in the toasty style); Pinot Noir-Beckstoffer (also Carneros); and Pinot Noir–Heinemann Mountain Vineyard (from a hilly ranch on Spring Mountain, the leaner and more tannic of the two reds).

SEARIDGE WINERY Sonoma T $7–$15
Winemaker Daniel Wickham chose a seashell motif for Searidge's label because he is also a marine biologist. But he and partner Tim Schmidt buy grapes from vineyards that hug the Pacific Ocean shore because they believe that no other climate offers conditions cool enough for California-grown Chardonnay and Pinot Noir to echo counterparts from Burgundy. They built their winery in the same neighborhood to keep the faith. The first vintage was 80; production is at 5,000 cases a year, and growing slowly.

** Sonoma Coast Pinot Noir and Pinot Noir–Coastal Selection (the latter the reserve, only from favorable vintages . . . both dark, firm, well-wooded), and Sonoma Coast Chardonnay–Mill Station Vineyard (toasty-buttery style). At the winery only: Sonoma Coast Zinfandel–Porter-Bass Vineyard and Sonoma Coast White Riesling–Hirsch Vineyard (off-dry).

SEBASTIANI VINEYARD Sonoma T,S,D
$5–$17.50 The venerable winery takes one major turn per generation. Founder Samuele Sebastiani produced nothing but bulk wine beginning around 1904. His son, August, launched a label focused on jug wines in the 1950s. August's sons—first Sam, then Don—have pushed into the fine varietal market ever since the late 1970s. The Sebastiani family has 300 acres in vineyard as an anchor for its top-of-the-line, Sonoma Valley varietals. It buys both grapes and wines for a complex web of labels that tot up, all together, to 3.8 million cases per year.

[**] Zinfandel (long-aged in old cooperage, supple, complex), Barbera (ditto), Cabernet Sauvignon (quicker to bottle after time in newer oak), Merlot (same program as Cabernet), Amore Cream Sherry (only at the winery).

** Chardonnay, Dry Chenin Blanc, Sauvignon Blanc, Eye of the Swan (blush from Pinot Noir), Gamay Beaujolais, Black Beauty (proprietary Pinot Noir).

* August Sebastiani Country wines (Chardonnay, Fumé Blanc, Johannisberg Riesling, White Zinfandel, White Cabernet, Cabernet Sauvignon, Pinot Noir, Zinfandel, all 1.5 liters).

NYR: Kinneybrook, Clark Ranch, Wilson Ranch, and Niles Chardonnays (all individual-vineyard bottlings launched with 86s); Bell Ranch and Cherryblock Cabernet Sauvignons (again individual-vineyard wines, started with 85s); and Richard Cuneo sparkling wine.

SEC
See CHAMPAGNE.

SEGHESIO WINERY Sonoma T $5–$11
The post-Prohibition, family-owned Sonoma winery waited until 1980 to turn from bulk to bottled wines. Once the Seghesios got going, they played catch-up well. Annual production at the Healdsburg cellars now stands at 85,000 cases and is pushing to reach 100,000. Nearly all of the grapes for the varietals come from 350 acres of family-owned vineyards (four in Alexander Valley, one in Dry Creek Valley, one in Russian River Valley).
*** Pinot Noir (textbook lesson in Pinot flavors but complex and supple after long wood-aging) 81 83 84 86.
[**] Zinfandel (same vein as Pinot for style); Cabernet Sauvignon (ditto); Chardonnay (pleasing fruit, gently balanced); White Zinfandel; red table wine (fine fruit plus bouquets from wood-aging); white table wine.
NYR: Reserve Pinot Noir, Reserve Zinfandel, Reserve Chardonnay (all scheduled for debut release during 1989).

SELLARDS WINERY, THOMAS Sonoma T
$7–$12.50 Sellards is another home winemaker turned professional, one of many in the state, but beginning to be one of the more durable ones. He has been commercial since 80 and now makes 1,000 cases a year, all from bought-in Alexander Valley, Dry Creek Valley, and Russian River Valley grapes.
• Chardonnay, Zinfandel, and Cabernet Sauvignon. Sauvignon Blanc, last made in 86, may or may not stay in the list.

SEMILLON
The Rodney Dangerfield of white varieties and varietal white wines. The grape appears to be related to its companion from Bordeaux, Sauvignon Blanc, but differs in California in having markedly subtler varietal flavors, and also in yielding fuller-bodied wines. Much of the state total of 2,725 acres was planted to provide a softer blending agent for Sauvignon Blanc, as in Graves, but a hardy few producers insist on offering it as a varietal. The plantings are scattered very evenly through the coast counties—Alameda (120 acres), Monterey (510), Napa (270), and Sonoma (280)—and the San Joaquin Valley—Fresno (155), Kern (205), Madera (125), and Stanislaus (240). The most impressive wines have come from Alameda, Napa, Sonoma, and Yolo.

SEQUOIA GROVE Napa T $12–$18
Ex-Coloradan James Allen settled on Cabernet Sauvignon and Chardonnay long before they became chocolate and vanilla, and he has devoted the vintages since 79 to polishing his skills in making the big two. Allen makes estate bottlings of both from his 22 acres at Rutherford, and a virtual estate bottling of Chardonnay from a Carneros vineyard in which he is a partner. Current volume is 16,000 cases, on the way to a planned maximum of 25,000.
** Chardonnay (big, sometimes a bit heady, always noticeably perfumed by new wood); Cabernet Sauvignon (same bold approach to reds as to whites).

SHADOW BROOK   Napa   T $9.50
Chardonnay is the main event at Emil Hoffman's 7,000-case winery just s. of St. Helena. The grapes come from Hoffman's three vineyards, one at the winery, the other two nearer Napa city. His first vintage was 84.
NYR: Chardonnay, Cabernet Sauvignon.

SHADOW CREEK
The label became a second line for Domaine Chandon in 1988. It was started with 80s as an independent champagne-method sparkler in Sonoma; in 1983 it moved to San Luis Obispo as a subsidiary of Corbett Canyon Vineyards. Domaine Chandon is making Shadow Creek at its Napa cellars using other-than-Napa (mostly Santa Barbara and Mendocino) grapes. Recent sales have been 23,000 cases a year.
NYR: Brut.

SHAFER VINEYARDS   Napa   T $13.50–$24
John Shafer started out as a grower in the early seventies, and like many before and since, he added a winery not long after. The winery has grown to 16,000 cases (from about 3,000 of the start-up 78s). In 1988, Shafer bought 70 acres in Carneros, more than doubling his existing 65 acres in the Stag's Leap district. The combined ranches could make the winery all estate-grown, but the Shafers will continue to buy from neighbors in Stag's Leap because they like the grapes.
*** Cabernet Sauvignon (ripe, husky, full of Cabernet fruit) 83 84 85 86; Cabernet Sauvignon–Hillside Select (same style but more intense); Merlot (firmly structured, rich with fruit flavors) 85 86 87; and Chardonnay (once pale and lean, it has turned deeper gold, showed slightly more new wood tones, and fattened up a bit in 86 and 87).

SHAW VINEYARDS & WINERY, CHARLES F.   Napa   T $5.99–$14.99   Shaw came to the Napa Valley with a fondness for Beaujolais of all stripes and a plan to make California Gamays as able challengers to them. This he has steadily done since the 79s, but without provoking the clamor that accompanies Cabernet Sauvignons or Chardonnays. And so his 40,000-case winery has Chardonnay and Sauvignon Blanc as additions to its roster. All are estate wines, the Sauvignon and Gamay from 50 acres at the cellar n. of St. Helena, the Chardonnay from a jointly owned vineyard at Rutherford.
** Gamay–Harvest Wine (fat, full of the flavors of both Gamay and carbonic maceration, was called Nouveau through 87); Gamay Beaujolais (fat, ripe, designed to compete with Beaujolais-Villages); and Gamay–Domaine Elucia (the flagship, rich with fruit, faintly touched by oak, meant to age a bit in the same way as its models, Morgons and the other Crus).
NYR: Sauvignon Blanc (melony, nicely balanced), and Chardonnay (dark gold, oaky from 83 until paler, subtler 87).

SHENANDOAH VALLEY-CALIFORNIA AVA
A shallow, gently sloped bowl just e. of the Amador County town of Plymouth holds about 700 acres of vineyards, much of the total old-to-ancient Zinfandel. Miners in the Gold

Rush era planted the first vines, a few of which still produce grapes at ages of 80 to 120 years. The valley is one of the lower and warmer vineyard districts in the Sierra foothills, able to turn out slightly raisiny, slightly thick, distinctly heady Zinfandels as a matter of course. Sauvignon Blanc is the white grape of choice. "California" must accompany the name on lables to avoid confusion with Virginia's Shenandoah Valley.

SHENANDOAH VINEYARDS Amador T,D
$5.75–$12 Zinfandel and the other table wines form the basis of the roster at Leon and Shirley Sobon's winery e. of Plymouth in this Shenandoah Valley winery, but their dessert wines contribute heftily to the label's reputation. Production has climbed from a tiny start in 1977 to its planned maximum of 60,000 cases. All are Sierra-foothill grapes, nearly all Amador (the exception a property within sight of the winery but across the line in El Dorado County). The Sobons have 32 acres planted, and 10 more to go. They also have leased 15 acres of old Zinfandel vines in the Fiddletown AVA.
** Vintage Port, Zinfandel Port, Orange Muscat, Black Muscat; Zinfandel (a bit weighty and heady but full of ripe Zinfandel flavors); Cabernet Sauvignon (echoes the Zinfandel).
*→** Sauvignon Blanc (ultraripe, slightly heavy as most Amador Sauvignons are) and White Zinfandel.

SHERRILL CELLARS Santa Clara T $5–$12
Jan Sherrill draws grapes to her Santa Cruz Mountains winery above Palo Alto from the home county and San Luis Obispo County. Production is a steady 2,500 cases, much of it vineyard designated. All sales are local on the San Francisco peninsula and have been since the start in 1973.
** Santa Cruz Mountains Chardonnay–Buhlmann Vineyard, Paso Robles Sauvignon Blanc–Shell Creek Vineyard, Paso Robles Gamay Blanc, Santa Clara Cabernet Sauvignon–Wiedeman Vineyard, Santa Cruz Mountains Cabernet Sauvignon–Luchessi Vineyard, Paso Robles Petite Sirah, and Paso Robles Zinfandel (all burly in texture and assertive in flavor).

SHERRY
A generic label term for a varied style ranging from barely dry appetizer wines to those outright dessert sweet. In California, the name most commonly refers to wine first fortified to 17 to 20% alcohol, then exposed to air in a warmed tank to produce characteristic oxidized flavors. Some more expensive bottlings, closer in technique to Spanish models, are produced by blending younger and older wines oxidized only through long aging in wood. A few dry sherries are marked by the distinctive flavor of a yeast called FLOR. The name usually is modified to describe sweetness: Dry or Cocktail Sherry (2.5% r.s. or less), Medium or Golden Sherry (2.5–4% r.s.), or Sweet or Cream Sherry (4% r.s. or more). In most cases this degree of sweetness is controlled by the timing of fortification with brandy.

SIERRA VISTA El Dorado T $5.50–$10
John and Barbara MacCready's winery, set amid vines that
look up to some of the most scenic peaks in the Sierra, has
grown from 400 cases of 77s to 6,000 cases of 88s, all of the
latter vintage from the winery's 30 acres.
** Chardonnay (pleasing fruit flavors); Fumé Blanc (leaner,
crisper than most foothills Sauvignons); White Zinfandel;
Cabernet Sauvignon (textbook Cabernet flavors, well-
balanced); and Zinfandel (straightforward).
NYR: Syrah. An unnamed Rhône-inspired blend is in the
works.

SIGNORELLO Napa T $8.25–$13.75
Ray Signorello has planted 30 acres of vines at the southern
tip of the Stag's Leap district since 1979 and has room to
plant another 70. His all-whites first vintage was 85. Production approaches 5,000 cases; as reds join the list, the
maximum will be 13,000.
NYR: Sauvignon Blanc (impressively flavorful debut 86),
and Chardonnay (dark, toasty-woody 85). Still to come:
Cabernet Sauvignon and Pinot Noir beginning with 88s.

SILVER MOUNTAIN VINEYARDS Santa Clara T
$7–$10 Chardonnay and Zinfandel dominate the short
list of Jerry O'Brien's weekend winery in the Santa Cruz
Mountains. He buys grapes from the home county, Monterey, and Sonoma. Production is 2,000 cases; the first vintage was 79.
• Chardonnay (usually Monterey, more recently Santa Cruz
Mountains); Zinfandel (Sonoma). Occasional Cabernet
Sauvignon and Petite Sirah have rounded out the list. Primitivo (semiproprietary, usually based in Zinfandel but
styled to be different from any varietal bottling) is becoming
a regular.

SILVER OAK CELLARS Napa T $22–$40
The only wine is Cabernet Sauvignon, but it comes in three
forms from a handsome stone cellar e. of Oakville. The label
began with one 73. Annual production has reached 24,000
cases, much of that from Sonoma's Alexander Valley (where
the winery bought 150 acres in 1988). A small lot of Napa
Valley comes from bought-in grapes, and a tiny bit of
vineyard-designated Napa Valley from 4 acres at partner
and winemaker Justin Meyer's homesite near the cellars.
*** Napa Valley Cabernet Sauvignon–Bonny's Vineyard
(big, firmly structured, well kissed by new American oak but
full of Cabernet flavors as well) 79 83; and Napa Valley
Cabernet Sauvignon (a slightly less forceful echo of the Bonny's) 79 83 85.
** Alexander Valley Cabernet Sauvignon (supple to soft,
more powerfully perfumed by new American oak barrels
than by Cabernet grapes).

SILVERADO HILLS Napa T $13
The label has been on the Atlantic seaboard since the 79s
emerged; Californians will recognize the wine sooner as
Pannonia, or Louis K. Mihaly. The 24,000-case winery Mihaly built n.e. of Napa city now belongs to Minami Kyushu

Co., as does a 36-acre vineyard that supplies almost half its grapes.

** Estate Chardonnay and Napa Valley Chardonnay (distinct fruit overlain with smoky note from toasty French oak in both). Sauvignon Blanc is disappearing from the list.

SILVERADO VINEYARDS Napa T
$8.50–$13.50 Winemaker John Stuart hit the ground running at Lillian Disney's winery e. of Yountville and has picked up the pace each year since his 81s made their fine first impression. Production is at 75,000 cases and will be able to grow as newly bought vineyards bring the winery's estate acreage to 335. Two mature properties totalling 180 acres flank the winery; a Cabernet vineyard of 120 acres straight e. of Napa city was planted beginning in 1987; 35 acres in Carneros were beginning to be planted, primarily to Chardonnay, in 1988.

[***→****] Chardonnay (subtle marriage of Chardonnay and new oak, firm balance) 83 84 85 87; Sauvignon Blanc (light on the tongue, but saturated with Sauvignon flavors deftly enriched by new wood) 83 84 85 86 87; and Cabernet Sauvignon (supple, polished, utterly specific of its grape variety, balanced for long life) 84 85 86.
NYR: Merlot. Reserve Chardonnay 86 and Reserve Cabernet Sauvignon 86 inaugurated program of special bottlings.

SIMI WINERY Sonoma T $6–$25
Zelma Long brought a developed sense of style and superb technical skills to Simi in time to make an impressive collection of 80s. Since then her wines have gained steadily, as she has homed in on vineyards that give what she wants. For some years before Moët et Hennessey took control in 1981, Simi had bought all its grapes; the new owners of the historic Healdsburg winery now have 175 acres at the southern tip of the Alexander Valley under development for Cabernet Sauvignon, and they are looking for a property on which to develop Chardonnay. Simi will continue to buy Sonoma and Mendocino grapes. Production stands at 130,000 cases.

**** Mendocino-Sonoma Chardonnay (marries fruit, wood, and other flavors so seamlessly that you wonder where everything comes from, and is balanced to age); Sonoma Chardonnay–Reserve (the regular only more so) 80 81 83 84 85 86; and Sauvignon Blanc (silky, gentle, yet surprisingly rich in ripe Sauvignon flavors) 83 84 85 86.
→* Cabernet Sauvignon (balanced yet firm, it leans strongly to the herbaceous side of Cabernet as Alexander Valley grapes have been wont to do) 84 85; Cabernet Sauvignon–Reserve (surprisingly hard with tannins, but similar in flavors to regular); Chenin Blanc (off-dry, enticingly fruity sipper); and Rosé of Cabernet Sauvignon (catches fruit, not herbs).

SINSKEY VINEYARD Napa T $14–$17
An elaborate winery dug into a hillside in the Stag's Leap district is one property of Robert M. Sinskey, M.D., a Napa physician. Two Carneros vineyards totalling 105 acres are a separate but intertwined entity. The first vintage for Sinskey's label was 86, part of it from his 35 acres old enough

to bear fruit, part from bought-in grapes of neighbors in Carneros. Current volume is 8,000 cases on the way to a planned maximum of 26,000.

NYR: Chardonnay (full-bodied 86, marked by new oak), Pinot Noir, Merlot. An as-yet-unnamed Merlot-based proprietary is in development.

SKY VINEYARDS Napa T $10
The wine is Zinfandel, entirely from the owners' 12 acres right on the ridgepole of the Mayacamas Mountains. Lore Olds and Linn Breiner, both veteran Napa winemakers, produce 1,600 cases a year. The first commercial vintage for Sky was 81.
• Zinfandel.

SMITH & HOOK Monterey T $12
Sloping vineyards in hills w. of the Salinas Valley town of Soledad are planted to 250 acres of Cabernet Sauvignon going back to the early seventies. Wines from the property, starting with the 79, have led its owners to add an adjoining 330 acres, to be fully planted by 1990. Current production is a bit less than 10,000 cases per year under the Smith & Hook label and will stay close to that modest level; a second label, LONE OAK, will take the rest.
** Cabernet Sauvignon (well-balanced, smooth textures; intense regional vegetative flavors in early vintages seem to be moderating at least somewhat).
NYR: Merlot (start-up 86 to be released in 1989).

SMITH-MADRONE Napa T $7.50–$14
Since their inaugural 77s, Stuart and Charles Smith have been conducting a fascinating search for the balance point between powerful wines and subtler ones. Current volume is 6,000 cases from the owning brothers' hilly 38 acres high up on Spring Mountain.
*** Riesling (refined varietal flavors, excellent balance, capable of age) 85 86 87; and Chardonnay (has wavered between powerful and understated, with the current trend leaning to the side of powerful flavors and firm textures) 85 86.
** Cabernet Sauvignon (dark, ripe, woody, tannic). Pinot Noir drops from the list after the 85.

SODA CANYON Napa T $10
A small specialist in Chardonnay began making about 3,000 cases a year from his own vineyard in the canyon for which it is named, about midway between the town of Napa and the Stag's Leap district. John Furtado's first vintage was 1985, seven years after he planted his 10 acres.
NYR: Chardonnay (well-wooded 85, a bit hard).

SOLANO-GREEN VALLEY AVA
A small district anchored on the Solano County town of Fairfield has three wineries in it, and nearly all of the county's 1,200 acres of vineyard. Though inland from Napa, its climate is moderated by the Sacramento River more than those farther e. Too few wines have borne the appellation for much judgment to be made on the character of its grapes.

The most-planted varieties are Chenin Blanc (233 acres) and Cabernet Sauvignon (205 acres). The district is not to be confused with the SONOMA-GREEN VALLEY AVA.

SOLARI ESTATE
A grower label belonging to the descendants of Bruno Solari, who established 300 acres of vineyards on several ranches in the upper Napa Valley around Calistoga, and who died in 1984 before he could build a planned winery. The family is at present having wines made from his vines. The roster, introduced with 84s, includes Chardonnay–Four Fingers Vineyards, Sauvignon Blanc–Chino Flat Vineyards, and Cabernet Sauvignon–Larkmead Vineyards.

SONOMA COAST AVA
This curious hybrid of an AVA overlaps parts of the Russian River Valley, Sonoma Valley, and Carneros AVAs, and also extends northward along the coast from the Russian River Valley.

SONOMA-CUTRER VINEYARDS Sonoma T
$12–$19.50 Winemaker William Bonetti made a spectacular sequence of Chardonnays for Charles Krug between 1963 and 1968 and settled on that grape as his consuming interest. Now he has a winery in the Russian River Valley that makes nothing else, though there are three per year, all from winery-owned vineyards. The vintages from 81 onward say that Bonetti mastered all of his early lessons and learned still others in the interim. They also say that proprietor Brice Jones had a good eye for grape land. Production is 75,000 cases.
**** Chardonnay–Les Pierres (from the southern Sonoma Valley, firm, understated, slow to develop but hauntingly fine when it gets there) 81 83 84 85 86; Chardonnay-Cutrer (from a vineyard at the winery, a few microns softer, lighter in body and less intense in flavor) 81 83 84 85 86.
[***] Chardonnay–Russian River Ranches (four properties including Cutrer contribute to a wine in the style of the others, but lighter and quicker to develop) 81 83 84 86 87.

SONOMA-GREEN VALLEY AVA
This sub-AVA of well less than 1,000 planted acres of vines fits just inside the westernmost boundary of the larger Russian River Valley AVA. Its anchor point is the town of Forestville. Its fame comes from plantings of Chardonnay and Pinot Noir for both still and sparkling wines. The best-known names within it are Iron Horse and Domaine Laurier; Dutton Ranch also lies within its boundaries.

SONOMA HILLS Sonoma T $8.50–$10.50
Terry Votruba decided that wine would respond to tutelage quicker than school pupils ever could, so she retired from teaching in time to start her winery with an 83 Chardonnay. Production is at the planned maximum, 1,000 cases. All of the grapes come from vineyards a few miles s. and w. in the Sonoma Mountain AVA.
NYR: Chardonnay (debut 83 aged quickly but showed promise; 84 more sturdily attractive); Pinot Noir (added to the roster with an 86).

SONOMA MOUNTAIN AVA

On mostly steep slopes forming the w. side of the Sonoma Valley above the towns of Glen Ellen and Kenwood, the Sonoma Mountain AVA was formed to call particular attention to Cabernet Sauvignon growing there, but the district has also done well with Chardonnay, Pinot Noir, and Sauvignon Blanc. The elevation produces cooler days and warmer nights than the valley floor below; exposure toward the morning sun means early afternoon shade. Acreage slightly exceeds 600.

SONOMA VALLEY AVA

A long, skinny valley stretches from the Bay across from San Francisco n. almost to Santa Rosa, running exactly parallel to the Napa Valley one row of ridges to the e. Commercial winemaking in northern California started here—as early as the 1840s; a mission vineyard at Sonoma town goes back to 1825. Yet the curse of versatility keeps it from finding an exact role to play in an era when other regions are settling on a comparatively few varieties. A broad range thrives here because of consistent warming from s. to n., and steep slopes facing primarily e. and w. with very little floor in between (and most of that is taken up with housing). While the search for a narrower focus continues, the valley grows excellent Zinfandel around Sonoma town and at Glen Ellen, and equally fine Chardonnay to the s. and w. of Sonoma. Sauvignon Blanc, Gewürztraminer, and Cabernet Sauvignon perform well in scattered spots. In all, it has 6,000 acres of vineyard, and more than a dozen wineries call it home. Sonoma Mountain AVA is carved out of its western flank, and its southern end overlaps much of the Sonoma side of the Carneros AVA.

SONOMA VINEYARDS

Original name of firm now called RODNEY STRONG VINEYARDS.

SONORA WINERY AND PORT WORKS   Sonoma

D,T $8.50–$16   Home-winemaker-turned-pro Richard Matranga is of Portuguese descent. He started his 2,000-case winery s.e. of the town of Sonora in 1986 to satisfy a passion for making port, and added table wine to help the cash flow.
NYR: Vintage Port (made in 86 and 87 entirely from Portuguese varieties grown in Amador); vintage-character Port (made in 88, and whenever future seasons do not deliver Vintage quality); and Zinfandel (Amador and Dry Creek Valley grapes).

SOTOYOME   Sonoma   T $6–$8

John and Susan Mitchell, an Englishman and a Kansan respectively, new owners in 1988, have settled on making only red wines, and only from the 10 acres that came with the winery. Both vines and cellar perch on a knoll in the Chalk Hill AVA not far s. of Healdsburg. The label goes back to a trio of 74s made in the year William Chaikin built the winery on an old vineyard he had bought not long before. Chaikin got the volume up to 3,000 cases; the Mitchells plan to hold at about that level.
NYR: Petite Sirah, Syrah, Pale Syrah (fairly dry blush).

SOUVERAIN CELLARS
Former name of a cellar that had been founded as and is again operating as CHÂTEAU SOUVERAIN.

SPARKLING BURGUNDY
Once-common, now rarely used name for red sparkling wine.

SPOTTSWOODE VINEYARD & WINERY Napa T
$10–$25 Mary Novak restored one of St. Helena's grand historic estates to life as a winery in time to make 82 Cabernet Sauvignon. Sauvignon Blanc followed in 85. Winemaker Tony Soter selects lots from 40 estate acres sandwiched between the old residential quarter of St. Helena and a newer one at the foot of the w. hills to make just 3,500 cases a year.
NYR: Cabernet Sauvignon (82 and 83 by another winemaker fiercely tannic, all since wonderfully supple in texture and complex in flavor) 84 85; Sauvignon Blanc (as polished and agreeable as its red running mate) 85 86 87 88.

SPRING MOUNTAIN VINEYARDS Napa T
$9.50–$15 One of the Napa Valley's great showplace properties is also its most seen in its secondary role as Falcon Crest. Owner Michael Robbins has 24 acres in vines at the winery w. of St. Helena, at the base of Spring Mountain, and another 20 near the town of Napa; he sold a third vineyard e. of Rutherford in 1986. The winery buys Napa grapes to bring production to 25,000 cases a year. The label and Robbins's ownership go back to 68s produced at a different winery; the move onto Spring Mountain itself came in 1975. FALCON CREST is a second label.
** Chardonnay, Sauvignon Blanc, and Cabernet Sauvignon (all three sound, steady in recent vintages). Pinot Noir dropped from the roster after an 84.

STAG'S LEAP DISTRICT
A short stretch of benchland along the e. side of the Napa Valley between the towns of Napa and Yountville in 1989 achieved status as an AVA. The district is a source of outstanding Cabernet Sauvignon grapes. Clos du Val and Stag's Leap Wine Cellars provided the early impetus. The name comes from a craggy outcrop at the top of a wall of basalt towering over the vineyards.

STAG'S LEAP WINE CELLARS Napa T $8–$75
The winery of Warren and Barbara Winiarski became an instant success in the mid-1970s with grand showings in tastings in the U.S. and France, especially with Cabernet Sauvignon from the affiliated Stag's Leap Vineyard adjoining the cellar s.e. of Yountville. It has gone from strength to strength since the first vintage, 72. Of the winery's current annual production of 40,000 cases, a bit less than 10,000 is Cabernet Sauvignon from Stag's Leap Vineyard, which has been 44 acres but will expand as parts of the 78-acre former Fay Vineyard are incorporated into it. Grapes for other types on the roster are bought-in from Napa growers.
**** Cabernet Sauvignon–Stag's Leap Vineyard (supple, polished, saturated with the flavors of its grapes) 73 75 78

79 83 85; and Cabernet Sauvignon–Cask 23 (the special selection from Stag's Leap Vineyard is riper and fuller than its running mate, and much rarer; only in selected vintages).
*** Cabernet Sauvignon (the Napa Valley bottling often runs even with its more illustrious brethren); Merlot (soft, polished, understated); and Johannisberg Riesling (firm, redolent of the berryish side of Riesling). Late Harvest Johannisberg Riesling comes from time to time, as does Petite Sirah . . . though for different reasons.
** Chardonnay and Chardonnay-Reserve (sound, steady, leaned slightly toward the toasty school, ready early); and Sauvignon Blanc–Rancho Chimiles (intensely herbaceous, almost eucalyptuslike at times).

STAGS' LEAP WINERY   Napa   T $5–$15
The other Stags' Leap belongs to Carl Doumani, who bought 110 acres of vineyard directly n. of Stag's Leap Wine Cellars and started his label with 73s made in leased space. Doumani has grown slowly to a current production of 17,000 cases and plans to expand only to 25,000 with a new winemaker on board beginning in 1989. All of the reds have been and will continue to be estate grown; some grapes are bought-in for both of the whites.
[**] Petite Sirah (hearty, even a bit rustic, and virtually immortal); Burgundy (a less expensive, nonvarietal alternative to the Petite Sirah); and Chenin Blanc (just as hearty, though not to keep for the ages).
** Cabernet Sauvignon, Merlot, and Chardonnay.

STAIGER, P. & M.   Santa Cruz Mountains   T
$14–$15   Paul and Marjorie Staiger make about 400 cases of Chardonnay and Cabernet Sauvignon a year from their 5 acres well uphill from the town of Boulder Creek, adding a small lot of Pinot Noir when they can get grapes from a prized vineyard nearby. That is how it has been since the 73s, and how it will stay.
• Chardonnay, Cabernet Sauvignon, and Pinot Noir.

STEARNS WHARF VINTNERS
In essence a merchant label owned by the new-in-1988 proprietor of SANTA YNEZ VALLEY WINERY and used by him for similarly styled wines sold from tasting rooms in the Santa Barbara area.

STELTZNER VINEYARD   Napa   T $7.50–$16
Richard Steltzner grows Cabernet Sauvignon, smaller bits of Merlot, Cabernet Franc, and some Sauvignon Blanc in his 78-acre vineyard right at the heart of the Stag's Leap district. His label began with a 77 Cabernet Sauvignon. Annual production is at the winery's current capacity, 7,500 cases.
→* Cabernet Sauvignon (early vintages were rough; more recent ones have been more polished).
NYR: Sauvignon Blanc. A late-harvest Gewürztraminer comes when *Botrytis* visits the vineyards.

STEMMLER WINERY, ROBERT   Sonoma   T $20
Pinot Noir in California seems to exert an irresistible attraction on German-born, German-trained winemakers. Robert Stemmler is one of no fewer than three cases in

point. After several years as a winemaker in Napa, then Sonoma, he started his own cellar in Dry Creek Valley with 77s. In 1989, he sold himself as a sort of one-man subsidiary to Buena Vista with the single duty of producing distinctive Pinot Noir in the parent company's cellars. Current production is 12,000 cases, almost all from bought-in Russian River Valley grapes. (Stemmler and a partner still make small lots of other varietals for local sale at their Dry Creek cellar under the Bel Canto label.)

→* Pinot Noir (ripe Pinot Noir flavors plus unmistakable bouquets from winemaking).

STERLING VINEYARDS Napa T $6.25–$22.50
Since its founding in 1969, Sterling has followed all sorts of trails under a series of three owners—four founding partners, then the Coca Cola Co., and finally Seagrams Co., Ltd. Seagrams has put the dramatic hilltop winery on the intriguing track of emphasizing vineyard-designated wines from winery-owned or controlled vineyards. At its 20th birthday in 1989, Sterling had 1,100 acres of vineyard to feed its 150,000-case capacity. In all there are a dozen ranches from Calistoga down to Carneros, with Diamond Mountain, Three Palms, and Winery Lake the properties with their names on labels.

*** Chardonnay (took a sharp turn toward polish, finesse with 85) 85 86 87.

** Sauvignon Blanc (typically understated, a bit hard), Merlot, Cabernet Sauvignon, Sterling Reserve (consistently dark, tannic), and Cabernet Blanc.

NYR: Chardonnay–Diamond Mountain; Chardonnay–Winery Lake; Cabernet Sauvignon–Diamond Mountain (typically tough, tannic hillside Cabernet from a ranch in hills w. of the winery); Three Palms (from a vineyard just below the winery, a Merlot-based proprietary introduced with an impressively supple, complex 85). Pinot Noir–Winery Lake begins with an 86.

STEVENOT WINERY Calaveras T $4.50–$17.50
Owner Barden Stevenot has tinkered and fussed with the sources for nonestate wines under his label since the first vintage, 78, but never wavered about the home county. The prides of the house always come from his 27-acre vineyard at the winery, tucked in a deep canyon near a town called Murphys. The remainder of 50,000 cases comes from bought-in grapes, currently from Amador County and the Lodi AVA.

** Estate: Chardonnay, Fumé Blanc, Chenin Blanc, Cabernet Sauvignon, Cabernet Sauvignon–Reserve, and Zinfandel. Also: Amador Zinfandel, California White Zinfandel, California Chardonnay, and Muscat Canelli.

STONEGATE WINERY Napa T $8.50–$15
Since 1973, the winery of Barbara and James Spaulding and their winemaker-son David has inched patiently upward from small beginnings to 15,000 cases annual production, at the same time inching its way to virtual estate status. The Spauldings own 35 acres in hills w. of the winery, and 15 acres at the cellars just down-valley from Calistoga. They

control another 100+ acres of two neighbors up in the hills. Between them these properties yield all but a bit of one bottling of Chardonnay.

** Chardonnay, Chardonnay–Spaulding Vineyard, Estate Sauvignon Blanc (firm to steely, intensely herbaceous to almost eucalyptuslike), Estate Cabernet Sauvignon, Merlot–Spaulding Vineyard.

NYR: Late Harvest Sauvignon Blanc appears when a vintage permits, beginning with an 87.

STONY HILL VINEYARDS Napa   T $7–$16
One of the first Napa cellars, if not the first devoted to doing grand things on a small scale, Stony Hill has been a premier voice in Chardonnay since the mid-1950s. For all that time Eleanor McCrea's steeply sloping 42 acres on Spring Mountain has been the sole source of all the wines . . . until now. Beginning with an 87, there is a second-label Chardonnay (SHV), this one from Howell Mountain, in the e. hills almost straight across the valley from Stony Hill itself. It will hold annual production at 4,000 cases while parts of Stony Hill undergo replanting. Nearly all sales are to a mailing list of customers who are backed up by a longer list of hopefuls.

→* Chardonnay (a bit deeper colored, riper, and more noticeably touched by new oak in recent vintages than before 78, when the wines were pale, firm, and almost ageless) 78 79 81 84 85 86; White Riesling (off-dry but firmly structured, saturated with Riesling flavors, able to age) 84 85 86.

*** Gewürztraminer (only whispers at Gewürz flavors, but so sturdy and well-balanced that it drinks wonderfully well for years on end).

STONY RIDGE WINERY Alameda   T $4.99–$10
The story is getting to be a saga. The original Stony Ridge in Pleasanton lost its home to developers, moved, then closed in 1984, not long before another Pleasanton winery, Anthony Scotto's Villa Armando, shut its doors forever. In 1988 two of Scotto's children, Gregory and Monica, bought the Stony Ridge name and set about building a new winery just e. of Livermore. Bought-in wines and wines made in leased space are bridging the gap while they get their own cellar going.

NYR: Carneros Chardonnay, California Chardonnay, North Coast Cabernet Sauvignon, White Zinfandel, sparkling Malvasia Bianca, and a Charmat-process Brut.

STORRS WINERY Santa Cruz   T $7–$16
After eight years of working for other wineries Stephen and Pamela Storrs founded their own 1,500-case cellar in Santa Cruz in 1988. The grapes are all bought, primarily from the Santa Cruz Mountains AVA.

NYR: Santa Cruz Mountains Chardonnay, Santa Cruz Mountains Carbernet Sauvignon, Santa Clara Merlot, and Monterey White Riesling (impressive first vintage).

STORY VINEYARD Amador   T $4.45–$11
The winery and label in Amador's Shenandoah Valley date from 73, but the 35-acre vineyard of Zinfandel grapes that supplies it goes back a long way further into history. Story

was founded by a veterinarian of that name; after his death, it became the property of his wife, since remarried to John Ousley. Current production is 5,000 cases.

*→** Zinfandel, Private Release Zinfandel, White Zinfandel. Also: Small lots of Chenin Blanc and Zinfandel Nouveau.

STORYBOOK MOUNTAIN VINEYARDS Napa T $8.50–$16.50 The product is Zinfandel, most of it estate bottled from a hilly 36-acre vineyard n. of Calistoga and hard against the Sonoma County line. Owner/winemaker J. Bernard Seps launched his label with the vintage of 80. Current annual production is 6,000 cases. The site was the pre-Prohibition winery and vineyard of two brothers Grimm, nonwriters both, but worth the fanciful name anyhow.

** Estate Zinfandel (ripe, fleshy, markedly flavored by new oak); Estate Zinfandel–Reserve (exceeds the regular bottling on all counts). A third bottling from Sonoma grapes is fading toward disappearance.

STRATFORD Napa T $8–$10
Chardonnay is the main event for a label that was, in 1989, about to graduate from a leased-space operation to a full-fledged producing winery. The partnership began buying grapes throughout the coastal counties in time to make an 82. Most of the grapes come from Napa and Santa Barbara counties, with smaller proportions from Sonoma and Monterey. Current production of Stratford approaches 20,000 cases. There are much smaller volumes of a $5–$7 second label called CANTERBURY, and smaller volumes still of a prestige Chardonnay called CARTLIDGE & BROWN.

[**] Chardonnay (subtle, balanced); Sauvignon Blanc; Cabernet Sauvignon (textbook varietal, approachable); and Merlot.

STRAUSS VINEYARDS Napa T $11
The label, specializing in Merlot, operates from leased space using all bought-in Napa grapes. Current volume is 3,200 cases; the first vintage was 84.
NYR: Merlot.

STREBLOW VINEYARDS Napa T $12–$16
A 12-acre vineyard and 1,200-case winery on the lower slopes of Spring Mountain e. of St. Helena began with 85s. Cabernet Sauvignon is the main wine for Jack Streblow and family.
NYR: Cabernet Sauvignon and Chardonnay. Sauvignon Blanc launched the label, but has been dropped.

STRONG VINEYARDS, RODNEY Sonoma T
$5.50–$12 The name has changed from Tiburon Vintners to Sonoma Vineyards to Rodney Strong Vineyards, and the ownership has changed more than that, but the Russian River Valley–based winery has stayed with a strengthening resolve to produce vineyard-designated wines from its finest vineyards and good-value bottles from the rest, always under the direction of the man whose name the label has borne since 1984. Current production approaches 375,000 cases,

including a direct-sales-only second label, WINDSOR VINEYARDS. [**] Chardonnay–Chalk Hill (understated, peaks early); Johannisberg Riesling–Le Baron (fine varietal flavors); and Pinot Noir–River East (pale, subtle, approachable). ** Cabernet Sauvignon–Alexander's Crown (dark, tannic, often heady), Zinfandel, Chenin Blanc, Gewürztraminer. NYR: Merlot.

STUERMER WINERY Lake T $5.50–$15
Although the winery is called Stuermer after the owning family, and although pride of the house is a Lake County Cabernet Sauvignon labeled Stuermer, most of the wines from an 8,500-case cellar go forth under the name of Arcadia. The Stuermer name dates only from 1987; the business goes back to 1977, when the Stuermers founded it as Lower Lake Winery. All of the grapes are bought-in from local growers.
** Stuermer Cabernet Sauvignon (sturdy, intense of Cabernet in recent vintages as Lower Lake); Arcadia Sauvignon Blanc (has shown some polish to go with ripe Sauvignon flavors in recent vintages); Arcadia Cabernet Sauvignon. Arcadia Chenin Blanc and Zinfandel are available only at the winery.

SUGARLOAF RIDGE WINERY Sonoma T
$6.50–$9 After years of home winemaking, Dick and Joann Puttbach bonded a winery in hills above Glen Ellen, in the Sonoma Valley AVA, in time to make 85s. Production of 87s stood at 1,200 cases, double the start-up volume. NYR: Cabernet Sauvignon (gentle flavors, textures), Zinfandel.

SUISUN VALLEY AVA
A small AVA in Solano County, rarely on bottled wine to date.

SULLIVAN VINEYARD AND WINERY Napa T
$7.50–$29 A 4,500-case winery between Rutherford and St. Helena based in two small vineyards owned by James Sullivan and family. Their first vintage was 81.
• Cabernet Sauvignon, Coeur des Vignes (Cabernet-based proprietary), Merlot, Zinfandel, and Chenin Blanc.

SUMMIT LAKE WINERY Napa T $9.50
After a brief flirtation with Chardonnay, Zinfandel is the beginning and end of the list from an estate winery based in a 14-acre vineyard high up in the Napa Valley's Howell Mountain sub-AVA. Bob and Susan Brakesman made their first wine in 78, then skipped ahead to 82. They are producing 1,200 cases a year on the way to 2,500.
NYR: Zinfandel (sturdy, distinct Zinfandel fruit in 85).

SUNNY ST. HELENA WINERY Napa T
$5.25–$9.50 A rarity of rarities in the recent history of the Napa Valley, Sunny St. Helena was founded by a local partnership with the goal of offering value-for-money wines that lay no claim on the top rung of the social ladder, but have nothing to do with the bottom, either. Current production is 20,000 cases, all from Napa grapes. The first vintage: 86.

NYR: Chardonnay (plenty of fruit, a bit rough); Sauvignon Blanc; and Cabernet Sauvignon (showed a turn of speed in an 85 that may develop into something rather better than many more pretentious bottlings). Gamay Beaujolais Blanc, Sunny White, and Picnic (a blush) are sold only at the winery.

SUNRISE WINERY Santa Cruz Mountains T $7–$15 Winemaker Rolayne Stortz and business manager Ron Stortz have owned Sunrise since 1976, first in a mountaintop location above Boulder Creek, then—since 1983—a short way down Montebello Ridge from Ridge Vineyards. They grow Zinfandel on the first 3 acres of what they plan to become a 20-acre vineyard at the winery, buying the rest of their grapes in Santa Clara and Sonoma counties. Annual production is 2,500 cases, half the planned maximum.
• Santa Clara Pinot Noir and Sonoma Pinot Noir (the flagship varietal type), Pinot Blanc, White Riesling, Chardonnay, and Estate Zinfandel.

SUTTER HOME Napa T $4.50–$8.75
Once a clunky little 12,000-case country winery at the s. side of St. Helena, this label turned into a 3-million-case market giant when the owning Trinchero family discovered that what the American public really wanted was sweet White Zinfandel . . . and gave it to them. With the energy and cash flow thus generated, Bob and Roger Trinchero then bought 50 acres of Napa vineyard, 300 acres in Lake County, 640 acres in Glenn County, and 1,200 in Colusa County. Except for some Cabernet Sauvignon, Sauvignon Blanc, and Chenin Blanc in Napa and Lake, the plantings are—no surprise—mostly Zinfandel. In 1988 the Trincheros also acquired Amador's MONTEVIÑA WINERY and its vineyards.
** Amador Zinfandel–Reserve (big, bold, heady, the model for most Amador Zins of recent times); and California Zinfandel (a bit less forceful than the Reserve, but substantial).
[*] White Zinfandel (well off-dry to outright sweet, cleanly made, and true to the grape); and Sparkling White Zinfandel (the White Zin with bubbles).
NYR: Cabernet Sauvignon (added with 85, and still searching for its style); Sauvignon Blanc, Chenin Blanc, and Muscat of Alexandria.

SWAN VINEYARDS, JOSEPH Sonoma T $12–$18 The late Joseph Swan retired from airline flying to pursue an intensely personal style of winemaking in his 2,000-case cellar not far from Forestville in the Russian River Valley AVA. His son-in-law, Rod Berglund, has assumed the reins and continues to estate bottle Chardonnay and Pinot Noir from 10 acres just outside the cellar door, and to buy Zinfandel from neighbors. The label dates from 1969. Nearly all of the wine sells to a loyal mailing-list clientele.
** Zinfandel (ultraripe, tannic, heady, well-wooded).
• Pinot Noir, and Chardonnay.

SWANSON VINEYARDS Napa T $?
Grower Clark Swanson bought the onetime Cassayre-Forni

winery near Rutherford as a starting point for making wine from his 130 acres of vineyard (75 acres e. of Oakville, 65 acres s.e. of Rutherford). The first wines are 6,000 cases of 87s; the long range plan is to go to 50,000 cases.
NYR: Chardonnay, Sauvignon Blanc, Cabernet Sauvignon. Merlot is to join the roster in 90 or soon after.

SYCAMORE CREEK Santa Clara T $6–$18
Walter and Mary Kaye Parks rebuilt a onetime Hecker Pass jug winery into a modern 5,000-case cellar producing heavyweight varietals from grapes from an estate vineyard and independent growers in the Central Coast in time to make 85s. They sold the winery to a Japanese firm in 1989; the new plan is to turn the property into a sake plant. The last of the wines are still in the marketplace.
*→** Chardonnay, Sauvignon Blanc, Johannisberg Riesling, Cabernet Sauvignon, Carignane, and Zinfandel.

SYLVAN SPRINGS
A Heublein-owned label for $5 Chardonnay, Sauvignon Blanc, White Zinfandel, and Cabernet Sauvignon made at Madera.

SYLVANER
A white grape and its varietal wine. Sylvaner is secondary to Riesling in the Rhine, not even that close to it in California, where a star that never shone too bright has been fading for several years. Current acreage statewide is 725, less than a third of the peak total. Monterey has 340 of those acres, and Santa Barbara 140. A few producers persist in making a varietal wine from it, some under its alternative name, Franken Riesling.

SYMPHONY
Among the most recent of H. P. Olmo's crosses (Muscat of Alexandria x Grenache Gris), Symphony is at once more intense than most Muscats, and more complex. Acreage remains meager, but the varietal wine is beginning to enjoy a vogue.

SYRAH
A black grape variety and its varietal wine. This is the true Syrah of Hermitage and other Rhône wines, as distinguished from Petite Sirah, which has been fingerprinted now as Duriff. Though some North Coast plantings of Syrah are old, the distinction is recent, and so is the varietal wine as a type. To this point the wines have not made a clear statement about what sets them apart from half a dozen other tannic reds of less distinctive flavor than Cabernet Sauvignon and Zinfandel. Total plantings in the state are 120 acres, of which 34 are in Mendocino County, 30 are in Napa, and 34 are in San Luis Obispo (the latter all from an Australian source). More plantings are coming. Fast.

TAFT STREET Sonoma T $5.50–$10
Brothers John and Mike Tierney have switched from an eclectic list to one dominated by Chardonnay since they started their winery in 82 at Forestville in the Russian River Valley. Most of the grapes are bought-in from Sonoma

growers, some from Napa. Current production is 18,000 cases; the goal is 25,000.

[**→***] Sonoma County Chardonnay, Russian River Valley Chardonnay (rich Sonoma Chardonnay flavors, well-balanced, age-worthy) 85 86 87.

** Sauvignon Blanc (sometimes Sonoma, sometimes Napa, always focused on varietal flavors). Also very small lots of Cabernet Sauvignon and smaller ones of Merlot.

TALBOTT VINEYARD, ROBERT Monterey T
$20 Local businessman Robert Talbott II makes only Monterey Chardonnay at his winery high up in the Carmel Valley, but makes it in several guises. His first vintage was 83; production is at 2,200 cases and building toward 3,000.
NYR: Chardonnay (regular bottling from a Salinas Valley vineyard; beginning with an 88 comes the first tiny lot of a separate estate bottling called Diamond T Ranch). Second labels are Rosewood Cellars and Logan.

TALLEY VINEYARDS San Luis Obispo T
$5.50–$12 A major grower of several crops in the Arroyo Grande district in extreme southern San Luis Obispo County has built a small winery to begin showing off his 75-acre vineyard. All of the wines are estate, save for a White Zinfandel from a neighbor's grapes. The 2,500-case first vintage was 86.
NYR: Chardonnay, Sauvignon Blanc, White Riesling, White Zinfandel, Pinot Noir.

TAYLOR CALIFORNIA CELLARS
A $2.99–$4.99 brand founded by Seagrams is now owned by Vintners International Co., Inc. Most of the varietals, dominated by Central Coast grapes, are made and bottled at the sister Paul Masson winery in Monterey's Salinas Valley; the generics come primarily from San Joaquin Valley vineyards. Volume is about 6 million cases a year.
[*] Chablis, Rhine, Rosé, Burgundy, Chardonnay, Chenin Blanc, Cabernet Sauvignon, Zinfandel; Charmat Brut and Extra Dry.

TEMECULA AVA
California's southernmost substantial AVA has about 2,000 planted acres in the s.w. corner of Riverside County midway between the cities of Riverside and San Diego, at a spot where sea air moderates a potentially desertlike climate. In a short history since 1972, Sauvignon Blanc (760 acres) and Chenin Blanc (225 acres) have seemed particularly adapted, and Chardonnay (730 acres) has performed steadily. Cabernet Sauvignon (155 acres) has performed as well as any of the reds planted to date. A dozen wineries within the boundaries take nearly all of the crop.

TERRACES, THE
A Napa grower label introduced with a small lot of $12.50 Zinfandel from 85, made at Caymus Vineyards.

TIJSSELING VINEYARD Mendocino T,S
$6–$12.99 The prestige label among three produced in two separate wineries by two generations of the Tijsseling

family goes on wines made entirely from 300 acres of vines between Hopland and Ukiah. The first vintage was 82; production approaches 50,000 cases and is planned to grow.
** Brut (champagne-method sparkler); Blanc de Blancs (100% Chardonnay running mate to the Brut); Chardonnay (well-wooded); Sauvignon Blanc; Cabernet Sauvignon; and Dry White and Dry Red.

TYLAND is the other winery, Mendocino Estate the third label.

TINTA MADEIRA
A black grape and its varietal dessert wine. The Tintas have their origins in Portugal's Douro River Valley. Only 97 acres grow in California at present, most of them in the San Joaquin Valley, but some in Amador. The ranks of the Tintas are swelled just slightly by a few acres each of Tinta Cao, Touriga, and Souzao.

TINTA PORT
See PORT.

T.K.C. Amador T $7.50
Harold Nuffer is a consulting engineer for China Lake Naval Air Station weekdays and a winery owner/winemaker weekends. Shenandoah Valley AVA Zinfandel from bought-in grapes has been the whole show since the first vintage, 81, but Nuffer is looking into a white to balance out the list. Production is 1,500 cases a year and meant to grow when the proprietor retires from engineering.
** Zinfandel (rustic early, but showing polish and balance in recent vintages) 84.

TOGNI, PHILIP Napa T $11.50–$22
After three decades as a winemaker, Philip Togni established his own winery and label beginning with an 83 Cabernet Sauvignon. All of the grapes for 1,000 cases come from his 10 acres high up Spring Mountain. Maximum production is planned to be 2,000 cases when the vineyard matures fully.
NYR: Sauvignon Blanc (subtle, polished 86); Cabernet Sauvignon and Ca' Togni (an ultrasweet, high-alcohol proprietary based in Black Hamburg and most easily found in the Highlands on a luxury excursion train called the Royal Scotsman).

TOPOLOS AT RUSSIAN RIVER VINEYARDS
Sonoma T $6.50–$14 Mike Topolos grows a few acres of vines but buys most of his grapes from growers in the Russian River and Sonoma valleys to make 8,000 to 10,000 cases a year. The winery is at Forestville; Topolos's first vintage was 78.
*→→** Sonoma Zinfandel (the lightest model), Zinfandel (hearty, rustic), Petite Sirah (ditto), Alicante Bouschet (also), Chardonnay, Sauvignon Blanc, Cabernet Blanc, and Sonoma Blanc (a blend of Chardonnay and French Colombard).

TOTAL ACID (t.a.)
Natural fruit acids in grapes give (or fail to give) wine its

characteristic crispness of texture and freshness of flavor. In California, acids are usually measured as tartaric and are sometimes shown on back labels as percent or grams per liter. For reds, the desired range is 0.5 to 0.7%, for whites from 0.5 to 0.9%, depending on how much r.s. (residual sugar) there is to balance against the acids. Sparkling wines often reach or just exceed 1%; dessert types stay close to 0.4%.

TRANSFER PROCESS
A technique for bottle-fermenting sparkling wine that substitutes quick, cost-efficient, and homogenizing pressurized filtration for the riddling and disgorging processes required by the classic champagne method.

TREFETHEN VINEYARDS Napa T $5–$16.25
Some of the shortest stories are among the most impressive. From 650 family-owned acres just n. of the town of Napa, two generations of Trefethens choose enough grapes to make 70,000 cases of ever more highly regarded wines. The debut vintage was 74, from a historic vineyard the Trefethens were steadily replanting.
**** Chardonnay (richly varietal, so imperishably well-balanced that earliest vintages continue to hold near peak form) 78 80 81 83 84 85 86 87.
*** Cabernet Sauvignon (once dominant note of American oak toned back in recent vintages to reveal textbook varietal flavors; good tannic grip) 78 79 83 84 85; White Riesling (just off-dry, crackerjack with cold Dungeness crab) most recent.
** Pinot Noir.
[**] Eschcol White (Chardonnay press and other good wines go into it); Eschcol Red (Cabernet Sauvignon forms the backbone, Pinot Noir supplies the flesh).
NYR: Cabernet Sauvignon Reserve.

TREMONT WINERY Solano T $6
The winery, not far w. of the University of California campus at Davis, was built to explore the possibilities of grape varieties developed by Dr. H. P. Olmo during his career at the school. One of his students, Justin Meyer (of Silver Oak Cellars), became the winemaker in time to do the 88s; the first vintage was 82. Volume is 1,500 cases, some from the winery's own 5 acres, some from bought-in grapes.
NYR: Emerald Riesling, Flora, Symphony, Carmine, Carnelian, and Centurion.

TRENTADUE WINERY Sonoma T $3.50–$12
This family-owned, 25,000-case winery and 145-acre vineyard in the Alexander Valley near Geyserville has had its ups and downs since opening in the mid-1970s. Consulting winemaker Chris Bilbro (MARIETTA CELLARS) steers it now on one of the ups.
** Red, White, and Blush are the mainstays; small lots of Petite Sirah; Carignane; Merlot; Cabernet Sauvignon; Old Patch Red (from a block of 103-year-old mixed blacks); Sangiovese; and Aleatico. From time to time there are tiny lots of Chardonnay and Chenin Blanc.

TRIBAUT, M. Alameda S $12–$15
Two *Champenois,* Michel Tribaut and Bertrand Devavry, commute from France to Monterey during the crush and to Hayward the rest of the year to make a bit less than 10,000 cases annually of champagne-method sparkling wine in the most traditional ways. Their first vintage: 84.
NYR: vintage Brut (well received) and vintage Rosé (dry, traditional style). To come: nonvintage Brut, Blanc de Blanc, and Tête de Cuvée.

TUDAL WINERY Napa T $14.50
Arnold Tudal has concentrated on 2,500 cases a year of estate Cabernet Sauvignon from his 7 acres near Calistoga since the beginning 79, but he has had such good luck with Chardonnay when the Cabernet crop left a little room in the cellar that he is adding space enough to make the white a fixture.
*** Cabernet Sauvignon (dark, ripe, and tannic and yet all is balance and harmony) 79 80 82 83 84 85.

TULOCAY VINEYARDS Napa T $11–$12.50
Owner Bill Cadman wryly says he makes just enough wine to keep his barrels topped up. In fact he buys enough Napa grapes to produce about 2,400 cases a year of somewhat erratic but always intriguing varietals. The first vintage was 75.
→* Pinot Noir (rich varietal, well-balanced, sometimes strongly perfumed by new wood, sometimes deftly so).
[**] Cabernet Sauvignon–Egan Vineyard, Cabernet Sauvignon–Cliff Vineyard (firm, flavorful of Cabernet), and Chardonnay.

TWIN HILLS WINERY San Luis Obispo T $4.35–$8.75 Owner/winemaker James Lockshaw makes 15,000 to 20,000 cases of estate wine a year from his 100-acre vineyard n.w. of Paso Robles town. His first vintage was 81.
NYR: Chardonnay, Chenin Blanc, White Zinfandel, Zinfandel Rosé, Zinfandel.

TYLAND VINEYARDS Mendocino T $4.75–$10
Dick and Judy Tijsseling, the younger of two generations of growers n. of Hopland, operate a 12,000-case winery on the family property to make two separate lines of wines, a $4.75–$6 line called Mendocino Estates for the U.S. market, and a slightly more prestigious $6–$10 line called Tyland, which is sold only in Canada. *See also* TIJSSELING VINEYARDS.
** Mendocino Estates Chardonnay, Sauvignon Blanc, White Zinfandel, Cabernet Sauvignon, and Zinfandel; and Tyland Chardonnay, Sauvignon Blanc, White Zinfandel, and Cabernet Sauvignon (all steady, sound).

VALLEJO, M. G.
This merchant label based in General Mariano G. Vallejo's old hometown of Sonoma offers $4.49 California Chardonnay, Fumé Blanc, White Zinfandel, and Cabernet Sauvignon.

VALLEY OF THE MOON Sonoma T,D
$3.75–$12 One of the Sonoma Valley's durable (1944) family wineries has upgraded its core roster of wines in recent years, from jug generics to pricier varietals. All of the Enrico Parducci family's varietals—save a recently added Symphony—are from Sonoma grapes; reserve bottlings are almost always Sonoma Valley. The style is still sturdily rustic. Annual production is 30,000 cases.
*→** Chardonnay, Reserve Chardonnay, Sauvignon Blanc, Reserve Semillon, Cabernet Sauvignon, Reserve Cabernet Sauvignon, Reserve Pinot Noir, Zinfandel, Reserve Zinfandel, White Zinfandel, Private Stock White, Private Stock Red, Chablis, Burgundy, and Vin Rosé.
NYR: Symphony.

VAN DER HEYDEN Napa T $11.50
Andre van der Heyden makes 3,000 cases of wine a year from his vineyard. His first vintage was 84.
NYR: Chardonnay, Cabernet Sauvignon, and Zinfandel. A Late Harvest Semillon joins the list in favorable vintages.

VAN DER KAMP
The label fits somewhere between a merchant's and a winemaker's. Martin van der Kamp has his own winemaker, buys Sonoma Valley grapes, starts his *tirage* in one leased space, then has the final work done at a sparkling-wine specialist in the Russian River Valley. His first such vintage was 81. The roster, all priced at $14.75, is Brut, Midnight Cuvée (a Brut rosé), and Brut English Cuvée (more toasty in character than the regular Brut). Annual volume: 5,000 cases.

VARIETAL
Label term for wines named after individual grape varieties, made with a minimum 75% of the particular grape for wines bottled since 1983, 51% for those bottled earlier. Examples: Cabernet Sauvignon, Chardonnay, Zinfandel.

VEGA VINEYARDS & WINERY Santa Barbara T
$4.50–$11 A family-owned, 10,000-case winery at the outskirts of Buellton that has its base in two mature Santa Ynez Valley vineyards totalling 30 acres, and one young one that will up the number to 45 acres. The first vintage was 78.
• Chardonnay, Gewürztraminer, Pineau (a proprietary Pinot Blanc), Pinot Noir (slightly erratic, but worth a gamble for the times when it connects) 85. A Late Harvest Johannisberg Riesling comes when *Botrytis* hits.

VENDANGE
A second label for Sebastiani Vineyards covers $3.99 Chardonnay, Sauvignon Blanc, White Zinfandel, Cabernet Sauvignon, and Merlot.

VENTANA VINEYARDS Monterey T $5–$18
Doug Meador grows 400 acres of grapes in the Arroyo Seco AVA w. of Soledad, taking enough of his own fruit to make 42,000 cases of wine a year. The plan is to go to 60,000 as a new winery goes up. Ventana's first vintage: 78. Inciden-

tally, the name of the vineyard goes on many labels in addition to Meador's own.

** Chardonnay–Green Stripe (freshly fruity); Barrel Fermented Chardonnay (toasty, but still plenty of fruit); Sauvignon Blanc; White Riesling; and Gewürztraminer.

NYR: Magnus (proprietary red based in Cabernet Sauvignon) and Primrose (proprietary blush based in Riesling).

VERMOUTH
A generic flavored wine with origins in Italy. White vermouths are typically drier than reds; both are infused with proprietary formulas of herbs.

VIANO WINERY   Contra Costa   T $2.25–$5.50
Clem Viano is the owner/winemaker of one of a handful of surviving family-owned, drop-in, buy-at-the-door country wineries. He produces an annual 4,000 or so cases of wine from 60 acres at the nonindustrial southern outskirt of Martinez.

[*] Cabernet Sauvignon, Gamay, Zinfandel, Hillside Red, Chardonnay, Sauvignon Blanc, Hillside White (all ripe, round to soft, rustic, reliable).

VIANSA
For the moment, Viansa is Sam J. and Vicki Sebastiani's winemaker's label. Construction of the winery that goes with the name got underway in Sonoma's portion of the Carneros AVA during 1989. Meanwhile, Sam is producing 12,000 cases a year in leased space, deliberately blending Napa and Sonoma grapes. The first wines were 82s under the Sam J. Sebastiani label; the name shifted over to Viansa with the 84s.

NYR: Cabernet Sauvignon (supple, with layers of Cabernet flavors and deft touches of oak) 84; Reserve Cabernet Sauvignon; Grand Reserve Cabernet Sauvignon; Chardonnay (as polished and complex as the Cabernet) 85 86; Sauvignon Blanc (textbook varietal flavors) 85 86.

VICHON   Napa   T $7.50–$18
A 50,000-case winery founded by a partnership in 1981 was purchased from them by the Robert Mondavi family in 1985. Vichon at present buys all of its grapes from independent growers throughout Napa. The winemaking is independent, the style distinct from Mondavi's.

*** Chardonnay (ultratoasty in the early years, but now balanced, subtle, complex) 85 86 87; Chevrignon (a 50/50 Sauvignon/Semillon blend leans to Sauvignon's light body and grassy flavors) 83 84 85 86 87.

** Napa Valley Cabernet Sauvignon (gliding in an ever more stylish direction).

NYR: Merlot (introduced with an 85) and Cabernet Sauvignon–SLD (for Stag's Leap District, also introduced with an 85). A botrytised Semillon is fairly regularly on the list.

VILLA HELENA   Napa   T $10
Los Angeles engineer Don McGrath launched the winery as a weekend hobby with a bit more than 1,000 cases of 84s. He plans to up production a bit after he retires in 1989. All

of the grapes are bought-in to his cellar s. of St. Helena.
NYR: Chardonnay (the mainstay); Sauvignon Blanc, Pinot
Noir, and Late Harvest Amador Zinfandel are sometimes
items.

VILLA MT. EDEN   Napa   T $6–$16
In 1974 James and Anne McWilliams founded a small winery on an 87-acre, pre-Prohibition vineyard e. of Oakville.
In 1986 they sold the business and leased the property to
Stimson Lane, the owners of Château Ste. Michelle in Washington. Under the new proprietors, some Napa Valley
grapes are being bought-in to bring production to 24,000
cases. They have kept Michael McGrath as winemaker.
** Chardonnay (now in three bottlings—Carneros, Napa
Valley barrel-fermented, and Estate); Chenin Blanc; Cabernet Sauvignon and Reserve Cabernet Sauvignon; and Zinfandel (well-balanced as a hearty red in 86).

VILLA PARADISO   Santa Clara   T $6.50–$7.50
Hank and Judy Bogardus buy local and Paso Robles grapes
to produce 1,800 cases of wine a year at an old fortress of
a winery at the n. flank of the Hecker Pass district. Sales are
entirely local, mostly from the cellar door.
• Merlot, Zinfandel.

VINMARK
Second label of MARKHAM VINEYARDS.

VIÑA VISTA   Sonoma   T $9–$16
After a stop-and-go history that lasted from 1971 until 1983,
owner Keith Nelson has his winery steady at 4,000 cases a
year, all from bought Sonoma grapes, and programmed to go
to 10,000, some from winery-owned vineyards.
NYR: Chardonnay, Cabernet Sauvignon (straightforward,
attractive 85), and Merlot. Zinfandel joins with an 88.

VIOGNIER
A white grape variety and its varietal wine. Viognier, the
source of the Rhône's fabled Château Grillet, has just begun
to be planted in California. Three tiny trial plots in Napa
have yielded the first varietal wines.

VITA NOVA   Santa Barbara   T $10–$20
The claret house in a group of overlapping specialists (AU
BON CLIMAT for Burgundy types and QUPÉ for Rhône-
inspireds). This one, owned by Jim Clendenen of Au Bon
Climat and Bob Lindquist of Qupé, is, like the others, lo-
cated in a winery at Sierra Madre Vineyards in the Santa
Maria Valley. The first vintage was 86. All of the grapes
come from Paso Robles and Santa Barbara.
NYR: Vita Nova (labeled with names of blended varieties in
order of volume), and Chardonnay.

VOLATILE ACID   (v.a.)
Technical term for acetic acid—the characteristic component of vinegar—present in minuscule amounts in all wines,
and in disagreeably noticeable amounts in a few.

VOSE VINEYARDS
Hamilton Vose has sold his cellar and vineyard on Napa's

Mt. Veeder, but will continue to sell bottled wine until the last of the 85 reds are gone.

WALKER WINERY Santa Cruz T $5.99–$10.00 Electronics executive Russ Walker is his own winemaker in a 1,000-case-a-year weekend winery in Felton. He buys white grapes in Monterey, reds in Santa Cruz, San Luis Obispo, and Napa. His first vintage was 79.
• Chardonnay, Sauvignon Blanc, Cabernet Sauvignon, Petite Sirah, and Pinot Noir.

WEIBEL CHAMPAGNE VINEYARDS Alameda/ Mendocino S,T,D $2.59–$12.99 Though the name says sparkling wine, the Weibel family makes a bit of everything. Table and sparkling wines come mostly from Mendocino grapes, including 450 owned acres, fermented at a winery near Ukiah but bottled at the old home cellars at the s. end of San Francisco Bay, in a district called Warm Springs. Annual production is 750,000 cases. Stanford is a second label for Charmat sparklers. The winery sells older wines under a reserve label.
[**] Dry Bin Sherry, Amber Cream Sherry, Rare Port, and Cream of Black Muscat.
** Brut and Blanc de Noirs (both champagne-method); Cabernet Sauvignon and Pinot Noir.
*→** Chardonnay, Green Hungarian, Chenin Blanc, White Pinot Noir, White Cabernet Sauvignon, White Zinfandel, Refosco, White Table Wine, Red Table Wine, Rosé, Hofberg May Wine, Wine Snob White, Wine Snob Red, Sparkling Green Hungarian, and Sparkling White Zinfandel.

WEINSTOCK CELLARS
One of the younger members of a cluster of kosher wine companies that use classic wine grapes for a whole new breed of sacramental wines. Weinstock buys Sonoma grapes and makes the wine in leased space near Healdsburg. The first vintage was 84. Annual production is a bit more than 30,000 cases of NYR $4.50–$6 Chardonnay, White Zinfandel, and Gamay Beaujolais.

WENTE BROS. Alameda T,S $3.99–$12.99 In Wente family hands since its founding in 1881, the 300,000-case winery has two cellars (one for still wine, one for sparkling) and 1,300 acres of vineyard in its traditional home, the Livermore Valley, but also grows 700 acres of grapes in Monterey's Arroyo Seco AVA.
→*** Sauvignon Blanc (estate bottling from Livermore wonderfully specific in varietal character; other bottlings from Chalk Hill and Napa Valley more modest in both flavor and texture); Semillon (pungent of its variety, fuller-bodied than the Sauvignon).
** Chardonnay (to be the mainstay white after Sauvignon), Gewürztraminer, Grey Riesling, Johannisberg Riesling, Blanc de Blanc (mostly Ugni Blanc), Cabernet Sauvignon (new emphasis on making it the premier red), Merlot, Petite Sirah, Zinfandel, and White Zinfandel.
NYR: Brut, Blanc de Blanc, Blanc de Noir (since debut 80s,

all three curiously toasty, somehow more reminiscent of good Spanish *cava* than any other Californian).

WERMUTH WINERY   Napa   T $8–$9
Frank and Smitty Wermuth make 3,000 cases of Napa varietals a year at their cellar near Calistoga. The first vintage was 83; the grapes are all bought-in from near neighbors. NYR: Dry Colombard, Sauvignon Blanc (beginning with 87s, two vineyard-designateds, Williams and Bone), and Cabernet Sauvignon. Wermuth makes an occasional barrel of another variety from time to time—usually Gamay.

WHALER VINEYARD   Mendocino   T
$5.25–$7.50   Russ and Annie Nyborg make 4,400 cases of wine a year, all from their rolling 23 acres of Zinfandel on the e. side of the Russian River between Talmage and Hopland. The name pays tribute to Russ Nyborg's career as a sea captain and San Francisco Bay pilot. They bought the property in 1972; their first vintage was 81.
[**] Zinfandel (well-balanced, packed with berrylike fruit flavors); White Zinfandel (off-dry, affably fruity).

WHEELER WINERY, WILLIAM   Sonoma   T
$6–$12   Once a label reliable for heady heavyweights, Wheeler has adopted a substantially more moderate style in recent years. The debut vintage was 79. Current production is 19,000 cases, all from Sonoma. Bill and Ingrid Wheeler founded the winery on 32 acres they call Norse Vineyard in the Dry Creek Valley AVA, from whence comes all of the Cabernet Sauvignon and some of the White Zinfandel. French-owned Domaines Paribas bought the winery in 1989.
→* Sauvignon Blanc (refined flavors, graceful balance since 83); and White Zinfandel (fresh, lively, just off-dry).
** Cabernet Sauvignon (dark, heady, tannic for years, possible change of pace with 84); Chardonnay (pleasantly varietal, a hint weighty at times).

WHITE OAK VINEYARDS   Sonoma   T $6.50–$18
This 11,000-case winery in Healdsburg buys a long half of its grapes in the Alexander Valley (and still others elsewhere in Sonoma), but draws on owner Bill Myers's 6-acre vineyard there for the heart of a startlingly rich Private Reserve Chardonnay that is its mainstay. The first vintage was 81.
*** Private Reserve Chardonnay (bold fruit flavors, rich textures) 83 84 85 87.
→* Myers Limited Reserve Chardonnay, Sonoma Chardonnay (near echoes of the leader).
** Chenin Blanc, Sauvignon Blanc.
NYR: Myers Limited Reserve Cabernet Sauvignon, Zinfandel.

WHITE PORT
Generic dessert-wine type, usually inexpensive to outright cheap for curbstone consumption, very sweet, and made with a high proportion of Muscat grapes.

WHITE RIESLING
A white grape variety and its varietal wine more often

known by the synonym Johannisberg Riesling, but increasingly as just Riesling. Total acreage has been eroding slowly; the 1988 level is 8,450. Monterey (2,875 acres), Mendocino (325), Napa (1,140), Santa Barbara (1,860), and Sonoma (1,100) have most of it. Typical table wines are off-dry, and quick to age. Since 1972 a proportion of the crop has been dedicated to *Botrytis*-affected wines whenever weather cooperates; r.s. typically ranges from 6% to as high as 35%; the record is 54%.

WHITE ROCK VINEYARDS Napa T $?
Henry and Claire Vandendriessche made the first wines from their 35 acres n.e. of the city of Napa in 86, then had their caves dug in time to make the 88s on the estate. Annual production is planned to grow from 2,000 cases to 6,000.
NYR: Chardonnay, Claret (Cabernet-based blend with Merlot, Petit Verdot, and Cabernet Franc).

WHITE ZINFANDEL
A varietal wine type made from Zinfandel grapes using white-winemaking techniques. Most examples are BLUSH rather than truly white, and styled off-dry to outright sweet.

WHITEHALL LANE WINERY Napa T
$5.95–$16 Founded as a family-owned winery in 1980 by the brothers Alan Steen and Art Finkelstein, Whitehall Lane acquired a Japanese owner, Hideaki Ando, in 1988. The original proprietors continue to operate the 20,000-case winery, which supplements 22 acres of estate vineyard near St. Helena with bought grapes from Napa and Sonoma.
*** Pinot Noir (made to show off Pinot Noir's fruit early and its bouquets late, a success on both counts) 82 84 85.
** Chardonnay (round to soft, noticeably touched by wood); Merlot (from Knights Valley grapes, big, often a bit heady, always full of flavor); Cabernet Sauvignon; Chenin Blanc; and Blanc de Pinot Noir.

WHITFORD CELLARS Napa T $10
Chardonnay is the only wine from Duncan Haynes's 38-acre vineyard e. of the city of Napa. The first was an 83 sold under the Coombsville Vineyard label; the Whitford label started with an 84. But the vineyard property has been in family hands for more than a century. Volume: 1,000 cases.

WILD HORSE VALLEY AVA
This tiny, 3-vineyard AVA straddling the Napa-Solano county line e. of Napa city was approved only in 1988. A winery is under construction on one of the properties.

WILD HORSE WINERY San Luis Obispo T
$9–$12 Owner/winemaker Ken Volk launched his 15,000-case winery in the Paso Robles district with fewer than 1,000 cases of 83s and grew on the particular strength of his Pinot Noirs. Volk grows 38 acres of grapes at Paso Robles and buys grapes there and in the Santa Maria Valley.
NYR: Santa Maria Pinot Noir (intensely flavorful, well-balanced in 84, 85); Paso Robles Pinot Noir; Cabernet Sauvignon (estate and nonestate bottlings); Paso Robles Merlot; Chardonnay (estate).

WILDCAT Sonoma T $6–$12.50
Charles Illgen grows his own Sonoma Valley Merlot on a small property near the original Buena Vista and buys the rest of his grapes from local growers. The first wine was a Merlot 84. Production—in leased space—is at 4,000 cases and planned to grow slowly. The name, incidentally, translates the much-used *mayacamas* from a local Indian language. NYR: Chardonnay, Gewürztraminer, Gamay Beaujolais, and Merlot.

WILE & SONS, JULIUS
A merchant label belonging to the New York importing firm offers a $5.99–$6.99 line called the Napa Valley Estate Collection, produced in space leased from the Napa Valley Co-operative Winery at St. Helena from grapes grown by members of the co-op. The first vintage was 85 for Cabernet Sauvignon, and 86 for Chardonnay and Sauvignon Blanc.

WILLIAMS & SELYEM Sonoma T $12.50–$25
The two-man partnership struck a responsive chord with its first Sonoma Pinot Noir, an 81 labeled Hacienda del Rio, and has been on a roll ever since. Annual production is 2,000 cases—in 88 divided into a potential 7 lots of Pinot Noir plus one of Zinfandel.
** Sonoma Pinot Noir–Rochioli Vineyard, Sonoma Pinot Noir (both full-bodied, firmly marked by new oak, and deeply flavored by their grape variety); other vineyard-designated Pinots of more recent origin are Howard Allen (87) and Summa (88) . . . and Zinfandel (same big, woody style as the Pinots).

WINTERBROOK VINEYARDS Amador T
$5–$15 The label began with an 81; the winery near Ione dates from 1983; current owners Maurice and Nancy Guiridi bought the winery and its 60-acre vineyard in 1986. They also established Sierra Foothill as a second label. Production is 40,000 cases and growing.
NYR: Vintage Port (estate-grown, made in 80, 85, and 86), Chardonnay (also estate), White Zinfandel, and Zinfandel.

WINTERS WINERY Solano T $6–$8
Proprietor John Storm has looked increasingly to reds as his winery has developed from beginnings in 1980. All of the wines come from 21 acres at Winters that Storm owns or manages. Production approaches 7,000 cases.
• Sauvignon Blanc, Petite Sirah, Pinot Noir, and Zinfandel.
NYR: Barbera is to join the list.

WOLFESPIERRE
Wolfespierre is the blanket name for a complicated combine of four $10–$18 Sonoma Mountain grower labels, all four wines made by one winemaker in a single leased cellar. The names are Wolfespierre Chardonnay, Berlin Sauvignon Blanc–Semillon, Steiner Cabernet Sauvignon, and Farina Pinot Noir. Aggregate production approaches 2,500 cases. The project has its roots in a Steiner Cabernet Sauvignon 85.

WOLTERBEEK-WESTWOOD El Dorado T
$6.50–$15 Two wineries for the price of one. Wolter-

beek is the label for 1,000 cases of organically grown Sauvignon Blanc from Teddie and Al Wolterbeek's 8 acres at Shingle Springs. The Westwood label belongs to winemaker Bert Urch, who buys grapes in El Dorado to make 1,500 cases a year. His first vintage was 84.

NYR: Wolterbeek Sauvignon Blanc (started with an 85).

NYR: Westwood Chardonnay, Pinot Noir, and smaller lots of Cabernet Sauvignon and Charbono.

WOODBURY WINERY Marin D,T $4.50–$8
Russ Woodbury buys mostly Alexander Valley grapes to make an annual 2,000 cases of wine. The focus is on port types of varying style. His first declared vintage was 77.

** Vintage Port (distinctive with flavors akin to Cabernet though that grape is not used).

Also: Chardonnay, Johannisberg Riesling.

WOODEN VALLEY WINERY Solano T $1.50–$3
A buy-at-the-door cellar near the town of Fairfield offers about 35,000 cases a year of a long list, all from its own 225 acres of vineyards plus another 100 the owners lease nearby. The winery dates from 1932 and is owned by the family of its founder, the late Mario Lanza.

• Chardonnay, Sauvignon Blanc, Johannisberg Riesling, White Zinfandel, Green Hungarian, Gewürztraminer, French Colombard, Chenin Blanc, Zinfandel, Cabernet Sauvignon, Gamay Beaujolais, Pinot Noir, Chablis, Rhine, Vino Bianco, Haut Sauterne, Petite Rosé, Vin Rosé, Burgundy, Chianti, Vino Rosso.

WOODSIDE VINEYARDS Santa Cruz Mountains T $8–$11 Miniaturists Bob and Polly Mullen use part of once-famed Rixford Vineyard at Woodside for tiny lots of Cabernet Sauvignon, and grapes bought locally and in Monterey for their other wines. Annual production is a shade more than 1,000 cases. The first vintage was 60.

** Chardonnay, Cabernet Sauvignon, and Zinfandel.

YORK MOUNTAIN AVA
In essence a one-winery sub-AVA in hills on the w. flank of the PASO ROBLES AVA.

YORK MOUNTAIN WINERY San Luis Obispo T,S $3.95–$12 A family named York ran the winery in steep hills w. of Paso Robles from the 1880s until 1970, when the last of the Yorks sold to Max Goldman. Goldman's son, Steve, is now in charge of making the annual 5,000 cases of wine, all from purchased Central Coast grapes.

*→** Chardonnay, Cabernet Sauvignon, Merlot, Pinot Noir, and Zinfandel, plus white and red table wine.

NYR: champagne-method sparkler (Max's original dream).

Z-D Napa T $12–$18.50
Chardonnay has been the signature wine since the late Gino Zepponi and Norman de Leuze founded the label in Sonoma in 1969. They moved to Napa in 1979. The winery buys grapes widely to make an annual 18,000 cases at a cellar e. of Rutherford.

** California Chardonnay (strong American-oak note

overshadows fruit flavors in a soft, curiously sweet, quickly mature wine from Napa + Santa Barbara grapes); Napa Pinot Noir (big, dark, woody); Santa Maria Pinot Noir (ditto); and Napa Cabernet Sauvignon (follows the style). Select Late Harvest White Riesling comes with cool, damp harvests.

ZACA MESA Santa Barbara T $5.50–$15
The winery had a brief identity crisis over size, but has settled down to being an always reliable, often impressive producer of 60,000 cases of Santa Barbara varietals. All of the grapes come from the 235-acre Zaca Mesa ranch in the Santa Ynez Valley, and the 650-acre Sierra Madre Vineyard (in which it is a partner) in the Santa Maria Valley. The firm was founded in 1978 and came under the control of present owner John Chrisman in 1985.
*** Chardonnay and Chardonnay–Barrel Select (both subtly fruity, with deft toasty overtones) 84 85 86 87; Pinot Noir (striking varietal, intriguing regional flavors) 81 84 85.
** Johannisberg Riesling, Sauvignon Blanc (cooked-asparagus flavors of the region); Cabernet Sauvignon (distinctly regional); Syrah; and White Zinfandel. Late Harvest Johannisberg Riesling made when possible.

ZELLERBACH VINEYARD, STEPHEN
See ESTATE WILLIAM BACCALA.

ZINFANDEL
A black grape and its varietal red wine. Zinfandel's origins remain shrouded in mystery, but it appears closely related to a present-day Italian variety called Primitivo. The much-planted grape (25,800 acres) grows well in most of California, reaching its zenith in Sonoma County (4,420 acres), which is closely challenged by Mendocino (1,475), Napa (2,060), San Luis Obispo (1,235), and the Sierra foothills (1,240). As red wine, Zinfandel ranges in style from light and zestfully fruity to thick, almost portlike. The most age-worthy bottlings tend to be restrained middleweights. Zinfandel's berrylike flavors also lend themselves to paler wines such as WHITE ZINFANDEL and ZINFANDEL ROSÉ.

ZINFANDEL ROSÉ
A varietal rosé type, usually off-dry but sometimes bone-dry.

VINTAGE NOTES

W ith the profusion of young wineries has come height-
ened awareness of vintage variations in California.
Distinctions once lost in multiple-vineyard blends now stand
out, especially in reds but also in whites.

The range of quality among vintages is narrow compared to most of the world. California rarely fails to ripen
its grapes; the main variable, thus, is between vintages to
drink young and vintages to keep. To date only Napa and
Sonoma have enough wineries and enough history to allow
reasonable speculation, so these notes apply mainly to those
regions.

CABERNET SAUVIGNON

88 The first word is that they will be charming early, not
   great keepers.
87 Promising as they approach bottling.
86 Well flavored but still showing a lot of baby fat.
85 Pleasing early; perhaps much like 78s.
84 As big and showy as the 74s were.
83 Hard, slow-developing in spite of favorable weather.
   Best should keep very well.
82 Warm season led to soft, approachable wines. Many
   drinking well right now. Not a vintage to cellar.
81 Heat, especially at harvest, casts doubts, but wines
   emerged complex in flavor, fairly well-balanced. Na-
   pans at peak now; Sonomans have slipped onto the
   downslope.
80 Enigmatic. Either closed or dull, probably the latter.
79 Cool year yielded firm, deeply flavored wines. Great bets
   for long keeping.
78 Full of charm early, then have hung on surprisingly well
   from Napa, less well from Sonoma.
77 Few if any remain at top of mediocre form.
76 Drought, heat overconcentrated most. At or past peak
   now.
75 Cool year yielded firm, richly flavored wines still at top
   of form; many can last longer.
74 Benign year yielded showy wines; most better earlier but
   few finest remain in fine fettle.
73 Overlooked early; aging beautifully now.

PINOT NOIR

88 No early book yet, except Central Coast growers happy.

87 Some promise on verge of bottling.

86 First few show depths of flavor, good balance.

85 A shade light all around, but full of charm for early drinking.

84 Sturdy, flavorful; one of the best bets for aging since 79.

83 Middle of the pack in the North Coast; Central Coast suffered difficult weather and fared even less well.

82 Ups and downs in the North Coast, with most charming at the least. Quite good in Central Coast.

81 Serviceable but in the pack then and now.

80 Hard, understated; still demanding more time.

79 Rich, firm; best agers of recent times; still going strong.

ZINFANDEL

88 Splendid flavors, promising balance in North Coast.

87 Sound, solid.

86 Fine berryish flavors make cellaring seem needless, but the prospects of some rewards are there. May surpass 85.

85 Outstanding in entire North Coast; can drink now or wait.

84 Sonomans big, sometimes a bit stolid; Dry Creek Valley finer. Napa another step ahead.

83 Steady wines, aging fairly well.

82 Many got away, ending up thick and heady. A few were fine, especially in Sonoma Valley and Napa.

81 Middle of the pack.

CHARDONNAY

88 Tiny crop, but good flavors. Room to hope.

87 Steady, agreeable wines as they went to bottle.

86 Big and bold, sometimes too much so. Carneros, Anderson Valley better bets than rest of North Coast; Central Coast at its peak thus far.

85 Splendid wines just settling into stride; some have years to go yet. Probably the vintage of the eighties.

84 Consistently attractive, and holding fairly well.

83 Most a bit soft, overripe; very few remain in top form.

82 A difficult growing season made this a handicapper's nightmare. Some of everything, but just enough outstanding examples to demand attention.

81 Scorned early because of harvest heat, the wines turned out splendidly. A few of the best remain in top form.

BOTRYTISED WHITE WINES*

88 Very few from a dry, warm harvest, but a couple of promising tries with Riesling.

87 Not many attempted, but a few from Mendocino and Sonoma.

86 Some promising efforts, especially in Riesling and Gewürztraminer.

85 Most favorable year since 82 for Mendocino and Sonoma Rieslings and Traminers; best year ever for Sauvignon-Semillon throughout North Coast.

* Central Coast produces *Botrytis* almost at will, so notes apply only to North Coast.

84 A handful tried, but the harvest was too warm and dry for any but slightly botrytised types.

83 Anderson Valley did well with Riesling, Gewürztraminer; most others hard put.

82 Splendid year all around, including first widespread tries with Semillon and Sauvignon Blanc.

81 Good vintage for the type.

80 Good vintage for the type; most now past their best days.

WINE AND FOOD

T he best part about drinking wine is to discover which ones add the most pleasure to favorite dishes. This is an altogether personal enterprise not subject to rules, and barely subject to suggestion. Still, the experience of others can provide at least a few useful signposts.

Most of the combinations in this section follow convention. They represent consensus to the extent that it exists. A few personal choices are tossed into the pot to help challenge such weary wisdom as red wine with red meat and white wine with fish. As California continues explosive expansion with new wineries, new districts, even new grape varieties, there is much to be gained through exploration. The recommendations here should serve only as departure points for more wide-ranging looks at what is possible.

The use of stars follows the same rating system used throughout the A–Z section (see page 14).

APPETIZERS

Beef carpaccio Cabernet Rosé or Sauvignon Blanc.

Caviar *** or **** Brut or Natural Champagne.

Cheese pastries Dry Sherry or any favorite white wine.

Cheeses See page 195.

Clams, smoked Dry Sherry.

Cream molds Fragrant off-dry whites such as Colombard.

Crêpes, mushroom ** or *** Sauvignon Blanc or White Riesling.

Fondue Pinot Blanc or dry Chenin Blanc.

Gougère Pinot Noir Blanc, Gamay, or modest Pinot Noir.

Liver pâté *** Gewürztraminer, White Riesling, or Champagne.

Mushrooms

plain Pinot Blanc or dry white table wine.

stuffed Dry Sherry, dry rosé or blush, or Gewürztraminer.

morels sautéed in butter Champagne.

Oysters on the half shell *** or **** Brut Champagne or understated, tart Chardonnay or Pinot Blanc.

Smoked salmon, trout, or sturgeon Champagne.

Vegetables, raw, with dip Dry rosé or blush.

FIRST COURSES OR LUNCHEONS

Artichokes
> **with lemon and butter** Dry to off-dry, full-bodied white wine.
>
> **stuffed with bread crumbs** Grignolino Rosé or other dry rosé.

Asparagus ** Chardonnay for the echo of flavor, dry rosé for contrast, or dry White Riesling as a German classic.

Avocado and seafood stuffing *** Pinot Blanc or Sauvignon Blanc.

Clams baked and seasoned *** Dry Chenin Blanc or Pinot Blanc.

Crab cakes, Maryland Champagne.

Salmon mousse Light, understated Chardonnay.

Pastas, rices, etc.
> **cream sauce or creamy casserole** Dry Chenin Blanc or Pinot Blanc, Zinfandel, or Merlot.
>
> **clam sauce** ** or *** Chenin Blanc or White Riesling.
>
> **herb sauce** Zinfandel or Grignolino.
>
> **lasagne** Any hearty red.
>
> **lentils baked with cheese** Dry Blush or Gamay.
>
> **pesto sauce** Sauvignon Blanc.
>
> **polenta** Zinfandel, White Zinfandel, or modest Chardonnay.
>
> **polenta-fried** Merlot.
>
> **raviolis** Sauvignon Blanc, Zinfandel, or red table wine.
>
> **risotto with 4 cheeses** Pinot Noir or Zinfandel.
>
> **risotto with mushrooms** Sauvignon Blanc or Zinfandel.
>
> **tomato and meat** Barbera.
>
> **tomato-sauced** * to *** generic red or Zinfandel, depending on how delicate the sauce and how fancy the dinner.

Prosciutto with melon ** or *** White Riesling or Gewürztraminer sweet enough to play against the salty meat.

Quiche
> **Lorraine** White Riesling or dry rosé.
>
> **shellfish** *** Off-dry White Riesling.
>
> **vegetable** ** Off-dry White Riesling to contrast fruit with vegetable, or Sauvignon Blanc to echo the vegetable.

Salads
> **Cobb** Sauvignon Blanc, Semillon, or dry rosé.
>
> **duck breast** (warm) Older Cabernet Sauvignon or Merlot.
>
> **fresh fruit** Off-dry to sweet blush or rosé.
>
> **greens with blue cheese dressing** Light, young red.
>
> **greens with vinegar or lemon dressing** Murderous to all wines.
>
> **Nicoise** Melony Sauvignon Blanc.
>
> **Oriental chicken** Off-dry White Riesling or Gewürztraminer.
>
> **pasta** Semillon, Sauvignon Blanc, or blush.
>
> **wild rice** White Riesling or light red.

Soups
> **black bean** Gewürztraminer or Pale Dry Sherry.

carrot, puréed White Riesling.

chili con carne Red table wine if one must, but beer is better.

consommé Pale Dry Sherry.

cream of vegetable Melony Sauvignon Blanc or dry Chenin Blanc.

French onion Fruity white table wine or Zinfandel Rosé.

gazpacho White Riesling.

green pea with ham Sauvignon Blanc or blush.

lentil and sausage Gamay, dry blush, or Sauvignon Blanc.

meat and vegetable Blush or light red table wine.

minestrone Sauvignon Blanc, dry or off-dry blush.

mulligatawny Sauvignon Blanc or dry White Riesling.

oyster stew Chardonnay.

seafood chowder or bisque White Riesling, Chablis, or, for Sunday best, light, fruity Chardonnay.

ENTRÉES—FISH AND SHELLFISH

Abalone *** Off-dry White Riesling or Sauvignon Blanc.

Bass, perch, et al. Pinot Blanc or light, crisp white table wine.

Blackened redfish Reddened Zinfandel or melony Sauvignon Blanc.

Catfish Cabernet Rosé or Sauvignon Blanc.

Clams

steamed Off-dry Gray Riesling, Sylvaner, or Emerald Riesling.

fried Colombard or fragrant White Riesling.

Cod, sea bass, rockfish, et al. Wide range of dry or off-dry white varietals or white table wines.

Crab

cioppino Zinfandel, or Barbera if sauce is thick.

Dungeness, cold cracked *** Off-dry White Riesling.

Dungeness, sauced or in casserole Chardonnay.

Eastern (or blue) White Riesling.

king or snow ** Chardonnay with little or no oak, or dry Chenin Blanc.

Louis White Riesling or Colombard.

Crayfish, boiled Off-dry White Riesling.

Halibut, grilled or poached, with lemon butter Sauvignon Blanc or Chardonnay.

Lobster, whole or tails, with drawn butter **** Chardonnay, preferably with bottle age.

Monkfish Semillon or Chardonnay.

Mussels Crisp, light Chardonnay or understated White Riesling.

Oysters

baked *** Chardonnay, preferably tart.

fried Dry Chenin Blanc or dry white table wine.

Sablefish Dry Semillon.

Salmon

> **baked** (plain or with cream or wine sauce) *** or **** Chardonnay, preferably full-bodied and ripe.
>
> **baked with herbs** *** or **** Chardonnay or well-oaked Sauvignon Blanc.
>
> **barbecued** Surprise! Supple, subtle Zinfandel with a bit of age, à la Louis M. Martini.
>
> **butter-sautéed steaks** Wide range of dry whites.
>
> **Gravlax or lox** **** Blanc de Noir Champagne. Or Pale Dry Sherry or Gewürztraminer, or other flavorful wine, to be taken alternately more than together.

Scallops Very difficult. Best hope is understated white.

Shad roe Chardonnay with little or no oak.

Shrimp or prawns

> **fried in butter** Chardonnay.
>
> **Louis** Colombard or other off-dry white.
>
> **plain** Wide range of off-dry whites.

Snapper

> **blackened** Fruity Zinfandel.
>
> **filets baked with butter and parmesan** Sauvignon Blanc or Semillon.
>
> **filets baked Vera Cruz style** Grassy Sauvignon Blanc.
>
> **grilled** Sauvignon Blanc or light Chardonnay.

Sole, petrale, sand dabs

> **baked** Dry Chenin Blanc or dry white table wine.
>
> **fried or grilled** Gray Riesling, Sylvaner, or white table wine.
>
> **poached** Folle Blanche or Dry Chenin Blanc.

Squid (calamari), baby octopus

> **fried** Colombard or other fruity white.
>
> **marinated** Colombard or other fruity white.
>
> **stewed, with tomatoes and garlic** Grignolino or other fresh, dry red, or Sauvignon Blanc.

Trout ** or *** barely off-dry White Riesling or white table wine.

Tuna steaks

> **broiled, with bacon** Rich Chardonnay.
>
> **grilled, rare with ginger** Rich Chardonnay.

ENTRÉES—POULTRY

Chicken

> **barbecued** Any youthful dry white or red, but especially Gamay, Chenin Blanc, or Riesling priced to fit the solemnity of the occasion.
>
> **fried** Any dry or off-dry white.
>
> **whole roasted** Understated, bottle-aged Zinfandel or Cabernet Sauvignon, or dry Chenin Blanc, or ** Chardonnay.

Quail Aged Pinot Noir.

Roasted duck *** or **** Cabernet Sauvignon, well aged, no matter which sauce.

Roasted goose *** or **** Cabernet Sauvignon or Petite Sirah with enough bottle age to be subtly flavored, but still some tannin to cut the fats.

Squab **** Chardonnay or aged Cabernet Sauvignon, depending on preference for white or red.

Turkey
> roasted, with all the trimming Chardonnay or well-aged Cabernet Sauvignon for fancy company, dry Chenin Blanc or Gamay for less stately occasions.
>
> smoked *** blush or richly flavored White Riesling.

ENTRÉES—PORK

Chops
> baked Gamay or other fruity red.
> fried Red table wine, dry rosé, or blush.
> stuffed ** or *** Zinfandel or Sauvignon Blanc.

Ham A ham is a ham is a ham. Drink rosé.

Loin, roasted
> plain ** or *** Chardonnay or Pinot Noir with some bottle age.
> with prune stuffing Dry Sauvignon Blanc of intense varietal character, or subtle Zinfandel.
> with sage dressing *** Zinfandel with some bottle age.

Sausages, baked, broiled or barbecued Gamay, Zinfandel, dry rosé, or Gewürztraminer.

Spareribs
> baked, plain Frisky young red, especially Zinfandel or Grignolino.
> with sauce Tannic Petite Sirah or crisp blush.

ENTRÉES—LAMB

Chops ** Dry red, especially Zinfandel or Petite Sirah, or perhaps a big, toasty Chardonnay.

Crown roast or rack *** Older Zinfandel or Cabernet Sauvignon.

Kebabs * to *** Zinfandel or red table wine.

Leg, whole roasted, butterflied, and grilled Petite Sirah, husky Zinfandel, or young Cabernet Sauvignon.

Moussaka ** Soft red, especially Merlot.

Nicoise ** Zinfandel in its frisky youth.

Shanks, baked in wine Stout red, especially Barbera or Petite Sirah.

ENTRÉES—BEEF

Hamburger, meat loaf Gamay, lighter Zinfandel, red table wine.

Liver ** Merlot or subtle, soft Zinfandel.

Oxtail ** Zinfandel or Petite Sirah with some tannic backbone to help cut the fatty qualities.

Prime rib or roast *** or **** Pinot Noir because Pinot and beef enrich each other.

Steak Favorite red.

Stew (bourguignon or other) A red every bit as good as the one in the recipe, or a little better.

Stroganoff Gamay, Zinfandel, or red table wine.

Tongue, smoked Well off-dry, rich White Riesling.

ENTRÉES—VEAL

Kidneys *** Merlot or a less tannic Cabernet Sauvignon.

Osso buco *** Zinfandel.

Parmigiana ** or *** Zinfandel of character.

Roast *** Zinfandel or Merlot of finesse and some age.
Many prefer fine dry whites.

Scallopini *** White Riesling, just off-dry. Dry Sauvignon
Blanc or Chenin Blanc is almost as flawless a match.

Stew, with mushrooms ** Zinfandel or red table wine.

Sweetbreads *** or **** Cabernet Sauvignon aged to maturity, especially if the sauce is Madeira.

ENTRÉES—GAME

Duck, wild *** or **** Cabernet Sauvignon, preferably
mature.

Frogs' legs **** Chardonnay, partly in tribute to the price.

Pheasant *** or **** Pinot Noir, preferably mature.

Rabbit
in wine stew Fruity Merlot, Zinfandel, or Gamay.
with prunes Pinot Noir.

Venison ** or *** Zinfandel is the middle ground. Sea-
sonal flavors from forage as well as quality of cut suggest a wide range of wines, but dry and intensely flavorful are the common qualities.

ENTRÉES—EGGS

Omelets Depends entirely on amount and flavor of stuffing;
best bets for seafood or herb omelets are off-dry whites
such as Sylvaner and Gray Riesling.

Scrambled Choose wine at your own risk; eggs taste sulfu-
rous because they have a natural amount of it, so they
make a wine taste that way, too.

Soufflés Much the same as for omelets, except Champagne
for fancy occasions.

ENTRÉES—VEGETABLES

Cabbage, stuffed Gewürztraminer or Gamay Beaujolais.

Calzone Zinfandel or a dry White Zinfandel.

Cassoulet Cabernet Sauvignon mellowed by time.

Onion tart or quiche White Riesling or Gewürztraminer.

Roasted red peppers and basil in quiche or a risotto Sauvignon Blanc.

Vegetable frittata Cabernet Sauvignon Rosé or Sauvignon
Blanc.

Wild mushrooms
and pasta Cabernet Sauvignon.
in risotto Pinot Noir.

ENTRÉES—ETHNIC OR REGIONAL

Baked pork chimichangas *** Cabernet Sauvignon with
some age.

Cashew chicken Gewürztraminer, Chenin Blanc, blush.

Corned beef and cabbage Young Gamay Beaujolais.

Creole catfish Zinfandel or dry White Zinfandel.

Fajitas, beef Young, fruity Zinfandel.

Indian curries Blush, Gamay, or Sauvignon Blanc.

Mu siu pork Gewürztraminer or understated Zinfandel.

Oyster beef, green-pepper beef, beef chow mein Young Zinfandel.

Paella Offer both a Chardonnay and a light Zinfandel.

Peking duck Older *** Cabernet Sauvignon.

Sashimi Champagne.

Tacos, enchiladas Off-dry blush or young Zinfandel if guests will not accept beer.

Teriyaki beef Soft Zinfandel or Merlot.

Teriyaki chicken Chenin Blanc or blush.

SAUCES

Brown Wide range of reds; choice depends largely on the meat.

Cheese Red or white from the lighter end of the spectrum.

Curry Gewürztraminer or off-dry White Riesling if no beer is to be found.

Garlic Grassy Sauvignon Blanc of the most intense character for white meats, Merlot for red meats.

Herb Sauvignon Blanc for white meats, Zinfandel for reds.

Hollandaise Dry Chenin Blanc or other fruity white.

Lemon Uncommonly difficult to match. If not too citric, a Colombard or Folle Blanche.

Mustard Gamay or other not-too-tannic red, or White Riesling.

Onion Red or white depending on the meat, but intensely fruity in either case.

Red wine The same wine as in the sauce, or one shade finer.

Seafood Johannisberg Riesling, or a lighter Chardonnay.

Sweet and sour Gewürztraminer, rosé, or blush.

Tomato-cream Dry Chenin Blanc, Pinot Blanc, or Chardonnay, depending on the elegance of the dish.

White Chenin Blanc, White Riesling, or Sauvignon Blanc.

White wine The same wine as in the sauce, or one shade finer.

CHEESES

Blue cheeses

>Oregon, Danablue, sweet Gorgonzola Pinot Noir or Tinta Port.

>Roquefort, Stilton Late-harvest or other heady Zinfandel, and better young than old.

Brie, Camembert Slightly underripe, they go with every fine wine, but especially Pinot Noir. Ripe or overripe, they wipe out every wine.

Chêvre (fresh goat cheese) Gamay Beaujolais or Pinot Noir.

Cheddar and cheddar types *** older Cabernet Sauvignon or Petite Sirah for milder-flavored ones, or Dry Sherry if as an appetizer; ** zesty young Zinfandel for sharper, aged types. Ports may also do well.

Cougar Gold Merlot or Cabernet Sauvignon.

Hard cheeses: Asiago, Pecorino, Kasseri Zinfandel, Petite Sirah, or Syrah.

Semisoft, full-flavored: Port Salut, Esrom, Muenster Wide range of young reds, or possibly, blush or White Riesling if as appetizers.

Semisoft, mild: Edam, Gouda, Fontina, Jack Old red of quality, or old Port. Pale Dry Sherry if as appetizer.

Sonoma Dry Jack Every good red, especially Charbono.

Swiss types: Gruyère, Samso ** or *** young Pinot Noir.

DESSERTS

Rich desserts and sweet wines are almost impossible to balance and sate too soon even if they can be brought into harmony. Better to choose one or the other, especially where there is chocolate. If you choose wine, contrasting accompaniments can please.

Late-harvest Johannisberg Riesling The sweeter they are the better they stand alone, but a simple butter cookie if you must.

Light, sweet Muscat Cashew or macadamia nuts, pound cake, peaches or small melons, apple pie.

Sec Champagnes, sparkling Muscats Wafers, fresh strawberries, hazelnut torte, medium-sweet soufflés.

Port Plain butter or nut cookies, pears, apples, nut breads, pistachios, roasted chestnuts.

Cream Sherry Plain or nut cookies, toasted almonds or walnuts, apple-nut cake, apple pie or cobbler, zabaglione.

Angelica Pound cake, nut breads, baked apple, fruitcake, mince pie.

Maps-

Districts and

Wineries

Mendocino-Lake

MENDOCINO AND LAKE AVAS

2 Anderson Valley
4 Clear Lake
* Cole Ranch
5 Guenoc Valley
* Mendocino
3 McDowell Valley
1 Potter Valley

*This symbol denotes AVAs too small to be indicated on the map.

MENDOCINO AND LAKE-BONDED WINERIES

Blanc Vineyards
Christine Woods
Dolan Vineyards
Fetzer Vineyard
Frey Vineyards, Ltd.
Greenwood Ridge
Guenoc Winery
Handley Cellars
Hidden Cellars
Husch Vineyards
Jepson Vineyards
Kendall-Jackson Vineyard
Konocti Cellars
Lazy Creek Vineyards
Lolonis Winery

McDowell Valley
 Vineyards
Mendocino Vineyards
Milano Winery
Navarro Vineyards
Olson Vineyards
Parducci Wine Cellars
Parsons Creek Winery
Roederer Estate
Rudd Cellars, Channing
Scharffenberger Cellars
Stuermer Winery
Tijsseling Vineyard
Tyland Vineyards
Whaler Vineyard

Sonoma

SONOMA AVAS

1 Alexander Valley
5a Carneros
4a Chalk Hill
2 Dry Creek Valley
3 Knights Valley
* Northern Sonoma
4 Russian River Valley
5 Sonoma Coast
4b Sonoma-Green Valley
* Sonoma Mountain
* Sonoma Valley

*This symbol denotes AVAs too small to be indicated on the map.

SONOMA-BONDED WINERIES

Adler-Fels
Alderbrook Vineyards
Alexander Valley Fruit &
  Trading Co.
Alexander Valley
  Vineyards
Arrowood Winery &
  Vineyards
Balverne Vineyards
Bandiera
Bellerose Vineyard
Belvedere Wine Co.
Benziger of Glen Ellen
Black Mountain Vineyard
Braren-Pauli Winery
Buena Vista
Bynum Winery, Davis
Carmenet
Caswell Vineyards
Chalk Hill Winery
Château de Baun
Château Diana
Chateau St. Jean
Château Souverain
Clos du Bois
Cohn Winery, B. R.
Coturri & Sons, H.
Dehlinger Winery
DeLoach Vineyards
DeLorimier
De Natale
Diamond Oaks Vineyards
Domaine Laurier
Domaine Michel
Domaine St. George
Dry Creek Vineyard
Duxoup Wine Works
Eagle Ridge Winery
Ferrari-Carano
Ferrer, Gloria
Field Stone Winery
Fisher Vineyards
Foppiano Wine Co.,
  Louis J.

Frick Winery
Fritz Cellars
Gan Eden
Geyser Peak
Glen Ellen Winery
Golden Creek
Grand Cru
Gundlach-Bundschu
  Vineyard Co.
Hacienda Wine Cellars
Hafner Vineyard
Hanna Vineyard
Hanzell Vineyard
Haywood Winery
Hop Kiln Winery at
  Griffin Vineyards
Iron Horse Ranch &
  Vineyards
Jade Mountain Winery
Johnson's of Alexander
  Valley
Jordan Vineyard and
  Winery
Kenwood Winery
Kistler Vineyards
Korbel & Bros., F.
La Crema
Lake Sonoma Winery
Lambert Bridge
Landmark Vineyards
Las Montanas
Laurel Glen
Lyeth Vineyard & Winery
Lytton Springs Winery
Marietta Cellars
Mark West Vineyards
Martini & Prati
Matanzas Creek Winery
Mazzocco Vineyards
Meeker Vineyard
Melim
Merry Vintners, The
Mill Creek Vineyards
Murphy-Goode

Nalle
Napoli Cellars
Pacheco Ranch Winery
  (Marin)
Pastori
Paulsen Vineyards, Pat
Pedroncelli Winery, J.
Piper-Sonoma
Pommeraie Vineyards
Porter Creek
Preston Vineyard &
  Winery
Quivira
Rabbit Ridge
Rafanelli Winery, A.
Ravenswood
Richardson Vineyards
River Road Vineyards
Rochioli Vineyards
Rose Family Vineyard
St. Francis
Sausal Winery
Searidge Winery

Sebastiani Vineyard
Seghesio Winery
Sellards Winery, Thomas
Simi Winery
Sky Vineyards
Sonoma-Cutrer Vineyards
Sonoma Hills
Sotoyome
Stemmler Winery, Robert
Strong Vineyards, Rodney
Sugarloaf Ridge Winery
Swan Vineyards, Joseph
Taft Street
Topolos at Russian River
  Vineyards
Trentadue Winery
Valley of the Moon
Viña Vista
Wheeler Winery, William
White Oak Vineyards
Williams & Selyem
Woodbury Winery
  (Marin)

Napa

NAPA

• Calistoga

Pope Valley

2

Chiles Valley

• St. Helena

• Rutherford
• Oakville
• Yountville

Napa Valley

Stag's Leap District

• Napa

3 *Carneros*

1 *Pope Valley*

NAPA AVAS

3 Carneros
2 Howell Mountain
1 Napa Valley
* Stag's Leap District
* Wild Horse Valley

*This symbol denotes AVAs too small to be indicated on the map.

NAPA-BONDED WINERIES

Acacia
Altamura Vineyards
Amizetta
Anderson Vineyards, S.
Arroyo Winery, Vincent
Arthur Vineyards, David
Atlas Peak Vineyards
Beaulieu Vineyard
Bergfeld 1885
Beringer Vineyard
Blue Heron Lake
   Vineyard
Bouchaine
Buehler Vineyards
Burgess Cellars
Cain Cellars
Cakebread Cellars
Calafia Cellars
Caporale
Carneros Creek
Casa Nuestra
Caymus Vineyard
Chappellet Vineyard
Château Boswell
Chateau Chevre
Chateau Montelena
Château Napa-Beaucanon
Chimney Rock
Christian Brothers
   Winery, The
Clos du Val Wine Co.
Clos Pegase
Conn Creek
Cosentino Wine Co.
Crichton Hall
Cuvaison, Inc.
Dalla Valle Vineyard
Deer Park Winery
DeMoor
Diamond Creek
   Vineyards
Domaine Carneros
Domaine Chandon
Domaine Karakash

Domaine Mumm
Domaine Napa
Dominus
Duckhorn Vineyards
Dunn Vineyards
Evensen Winery
Fairmont
Far Niente
Flora Springs Wine Co.
Folie à Deux
Forman Winery
Franciscan Vineyards
Freemark Abbey
Frog's Leap Wine Cellars
Girard Winery
Goosecross Cellars
Grace Family Cellar
Graeser Winery, Richard
   L.
Green & Red Vineyard
Grgich Hills
Groth Vineyards &
   Winery
Havens Wine Cellars
Heitz Cellars
Hess Collection
Hill Winery, William
Honig Cellars, Louis
Inglenook-Napa Valley
Jaeger-Inglewood
   Vineyard
Johnson-Turnbull
   Vineyards
Keenan Winery, Robert
Kornell Champagne
   Cellars, Hanns
Krug Winery, Charles
La Jota Vineyard Co.
La Vieille Montagne
Lakespring Winery
Lamborn Family Vineyard
Livingston
Long Vineyards
Markham Winery

Martini, Louis M.
Mayacamas Vineyards
Merlion
Merryvale Vineyards
Milat Vineyards
Mondavi Winery, Robert
Mont St. John Cellars
Monticello Cellars
Mt. Veeder Vineyard
Napa Creek Winery
Napa Valley Port Cellars
Napa Vintners
Newlan Vineyards and
  Winery
Newton Vineyards
Neyers Winery
Nichelini Vineyards
Niebaum-Coppola Estates
Opus One
Pecota Winery, Robert
Peju Province
Pepi Winery, Robert
Phelps Vineyards, Joseph
Piña Cellars
Pine Ridge
Plam Vineyards
Pradel Cellars, Bernard
Prager Winery
Quail Ridge
Rasmussen Winery, Kent
Raymond Vineyard &
  Cellar
Revere Vineyard
Ritchie Creek
Rombauer Vineyards
Round Hill
Rustridge
Rutherford Hill Winery
Rutherford Vintners
Saddleback Cellars
Sage Canyon Winery
St. Andrews Winery
St. Clement Vineyard
St. Supery Vineyards &
  Winery
Saintsbury
Sattui Winery, V.

Schramsberg
Schug Cellars
Sequoia Grove
Shadow Brook
Shafer Vineyards
Shaw Vineyards &
  Winery, Charles F.
Silver Oak Cellars
Silverado Hills
Silverado Vineyards
Sinskey Vineyard
Smith-Madrone
Soda Canyon
Spottswoode Vineyard &
  Winery
Spring Mountain
  Vineyards
Stag's Leap Wine Cellars
Stags' Leap Winery
Steltzner Vineyard
Sterling Vineyards
Stonegate Winery
Stony Hill Vineyards
Storybook Mountain
  Vineyards
Stratford
Streblow Vineyards
Sullivan Vineyard and
  Winery
Summit Lake Winery
Sunny St. Helena Winery
Sutter Home
Swanson Vineyards
Togni, Philip
Trefethen Vineyards
Tudal Winery
Tulocay Vineyards
Van der Heyden
Vichon
Villa Helena
Villa Mt. Eden
Wermuth Winery
White Rock Vineyards
Whitehall Lane Winery
Whitford Cellars
Z-D

Alameda – Santa Clara – Santa Cruz

SAN FRANCISCO BAY AREA AVAS

1 Livermore Valley
2 Santa Cruz Mountains

*This symbol denotes AVAs too small to be indicated on the map.

SAN FRANCISCO BAY AREA—BONDED WINERIES

Ahlgren Vineyards
Ashly
Audubon Cellars
Bargetto's Santa Cruz
  Winery
Bay Cellars
Bonny Doon Vineyard
Bruce Winery, David
Carrousel Cellars
Cline Cellars (Contra
  Costa)
Concannon Vineyard
Congress Springs
  Vineyard
Conrotto Winery, A.
Crescini
Cronin Vineyards
Devlin Wine Cellars
Edmunds St. John
Elliston Vineyards
Fenestra Winery
Fogarty Winery, Thomas
Fortino Winery
Gemello Winery
Grover Gulch Winery
Guglielmo Winery, Emilio
Hallcrest Vineyards
Hecker Pass Winery
Jory Winery
Kennedy Winery, Kathryn
Kirigin Cellars
Kruse Winery, Thomas
Live Oaks Winery
Livermore Valley Cellars

Lohr, J.
McHenry Vineyard
Mirassou Vineyards
Mount Eden Vineyards
Noble Hill Vineyards
Obester Winery
Page Mill Winery
Pedrizzetti Winery
Rapazzini Winery
Retzlaff Vineyards
Ridge Vineyards
River Run Vintners
Rosenblum Cellars
Roudon-Smith Vineyards
San Martin Winery
Santa Cruz Mountain
  Vineyard
Sarah's Vineyard
Sherrill Cellars
Silver Mountain
  Vineyards
Staiger, P. & M.
Stony Ridge Winery
Sunrise Winery
Sycamore Creek
Tribaut, M.
Viano Winery (Contra
  Costa)
Villa Paradiso
Walker Winery
Weibel Champagne
  Vineyards
Wente Bros.

Monterey–San Benito

MONTEREY-SAN BENITO AVAS

3 Arroyo Seco
1 Carmel Valley
2 Chalone
4 Cienega Valley
* Lime Kiln Valley
* Monterey
5 Paicines
* San Benito
* San Lucas

*This symbol denotes AVAs too small to be indicated on the map.

MONTEREY-SAN BENITO—BONDED WINERIES

Casa de Fruta
Chalone Vineyards
Château Julien
Cygnet Cellars
Durney Vineyards
Enz Vineyards
Georis Winery
Jekel Vineyard
La Reina

Masson Vineyard
Monterey Peninsula
  Winery
Monterey Vineyard, The
Morgan Winery
Smith & Hook
Talbott Vineyard, Robert
Ventana Vineyards

San Luis Obispo-
Santa Barbara

SAN LUIS OBISPO-
SANTA BARBARA AVAS

* Central Coast
2 Edna Valley
1 Paso Robles
3 Santa Maria Valley
4 Santa Ynez Valley
* York Mountain

*This symbol denotes AVAs too small to be indicated on the map.

SAN LUIS OBISPO-SANTA BARBARA—BONDED WINERIES

Adelaida Cellars
Arciero Winery
Au Bon Climat
Austin Cellars
Babcock Vineyard
Ballard Canyon
Baron & Kolb
Brander Vineyard, The
Byron Vineyard
Calera Wine Co.
Caparone Vineyards
Carey Cellars, J.
Chamisal Vineyards
Claiborne & Churchill
Corbett Canyon
Creston Manor
Eberle Winery
Edna Valley Vineyards
Estrella River
Firestone Vineyard
Foxen Vineyard
Gainey Vineyard, The

Houtz Vineyards
La Cascada
Maison Deutz
Martin Brothers
Mastantuono
Meridian Vineyards
Mission View Winery
Pesenti Winery
Qupé
Rancho Sisquoc Winery
Sanford Wines
Santa Barbara Winery
Santa Ynez Valley Winery
Saucelito Canyon
  Vineyard
Talley Vineyards
Twin Hills Winery
Vega Vineyards &
  Winery
Wild Horse Winery
York Mountain Winery
Zaca Mesa

Sierra Foothills

PLACER

EL DORADO

• Placerville

1

Plymouth • **2** AMADOR

• Sutter Creek

• Ione

CALAVERAS

Murphys •

SIERRA FOOTHILLS AVAS

1 El Dorado
* Fiddletown
2 Shenandoah Valley-California
* Sierra Foothills

*This symbol denotes AVAs too small to be indicated on the map.

SIERRA FOOTHILLS—BONDED WINERIES

Amador Foothill
Argonaut Winery
Baldinelli Vineyard
Black Sheep Vintners
Boeger Winery
Butterfly Creek Winery
Fitzpatrick Winery
Gerwer Winery
Gold Hill Vineyard
Granite Springs
Greenstone Winery
Karly Wines
Kenworthy Vineyards
Lava Cap
Madrona Vineyards
Monteviña

Nevada City Winery
Radanovich Winery
Renaissance Vineyard and
  Winery
Richards Winery, L. W.
Santino Winery
Shenandoah Vineyards
Sierra Vista
Sonora Winery and Port
  Works
Stevenot Winery
Story Vineyard
T.K.C.
Winterbrook Vineyards
Wolterbeek-Westwood

Southern California

SOUTHERN CALIFORNIA AVAS

2 San Pasqual Valley
* South Coast
1 Temecula

*This symbol denotes AVAs too small to be indicated on the map.

SOUTHERN CALIFORNIA—BONDED WINERIES

Baily Vineyard
Britton Cellars
Callaway Vineyards and
  Winery
Carrie Vineyards,
  Maurice
Cilurzo Vineyard and
  Winery
Culbertson Winery, John
Daume Winery
Donatoni Winery
Filippi Vintage Co., J.
Filsinger Vineyards &
  Winery

French Valley Vineyards
Galleano Winery
Hart Vineyards
Jaeger Winery, Thomas
Leeward Winery
McLester Winery
Menghini Winery
Mount Palomar Winery
Ojai Winery
Old Creek Ranch Winery
Palos Verdes Winery
Piconi Winery, Ltd.
Rolling Hills Vineyards
San Antonio

San Joaquin Valley

CENTRAL VALLEY AVAS

* Clarksburg
* Lodi
* Madera
* Merritt Island
* Solano-Green Valley
* Suisun Valley

*This symbol denotes AVAs too small to be indicated on the map.

CENTRAL VALLEY–BONDED WINERIES

Almaden
Anderson Wine Cellars
Bianchi Vineyards
Bogle Vineyards
Borra's Cellar
Cache Cellars
Cache Creek
Cadenasso Winery
Chateau de Leu
Cline Cellars
Cook Winery, R & J
Cribari
Delicato Vineyards
Ficklin Vineyard
Franzia
Gallo Winery, E. & J.
Giumarra Vineyards
Gibson Vineyards
Handel & Mettler

Harbor Winery
Heritage Cellars
Inglenook-Navalle
JFJ Winery
Las Vinas Winery
Lost Hills Winery
Lucas Winery, The
Nonini Winery, A.
Oak Ridge Winery
Orleans Hill Winery
Papagni Vineyards
Phillips Farms
Phillips Vineyards, R. H.
Quady Winery
Satiety
Tremont Winery
Wooden Valley Winery
Winters Winery

About the Author

Bob Thompson wakes up at night wondering if he has become a monomaniac. Since 1967 he has written—in round numbers—ten books, a hundred magazine pieces, and a thousand newspaper columns about wine. In addition, he has judged at fifty major national and regional wine competitions. He has been comforted to find that he still knows a little bit about tennis, cheese, Italian, flight, French, and jazz, and may be learning more.